Socio-Technical and Human Cognition Elements of Information Systems

Steve Clarke
University of Luton Business School, UK

Elayne Coakes
University of Westminster, UK

M. Gordon Hunter
University of Lethbridge, Canada

Andrew Wenn
Victoria University, Australia

 **Information Science Publishing**

Hershey • London • Melbourne • Singapore • Beijing

Acquisition Editor:	Mehdi Khosrowpour
Managing Editor:	Jan Travers
Development Editor:	Michele Rossi
Copy Editor:	Maria Boyer
Typesetter:	LeAnn Whitcomb
Cover Design:	Integrated Book Technology
Printed at:	Integrated Book Technology

Published in the United States of America by
    Information Science Publishing (an imprint of Idea Group, Inc.)
    701 E. Chocolate Avenue
    Hershey PA 17033-1117
    Tel: 717-533-8845
    Fax: 717-533-8661
    E-mail: cust@idea-group.com
    Web site: http://www.idea-group.com

and in the United Kingdom by
    Information Science Publishing (an imprint of Idea Group, Inc.)
    3 Henrietta Street
    Covent Garden
    London WC2E 8LU
    Tel: 44 20 7240 0856
    Fax: 44 20 7379 3313
    Web site: http://www.eurospan.co.uk

Library of Congress Cataloging-in-Publication Data

Socio-technical and human cognition elements of information systems / Steve Clarke ... [et al.].
    p. cm.
  Includes bibliographical references and index.
  ISBN 1-59140-104-6 (cloth)
    1. Information resources management. 2. Information technology--Social aspects. 3. Human engineering. I. Clarke, Steve, 1950-

  T58.64 .S68 2002
  303.48'33--dc21

                                            2002068788

eISBN 1-59140-112-7

British Cataloguing in Publication Data
A Cataloguing in Publication record for this book is available from the British Library.

Socio-Technical and Human Cognition Elements of Information Systems

Table of Contents

Section IV: Human Issues: The Lessons from and Applications of Social Theory

Preface

The 1980s and 1990s saw a growing interest in research and practice into information systems viewed from a combination of social, technical and cognitive perspectives. This edited book of contributed chapters by researchers and practitioners who utilise these perspectives in their work looks at some of the key developments in this domain. They also examine the extent to which it should be perceived as one in which technical, social or cognitive issues dominate, the main purpose being to present these three perspectives in a balanced way, giving equal emphasis to each of them.

The book is divided into four sections, each with a managing editor whose area of expertise is in that field.

In Section I, Elayne Coakes focuses on the socio-technical aspects of information systems, setting the scene for the rest of the text. Each of the four chapters in this section address this theme, and in their own way stress the holistic viewpoint necessary to the domain. The origins of information systems, viewed from this perspective, are seen to lie in the human resource: a view which stresses the ethical issues relating to participation in IS management.

In the next section, Gordon Hunter focuses on the individual within the socio-technical systems paradigm, aiming to "present a bridge between the comprehensive discussion of the socio-technical paradigm and the configuration of users/systems." Issues are discussed surrounding individuals through an exploration of their experiences within the social environment of the information technology profession. The discussion presents different perspectives of the individual within the socio-technical systems paradigm.

Andrew Wenn, in Section III, looks at how different configurations (of people and technology) enable work in different ways, but with each bringing its own concerns of, for instance, portability, access and ease of use. It is one of the themes of this section that the different configurations between the human and non-human actors bring a variety of issues to system adoption and use.

Andrew covers this topic, in his inimitable style, through observations about how we "have to learn how to interact with the technology," suggesting that "the user has been configured by the technology," and concludes by arguing for a more holistic, socio-technical approach to comprehending information systems.

Finally, in Section IV, Steve Clarke and Paul Drake propose a way in which critical social theory might be applied within the currently highly rule-based domain of information security. This is part of a larger research program, in which critical social theory and the ideas from critical systems thinking are being used to offer new insights to information management.

All that remains is for us to say that we have enjoyed the exercise of collating this text immensely, and particularly have enjoyed working with a group of contributors who have such diverse but also connected ideas. In the final analysis, however, it is up to you, as readers, to decide whether you see any of these perspectives as relevant to the context in which you undertake your work or study; we will be happy to hear your opinions.

Steve Clarke, Elayne Coakes, Gordon Hunter and Andrew Wenn
Editors

Acknowledgement

The editors would like to acknowledge the help of all involved in the collation and review process of the book, without whose support the project could not have been satisfactorily completed.

A further special note of thanks goes also to all the staff at Idea Group, whose contributions throughout the whole process, from inception of the initial idea to final publication, have been invaluable.

Section I

From Technical to Socio-Technical

Socio-Technical Thinking— An Holistic Viewpoint

Elayne Coakes
University of Westminster, UK

Introduction

In this book we set out to look at the socio-technical and human cognition elements of information systems. In this first section of the book, we look particularly at the socio-technical aspects of these information systems through four chapters submitted by leading researchers in the field and practitioners. We have, in this section of the book, a strong bias towards a discussion of how we can develop better information systems, especially those relying on computers, utilising insight from the social paradigm. These chapters provide a strong moral as well as theoretical foundation for the rest of the book. Later sections and chapters, where the holistic viewpoint offered by the socio-technical paradigm is emphasised, take up this morality theme.

Socio-Technical Thinking

Socio-technical thinking has been a significant element of the way we think about systems in organisations for some 50 plus years. Its origins lie in work done in the human resource and organisational management fields, especially relating to the way human psychology and technical artefacts inter-relate. In particular how humans react to technology of any type or form. Theoretically it combines the social and technical paradigms that come together to form the socio-technical paradigm. It has been described as *"the study of the relationships between the social and technical parts of any system"* (Coakes, 2002).

Socio-technical thinking has been attributed with a number of principles (see Cherns, 1976, 1987), which help organisations to explore and adjust to conflicts and complexity in the human, organisational and technical aspects of change. In particular these principles emphasise an ethical principle relating to the individual's participation in decision making and control over their immediate work environment. We see this ethical principle discussed and implemented in the chapters in this section.

Socio-technical thinking is holistic in its essence; it is not the dichotomy implied by the name; it is an intertwining of human, organisational, technical and other facets. In essence it is an approach to organisational change and analysis that looks at how people work together, how they organise themselves and how technology can support their work.

The Chapters in this Section

The four chapters in this section commence with a review and reformatting of the Multiview Information Systems Development Methodology by its authors David Avison and Trevor Wood-Harper. Avison and Wood-Harper begin with a discussion of how they came to devise the Multiview Methodology and their motivation for undertaking such a task. They then discuss how they revised and reformatted the original methodology to take account of changing information in the research field that has enlightened their thinking, and also as a result of action research in implementing the methodology in real-world cases, and the lessons learned from such experiences. Additionally, changing types of applications or fields of implementation have also occasioned reflection on the content of the methodology.

The philosophy that underlies the third stage of the original Multiview framework and the (P) stage, as it was reformulated in Multiview 2, is socio-technical. As Avison and Wood-Harper say, it is concerned with a belief *"that people have a basic right to control their own destinies"* and that participation in system design will enhance acceptance, operation and implementation of any such system.

The section continues with work by Neil Doherty and Malcolm King who have developed an organisational impact analysis procedure for the proactive treatment of organisational issues in the development and implementation of information systems. Typically, they comment, system developers have focused on the delivery of a technically effective system, on time andllah within budget, and have reacted to organisational issues when they have arisen rather than planning for organisational impacts.

Doherty and King also comment that on the whole, technical specialists are reluctant to experiment with organisational focused approaches and prefer to concentrate on technical tools and techniques with which they feel more comfortable. Socio-technical methods are seen to them as being untried and untested. The approach proposed in this chapter, it is suggested, may be more acceptable to the systems developer as it can be considered complementary to their normal development methods: being straightforward, proactive, comprehensive and flexible. It demonstrates that a socio-technical approach can lead to efficiency, profitability and a high-morale labour force, which, as they comment, Mumford (1997) recognised as the way forward for socio-technical approaches.

Niek du Plooy, in his chapter, discusses the social responsibility of IS developers to take cognisance of the social context of information systems. Du Plooy comments that that it is not only the introduction of information systems that changes the organisation but also the actual use of such systems. Adopting and using new technology changes the organisation into a new paradigm from which we cannot go back.

In his chapter, du Plooy discusses the assumptions, norms and values of information systems developers, which seem so often to be at odds with that of the organisation. He also looks at the goals for the introduction of these systems, which may be disparate from that of the developers. In short, it has generally been agreed that neglect of the human factors in system implementation has led to many systems failures, in particular where goals and assumptions are at odds. He therefore argues that information system adoption and use should be understood as an organisational intervention and thus the complex social factors that impact on any organisational change need to be understood by the developers, who will need to be trained appropriately. IS developers will need to take on the responsibility of cultivating and nurturing the human environment.

Finally the section closes with a look at IT in the construction industry by two Scandinavian authors Lauri Koskela and Abdul Kazi working in Finland, but drawing some generic conclusions across the sector that we can also extrapolate to other industry sectors.

Interestingly, they argue that the use of IT in the construction industry has brought with it negative impacts rather than the expected positive benefits. One of the arguments as to why this has occurred is that an excessive focus on technology has limited the understanding of the organisational context in which the technology is implemented. The socio-technical viewpoint as they point out and as exemplified in Niek du Plooy's discussion of IS developers' expectations as discussed above. Koskela and Kazi argue that the introduction of computers to construction is worthwhile only as far as it can contribute to the realisation of the principles of production, in a better way than other alternatives such as operations management. They conclude, among other things, that more emphasis needs to be placed on how organisational and managerial changes can be effectively supported by IT rather than by utilising IT as the driving force for organisational change. Their final research questions, in their chapter, echo the discussion above by Niek du Plooy, in which they ask, "How are information systems developed and implemented in practice? What actually happens when people are using information technology in construction?"

Conclusion

These four chapters set the tone for the book and the sections that follow. They ask relevant questions that the authors attempt to answer but also make important points about the social and organisational context in which information systems are developed and the result of not taking these into account during development.

They show how researchers and practitioners are exploring how we can develop systems that fit the organisation rather than fit the organisation to the system. This is of course the socio-technical viewpoint. How to jointly optimise both people and technology to introduce an improvement in the organisational work practices, products and services, communications and relationships, responsiveness to environmental change, are all key to socio-technical change initiatives.

The philosophical and research implications of these questions are still being explored and are worthy of yet more exploration both in this book and in future work. I welcome this future research and look forward to participating in it. The socio-technical paradigm is alive and well and still relevant to all that is to come in the field of information systems.

References

Cherns, A. (1976). The principles of socio-technical design. *Human Relations, 29*(8), 783-792.

Cherns, A. (1987). Principles of socio-technical design revisited. *Human Relations, 40*(3), 153-162.

Coakes, E. (2002). Knowledge management: A socio-technical perspective. In Coakes, E., Willis, D. and Clarke, S. (Eds.), *Knowledge Management in the Socio-Technical World*, 4-14. London: Springer-Verlag.

Mumford, E. (1997). The reality of participative systems design: Contributing to stability in a rocking boat. *Information Systems Journal, 7*(4), 309-321.

Chapter I

Bringing Social and Organisational Issues into Information Systems Development: The Story of Multiview

David Avison
ESSEC Business School, France

Trevor Wood-Harper
University of Salford, UK

ABSTRACT

Multiview is a framework to support the information systems development process. It was formulated originally in 1985, but has been developed and changed since that time. It was originally defined to take into account the human and organisational aspects of information systems development, as the alternative methodologies of the time–and most since that time–took a very technology-oriented approach. Furthermore, it is a contingency approach, and again this compares with the alternative bureaucratic and prescriptive methodologies. In this chapter, we describe the history of Multiview, and we reflect on the experiences of using it in action in many organisations.

THE MOTIVATION FOR MULTIVIEW

The authors had several years' experience as systems analysts in industry before joining Thames Polytechnic together in 1974 as lecturers in systems analysis. Our role was to teach systems analysis to undergraduates and post-experience students. The major part of this consisted of a basic course in information systems development. This was based on the National Computer Centre (NCC) course in systems analysis (Daniels and Yeates, 1971) that was used in the UK and elsewhere at the time. However, this provided a very technology-oriented understanding, and our experience suggested that for information systems to be successful this was a very narrow view. Further, the description of the process of information systems development as formal, step-by-step, almost 'scientific,' did not coincide with our experience developing information systems in practice, which was much more like a trial-and-error exercise. We felt that there was a major rift between both what was espoused with what was practised and what was espoused with what was desirable.

Our first move was to look as widely as possible so as to ascertain whether there were more enlightened approaches to information systems development. However the alternatives of the time did not provide a human or organisational view. Most were either data-oriented, such as D2S2 (MacDonald and Palmer, 1982) which was the basis for Information Engineering (Martin, 1990), or process-oriented (Yourdon and Constantine, 1978) or a combination of both, leading eventually to MERISE (Quang and Chartier-Kastler, 1991) and SSADM (Downs et al., 1991). There was no approach at that time which took human and organisation issues in information systems development seriously. The main motivation for Multiview was to include these human or organisational aspects fully into information systems development. But we also wanted to suggest that information systems development was not a step-by-step, prescriptive process, but iterative and sometimes applied differently as circumstances dictated. This reflected our real-world experience. Our definition of Multiview was more a contingency framework than a formal set of procedures. We show how Multiview was defined and developed in this chapter.

Our view was that this was not a theoretical exercise. We wanted to see if these ideas would work in practice. Thus our original definition of Multiview was tried out in a number of real-world situations, frequently working with practitioners. These experiences were very different and illustrated the contingent nature of the process. Further, in our teaching we used these experiences to expose the difficulties and practical problems of information systems work, frequently ignored in the texts of the time. We also discuss in this chapter the role of action research in defining and refining Multiview.

DEFINING MULTIVIEW

In defining Multiview (Wood-Harper et al., 1985), we proposed that the following questions ought to be addressed in information systems development:

1. How is the computer system supposed to further the aims of the organisation installing it?
2. How can it be fitted into the working lives of the people in the organisation that are going to use it?
3. How can the individuals concerned best relate to the machine in terms of operating it and using the output from it?
4. What information system processing function is the system to perform?
5. What is the technical specification of a system that will come close enough to doing the things that have been written down in the answers to the other four questions?

These five dimensions may now seem obvious to present readers, however at the time information systems methodologies addressed only question 5 (technical aspects) and question 4 (data and structured analysis) fully, and paid only lip-service to the human-computer interface (question 3) and even then in only some approaches. Indeed, it was the Alvey Commission in the UK, which in 1984 started to allocate government research monies to this latter issue. On the other hand, the issues of questions 1 and 2 were not addressed at all by conventional methodologies (nor the Alvey Commission).

In devising Multiview, we were most influenced by Checkland's work in addressing question 1 (Checkland, 1985) and Mumford (1981), Land and Hirschheim (1983), and the Tavistock School in general, regarding question 2. It should also be noted that the conventional way of teaching systems analysis in the 1980s was also to concentrate on, in descending order of magnitude, technical, data and process issues. Further, in our definition of Multiview, we could envisage occasions when systems analysis may not lead to computerised information systems at all (Episkopou and Wood-Harper, 1985), very unusual at a time when *computerising* clerical systems was the norm.

A full account of this early definition of Multiview is found in Avison and Wood-Harper (1990), and Figure 1 shows its diagrammatic representation at the time and how each phase addressed the five questions above. In the context of this present book, we provide a brief overview of these five stages. The first stage looks at the organisation–its main purpose, problem themes, and the creation of a statement about what the information system will be and what it will do. It is based on soft systems methodology (mode 1), described in Checkland (1981), using the techniques of rich picture building, CATWOE definition and the creation of root definitions, and conceptual models. Possible changes are debated and agendas

Figure 1: The original multiview framework

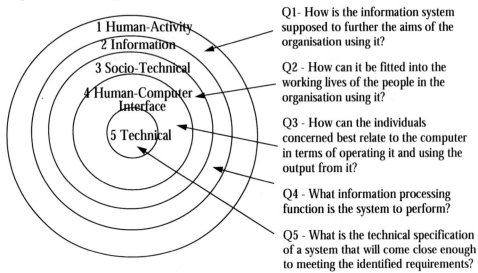

1 Human-Activity
2 Information
3 Socio-Technical
4 Human-Computer Interface
5 Technical

Q1- How is the information system supposed to further the aims of the organisation using it?

Q2 - How can it be fitted into the working lives of the people in the organisation using it?

Q3 - How can the individuals concerned best relate to the computer in terms of operating it and using the output from it?

Q4 - What information processing function is the system to perform?

Q5 - What is the technical specification of a system that will come close enough to meeting the identified requirements?

drawn up for change. The second stage is to analyse the entities and functions of the problem situation described in stage one. This is carried out independently of how the system will be developed. The functional modelling and entity-relationship modelling found in most methodologies are suggested as modelling techniques.

The philosophy behind the third stage is that people have a basic right to control their own destinies and that if they are allowed to participate in the analysis and design of the systems that they will be using, then implementation, acceptance and operation of the system will be enhanced. Human considerations, such as job satisfaction, task definition, morale and so on are seen as just as important as technical considerations. This stage emphasizes the choice between alternative systems, according to important social and technical considerations. The fourth stage is concerned with the technical requirements of the user interface. Choices between batch or on-line and menu, command or soft form interfaces are made. The design of specific conversations will depend on the background and experience of the people who are going to use the system, as well as their information needs. Finally, the design of the technical subsystem concerns the specific technical requirements of the system to be designed, and therefore to such aspects as computers, databases, application software, control and maintenance.

REFLECTIONS ON MULTIVIEW

In our case studies using Multiview in many real-world situations using action research, which we will discuss later, we gained much feedback in its use. In Wood-

Harper et al. (1985) we illustrated its original definition using one such case, and in Avison and Wood-Harper (1990) six such cases are described. We have been informed by many such cases involving ourselves and others. In reporting on our experiences in using Multiview across a range of projects, we have identified a series of lessons learned. Key observations among these are that:

- *A methodology takes time to learn*: There is a wide range and large number of techniques and tools available. Describing them all would result in an information systems development methodology that is long, complex and therefore difficult to learn and to master. Multiview is, perhaps, even more complex for two main reasons: (1) it combines 'hard' and 'soft' techniques and tools; and (2) it is a contingent approach and so does not follow a rigid, step-by-step prescription with specific techniques and tools to be used at each stage and well-defined deliverables to be produced following each stage.

- *The waterfall model is inappropriate for describing information systems development in practice*: This approach, as evidenced by the field work, does not, in practice, exhibit the step-by-step, top-down nature of conventional models, and none of the applications have exactly followed the framework as espoused in the main text (Avison and Wood-Harper, 1990). The users of the approach will almost certainly find that they will carry out a series of iterations that are not shown in the framework. Further, in some of the real-world cases undertaken, certain phases of the approach were omitted and others were carried out in a sequence different from that expected.

- *The framework is not a 'guarantor of truth'*: Images within the views of the approach are interpreted and selected depending on context. For example, in two cases described in the 1990 text, the social options of the socio-technical phase were either omitted or not fully explored. The appropriateness of using some techniques also varied.

- *The political dimension is important*: The manipulation of power, that is, the political dimension, is important in real-world situations. This transcends the rationale of any methodology. In most cases decisions were made in light of considerations beyond those implied by Multiview. For example, in one application computer equipment was purchased before requirements analysis had been undertaken fully. The reason concerned a fund of money in the organisation that was not available after a particular date (the 'year end'). This makes perfect sense in the particular context, but does not fit into the requirements of conventional approaches.

- *Responsible participation is contingent*: A high level of responsible participation is a positive ingredient of successful information systems development. Nevertheless, our experience suggests that the role of the facilitator is frequently that of 'confidence booster' rather than that of adviser or applications developer as usually described. The role of the facilitators proved crucial in most applications on both the people and the technical side of information systems development. However, participation is not always possible. For example, it depends on the organisation's structure and the attitudes of the people concerned.

- *The approach is interpreted by users/analysts*: People view each situation differently depending on their education, culture and experience. Users of Multiview (and conventional methodologies as well) interpret the approach and the problem situation uniquely. There is no such thing as a 'typical situation,' 'typical user' and 'typical analyst.'

REDEFINING MULTIVIEW AS MULTIVIEW2

Each reflection came from a lesson (or lessons) learned through experience. Each case has led to some modification of our definition of Multiview. These cases included those led by our colleagues Richard Vidgen, now at Bath University, and Bob Wood at Salford University. We have also been influenced by other writings, and these influences together have led to a new definition published as Multiview2 (Avison et al., 1998).

The original conception of Multiview posited a three-way relationship between the analyst, the methodology and the situation. We suggested that parts of this relationship were missing in many descriptions of information systems development, and that methodologies often contained unstated and unquestioning assumptions about the unitary nature of both the problem situation and the analysts involved in investigating it. Despite this criticism of other methodologies, the original definition of Multiview itself offered no further guidance on how any given instantiation of the triad (analyst-methodology-situation) might come about in actual practice. We observed that the multiple perspective approach described by Mitroff and Linstone (1983) can be used to inform the particular occurrence of Multiview2 under any given set of circumstances (Figure 2). The Multiview2 stages of technical design and construction (T), socio-technical analysis and design (P), and organisational analysis (O) align well with this approach.

Multiview2 offers a rich implementation of the multiple perspective approach as far as information systems development is concerned. As we have seen, in the original version of Multiview, we implemented such an approach through a five-stage methodology. These five stages were then typically presented as a waterfall structure. In Multiview2 the outcomes of information systems development are posited as consisting of three elements: organisational behaviours, work systems and technical artefacts, which are reflected in the stages of organisational analysis (O), socio-technical analysis and design (P), and technical design and construction

Figure 2: The interaction of situation, interveners (analysts) and methodology

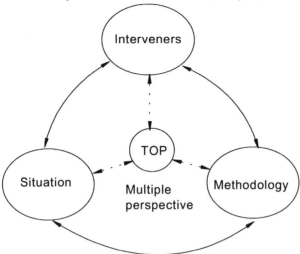

(T) respectively (Vidgen, 1996). The fourth stage of Multiview2, information modelling, acts as a bridge between the other three, communicating and enacting the outcomes in terms of each other (Figure 3). The proposed new framework for Multiview shows the four stages of the methodology mediated through the actual process of information systems development.

Together with the change in the Multiview2 framework go changes to the content of the four stages, reflecting the experiences of applying Multiview through action research and developments in IS theory and practice. The major amendments made in the content of Multiview2 are summarized in Table 1.

The Multiview2 stages of technical design and construction (T), socio-technical analysis and design (P), and organisational analysis (O) (see Figure 2) align

Figure 3: The Multiview2 framework

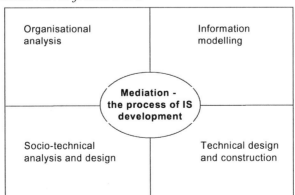

well with the multiple perspective approach put forward by Mitroff and Linstone (1993). However, there are important differences of emphasis and definition. For example, the T perspective is equated by Mitroff and Linstone with rationality and functionalism, whereas in Multiview2 the technical design stage is concerned with the detail of computer system design and construction. In unbounded systems thinking, therefore, it would be perfectly feasible to have a T perspective of the analysis of human activity. We consider it more insightful to apply the TOP multiple perspective as a basis for informing the *approach* taken to information systems development. In this way the stages of the Multiview2 methodology can be seen as methods appropriate to the analysis of the problem situation, given an overall multiple perspective approach.

The T perspective reflects a rational, engineering-based approach to systems development in which the aim is to produce technical artifacts that will support purposeful human and organisational activity. The O perspective is typified by the development of a shared understanding and organisational learning, within the process of information systems development. It can be visualized as a learning cycle including discovery, invention, production and generalization, as well as double-loop learning to bring about the surfacing and challenging of deep-rooted assumptions which were previously unknown or undiscussable (Argyris and Schön, 1978). The P perspective represents the fears and hopes of individuals within the organisation, and deals with situations of power, influence and prestige (Knights and Murray, 1994).

The TOP multiple perspective approach described by Mitroff and Linstone can be used to inform the different views that can be taken of the three sets of outcomes—organisational behaviours, work and technical artefacts—within any given problem context. As we have seen, traditional information systems development takes a singular T perspective of the system development process. Alternative life-cycle models, such as iterative and evolutionary development, although generally more sympathetic to the O and P perspectives, may still be reduced in practice to a T-dominant view of information system development in which it is believed that the 'real' requirements are 'captured' more effectively than with a waterfall life-cycle model.

Multiview2 offers a systematic guide to any information system development intervention, together with a reflexive, learning methodological process, which brings together the analyst, the situation and the methodology. However, although the authors recommend a contingent approach to information system development, Multiview2 should not be used to justify random or uncontrolled development.

The terms 'methodology' and 'method' tend to be used interchangeably, although they can be distinguished insofar as a method is a concrete procedure for getting something done while a methodology is a higher-level construct which

Table 1: The rationale of Multiview2

Stage	Change	Rationale
Organisational analysis	Inclusion of strategic assumption surfacing and testing (Mason and Mitroff, 1981)	To strengthen the conceptual analysis of SSM with real-world stakeholder analysis (Vidgen, 1994)
	Radical change and business process redesign	IT as business enabler, rapid change in business environments (Wood et al., 1995)
	Introduction of ethical analysis	Stakeholders can have different moral ideals (Wood-Harper et al., 1996)
	Consideration of non-human stakeholders	To support a symmetrical treatment of social and technological factors (Vidgen and McMaster, 1996)
	Inclusion of technology foresight and future analysis	Consider the impact of the intervention on stakeholders (Avison et al., 1994, 1995 and the potential role of technology
Information modelling	Migration to object-oriented analysis (from structured methods)	The principles of O-O are more compatible with systems thinking than are the process/data separation and data flow metaphor of structured methods (e.g., the notion of systemic transformation and state change)
Socio-technical analysis and design	Ethnographic approaches to supplement ETHICS	Ethnographic approaches to socio-technical design (Randall et al., 1994) (Avison and Myers, 1995) aid the analyst in understanding how work is accomplished (Sachs, 1995)
Technical design and construction	Construction of technical artefacts is incorporated within the scope of the methodology	Prototyping, evolutionary, and rapid development approaches to system development require that analysis, design and construction be more tightly integrated (Budde et al., 1992)

provides a rationale for choosing between different methods (Oliga, 1991). In this sense, an information systems methodology, such as Multiview2, provides a basis for constructing a situation-specific method (Figure 4), which arises from a genuine engagement of the analyst with the problem situation (Wastell, 1996).

Although Multiview has been in a continual state of development since 1985, the reflections on Multiview in action over the last 10 years have suggested this radical re-definition of Multiview into Multiview2 which takes these experiences into account, along with the more recent literature and recognizing the new 'era' of the domain of information systems. Change is the norm, and the rapidly changing environment in which information systems development takes place suggests that there will be a further major re-definition of Multiview in an even shorter time-space (Vidgen et al., 2002). Most recent cases have concerned the use of Multiview in

Figure 4: Constructing the information systems development methodology (adapted from Checkland and Scholes, 1990, and Wood-Harper and Avison, 1992)

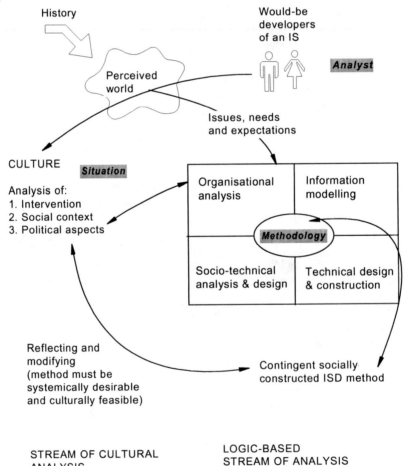

different contexts, for example, in developing countries (Kamsah and Wood-Harper, 1999) or for new application types, such as enterprise information systems (Kawalek and Wood-Harper, 2001) and Web development (Vidgen et al., 2002).

THE USE OF THE ACTION RESEARCH APPROACH

A second contribution of Multiview has been the use of action research, which led to its definition and redefinition, and the consequential spread of action research within the academic community of information systems (the authors have been part of a number of panels on action research at conferences such as ICIS and IFIP). Action research is one of a number of qualitative research approaches–others include case study, ethnography and grounded theory–which are particularly suited to application in natural settings, that is, to study social and cultural phenomena. As Myers and Avison (2002) show, action research has been accepted as a valid research method in applied fields such as organisational development and education, but in information systems it is only within the last decade that action research has started to make an impact. Action research combines theory with practice (and researchers with practitioners) through change and reflection in an immediate problematic situation. The use of Multiview can be said to be an 'exploration' in information systems development, and the action research cases provide an opportunity to see Multiview in operation in different situations.

Rapoport defines action research in the following way: "Action research aims to contribute both to the practical concerns of people in an immediate problematic situation and to the goals of social science by joint collaboration within a mutually acceptable ethical framework" (Rapoport, 1970, p.499). This definition draws attention to the collaborative aspect of action research and to possible ethical dilemmas that arise from its use.

Action research is often confused with case study research, but whereas case study research examines phenomena in their natural setting with the researcher as an independent outsider, in action research the researcher is also a participant. Grounded research might proceed through a series of interviews or observations to hypothesis formation. No hypothesis is assumed before the interviews in this case, thus attempting to avoid pre-judging the issues–it generates rather than tests theory. In participant observation (a research approach frequently associated with ethnography), although there is active involvement by the observer, that person does not seek to influence the situation more than would be expected from other participants. Action research is notable for the deliberate intervention of the researcher.

A brief overview of action research is provided by Susman and Evered (1978). Baskerville and Wood-Harper (1996) review the origins, techniques and roles associated with action research into information systems. This latter paper proposes what the authors call 'a rigorous approach' to action research and suggests certain domains of ideal use (such as systems development methodology as in the case of Multiview). As for many other exemplars mentioned in this paper, the authors discuss various problems, opportunities and strategies for those faced with conducting, reviewing or examining the research method.

As Avison et al. (1999) show, it is infeasible to design an appropriate methodology for information systems development in an academic's office without trying it out in many real-world situations. The academic may have read a lot about the subject, maybe having observed information systems development extensively in organisations and built up a series of case studies, and even developed a theory for information systems development–but this is not enough. In action research, the researcher wants to try out a theory with the practitioners in a real situation, gain feedback from this experience, modify the theory as a result of this feedback and try it again. Each iteration of the action research process adds to the theory, in this case a framework for information systems development, so that it is more likely to be appropriate for different situations.

However, there are problems as well as advantages of action research in information systems. On the positive side, action research allows the researcher great potential to utilise the ideas of users and change concepts and methods as the work develops. Researchers and 'subjects' cooperate in solving a real-life problem. It is particularly useful that action research allows work to take place in its natural setting and it gives the researcher an insight into real-life practical areas. Feedback from the practical application of techniques can be used to refine and improve those techniques and their description. Although the results of action research are of a qualitative nature, they do offer a degree of external validity because the theory developed can be interpreted and refined by others in other real-world situations.

Action research has proved helpful to the development of Multiview. The weaknesses in the descriptions of some of the techniques, such as data flow diagrams and entity life histories, was revealed when using them in early applications. The practicality of using techniques and tools contingent on a particular problem situation, as suggested by Multiview, can only be revealed by its use in different situations. Major omissions in the exposition of Multiview, such as the inadequacy of documentation procedures, project control and the lack of advice when selecting application packages, were revealed in the cases. Some assumptions in Multiview, such as the users' enthusiasm for participation and the low relative importance of the technical dimension, have also been questioned through this experience. The part played by researchers as active players in the problem situation (not merely 'impartial' observers), along with users and analysts, has meant that both researchers and practitioners have together influenced the practice (by implementing change in the problem situation) and the theory (by changing the Multiview approach).

CONCLUSIONS

Along with the contributions of other authors and practitioners, in defining Multiview, the authors have contributed to making information systems development a more balanced process of the technical on the one hand and human, social and organisational on the other. They have also made explicit the reality that information systems development is not a 'scientific,' prescriptive process, but a contingent one where the 'ideal' framework is interpreted for each combination of analysts, users and situation. The testing of the Multiview 'theory' in real-world situations through action research has provided us with many lessons about information systems development in practice as well as improved the definition of Multiview itself. The interest in Multiview over the years has had a secondary effect in promoting action research as a potentially valuable research approach in information systems.

However, there is presently a debate concerning information systems research, and in particular, perceived disadvantages of action research. The lack of impartiality of the researcher has led to its rejection by a number of researchers and academic departments. The lack of scientific discipline in such research makes it difficult for the work to be assessed for the award of research degrees and for publication in academic journals. A particular difficulty that universities have is persuading research-funding bodies that this type of research is as valid and as useful as conventional methods of scientific research. Further, although the researcher's intent is to conduct research while effecting change, the approach is sometimes branded with the description 'consultancy' and not research. The open-endedness of such research and the consequent flexibility necessary in writing a research proposal also provide additional difficulties. Further, a major consequence of the choice of the action research method is that the research is context-bound as opposed to context-free. It is difficult to determine the cause of a particular effect, which could be due to environment (including its subjects), researcher or methodology. This has been explicit in this research, but it can mean that action research produces narrow learning in its context because each situation is unique and cannot be repeated. This is a major criticism of action research–it does not easily produce generalisable learning.

However, in our research there has been an attempt to reconcile the potentially narrow learning from action research with the need for generalisable research. It is hoped that the generalised findings from our work will result in other researchers and practitioners applying the Multiview approach in other problem situations and will take into consideration the learning that emerges in the complex process of developing an information system. We believe that the definition and redefinition of Multiview, and its application in a number of real-world situations following the tenets of action research, has contributed to social and organisational aspects being included on the agenda in information systems development as much as technological and technical aspects. We claim that no other research approach could have led to the definition and refinement of Multiview as laid out in this chapter. Happily, the benefits of this research approach is now apparent to many IS academics, and action research has been the subject of papers in leading journals as well as conference panels.

ACKNOWLEDGEMENTS

We would like to acknowledge the contributions of many colleagues who have contributed to this research and, in particular, Lyn Antill, Richard Vidgen and Bob Wood.

REFERENCES

Argyris, C. and Schön, D. (1978). *Organisational Learning: A Theory of Action Perspective*. Reading, MA: Addison-Wesley.

Avison, D., Lau, F., Myers, M. D. and Nielson, P. A. (1999). Action research. *Communications of the ACM*, *42*(1), 94-97.

Avison, D. E. and Myers, M. D. (1995). Information systems and anthropology: An anthropological perspective on IT and organisational culture. *Information Technology & People*, *8*(3), 43-56.

Avison, D. E., Powell, P. L. and Adams, C. (1994). Identifying and incorporating change in information systems. *Systems Practice*, *7*(2), 143-159.

Avison, D. E., Powell, P. L., Keen, P., Klein, J. H. and Ward, S. (1995). Addressing the need for flexibility in information systems. *Journal of Management Systems*, *7*(2), 43-60.

Avison, D. E. and Wood-Harper, A. T. (1990). *Multiview: An Exploration in Information Systems Development*. New York: McGraw-Hill.

Avison, D. E., Wood-Harper, A. T., Vidgen, R. T. and Wood, J. R. G. (1998). A further exploration into information systems development: The evolution of Multiview2. *IT and People*, *11*(2), 124-139.

Baskerville, R. L. and Wood-Harper, A. T. (1996). A critical perspective on action research as a method for information systems research. *Journal of Information Technology, 11,* 235-246.

Budde, R., Kautz, K., Kuhlenkamp, K. and Züllighoven, H. (1992). *Prototyping– An Approach to Evolutionary Systems Development.* London: Springer Verlag.

Checkland, P. (1985). Systems theory and information systems. In Bemelmans, T. M. A. (Ed.), *Beyond Productivity: Information Systems Development for Organisational Effectiveness.* Amsterdam: North Holland.

Checkland, P. and Scholes, J. (1990). *Soft Systems Methodology in Practice.* Chichester: John Wiley & Sons.

Checkland, P. B. (1981). *Systems Thinking, Systems Practice.* New York: John Wiley & Sons.

Daniels, A. and Yeates, D. A. (1971). *Basic Training in Systems Analysis.* London: Pitman.

Downs, E., Clare, P. and Coe, I. (1991). *Structured Systems Analysis and Design Method: Application and Context.* Englewood Cliffs, NJ: Prentice Hall.

Episkopou, D. M. and Wood-Harper, A. T. (1985). The Multiview methodology: Applications and implications. In Bemelmans, T. M. A. (Ed.), *Beyond Productivity: Information Systems Development for Organisational Effectiveness.* Amsterdam: North Holland.

Kamsah, M. and Wood-Harper, A. T. (1999). EDI diffusion in Malaysia: Toward a multiple perspective framework. *Journal of Scientific and Industrial Research, 89,* 242-252.

Kawalek, P. and Wood-Harper, A. T. (2001). The finding of thorns: User participation in enterprise system implementation. *DataBase.*

Knights, D. and Murray, F. (1994). *Managers Divided: Organisation Politics and Information Technology Management.* Chichester: John Wiley & Sons.

Land, F. and Hirschheim, R. (1983). Participative systems design: Rationale, tools and techniques. *Journal of Applied Systems Analysis, 10.*

MacDonald, I. G. and Palmer, I. (1982). System development in a shared data environment, the D2S2 methodology. In Olle, T. W., Sol, H. G. and Verrijn-Stuart, A. A. (Eds.), *Information Systems Design Methodologies: A Comparative Review.* Amsterdam: North Holland.

Martin, J. (1990). *Information Engineering: Book 1 Introduction.* Englewood Cliffs, NJ: Prentice Hall.

Mason, R. and Mitroff, I. (1981). *Challenging Strategic Planning Assumptions.* New York: John Wiley & Sons.

Mitroff, I. and Linstone, H. (1993) *The Unbounded Mind, Breaking the Chains of Traditional Business Thinking*. New York: Oxford University Press.

Mitroff, I. L. (1983). Archetypal social systems analysis: On the deeper structure of human systems. *Academy of Management Review*, 8, 387-397.

Mumford, E. (1981). Participative systems design: Structure and method. *Systems, Objectives, Solutions*, *1*(1), 5-19.

Myers, M. D. and Avison, D. E. (2002). An introduction to qualitative research in information systems. In Myers, M. D. and Avison, D. E. (Eds.), *An Introduction to Qualitative Research in Information Systems: A Reader*. London: Sage.

Oliga, J. (1991). Methodological foundations of systems methodologies. In Flood, R. L. and Ackson, M. C. (Eds.), *Critical Systems Thinking: Directed Readings*. Chichester: John Wiley & Sons.

Quang, P. T. and Chartier-Kastler, C. (1991). *Merise in Practice*. Basingstoke: Macmillan.

Randall, D., Hughes, J. and Shapiro, D. (1994). Steps towards a partnership: Ethnography and system design. In Jirotka, M. and Goguen, J. (Eds.), *Requirements Engineering: Social and Technical Issues*. London: Academic Press.

Rapoport, R. N. (1970). Three dilemmas in action research. *Human Relations*, *23*(4), 499-513.

Sachs, P. (1995). Transforming work: Collaboration, learning, and design. *Communications of the ACM*, *38*(9), 36-44.

Susman, G. I. and Evered, R. D. (1978). An assessment of the scientific merits of action research. *Administrative Science Quarterly*, *23*(4), 582-603.

Vidgen, R. (1994). Research in progress: Using stakeholder analysis to test primary task conceptual models in information systems development. In *Proceedings of the Second Annual Conference on Information System Methodologies*, BCS IS Methodologies Specialist Group, Edinburgh.

Vidgen, R. (1996). *A Multiple Perspectives Approach to Information System Quality*, Unpublished PhD Thesis. University of Salford, Salford.

Vidgen, R. and McMaster, T. (1996). Black boxes, non-human stakeholders, and the translation of IT through mediation. In Orlikowski, W., Walsham, G., Jones, M. and DeGross, J. (Eds.), *Information Technology and Changes in Organisational Work*. London: Chapman & Hall.

Vidgen, R., Avison, D. E., Wood, R. and Wood-Harper, A. T. (2002). *Developing Web Applications*. Butterworth-Heinneman.

Wastell, D. (1996). The fetish of technique: Methodology as a social defence. *Information Systems Journal*, *6*(1), 25-40.

Wood, J. R. G., Vidgen, R. T., Wood-Harper, A. T. and Rose, J. (1995). Business process redesign: Radical change or reactionary tinkering? In Burke, G. and Peppard, J. (Eds.), *Examining Business Process Reengineering: Current Perspectives and Research Directions*. London: Kogan Page.

Wood-Harper, A. T., Antill, L. and Avison, D. E. (1985). *Information Systems Definition: The Multiview Approach*. Oxford: Blackwell Scientific Publications.

Wood-Harper, A. T. and Avison, D. E. (1992). Reflections from the experience of using Multiview: Through the lens of soft systems methodology. *Systemist*, *14*(3).

Wood-Harper, A. T., Corder, S., Wood, J. and Watson, H. (1996). How we profess: The ethical systems analyst. *Communications of the ACM*, *39*(3), 69-77.

Yourdon, E. and Constantine, L. L. (1978). *Structured Design*. New York: Yourdon Press.

Chapter II

From Technical Change to Socio-Technical Change: Towards a Proactive Approach to the Treatment of Organisational Issues

Neil F. Doherty and Malcolm King
Loughborough University, UK

ABSTRACT

The organisational application of information technology commonly evokes a wide variety of impacts upon the enterprise as a whole, and the individual members of staff affected by it. However, there is much evidence to suggest that the identification and management of such impacts, which is typically referred to as the treatment of organisational issues, is poorly handled in practice. The primary aim of the research project, described in this chapter, was to develop a proactive approach to the analysis of organisational impacts. The aim of the approach, which is presented as a flow diagram, is to clearly articulate the sequence of activities that have to be undertaken and the decisions that need to be addressed to ensure that all organisational issues are treated effectively. This approach has been formulated from an extensive review of the literature, and the authors' experience working in this domain for the past six years. It is argued that this approach may well succeed, where many of its predecessors have failed, as it complements, rather than replaces, existing development tools and methods. Moreover, as this approach adopts a common-sense perspective, it should be relatively easy to learn and apply.

Finally, it benefits from adopting a proactive, flexible and coherent approach to the treatment of organisational issues.

> *"There is nothing more difficult to plan, more doubtful of success, nor more dangerous to manage than the creation of a new system. For the initiator has the enmity of all who would profit by the preservation of the old system, and merely lukewarm defenders in those who would gain by the new one."*
>
> **Count Machiavelli (1513)**

INTRODUCTION

The implementation of information technology within organisations almost invariably results in a wide variety of impacts upon the design of the business, its economic performance and the working conditions of members of staff; technical change is the catalyst for organisational change. For example, the introduction of an enterprise resource planning system (ERP) within a manufacturing company is likely to have a significant impact on that organisation's business processes, structure, culture and enterprise level performance, as well as the motivation, job specifications and performance of individual employees. It is suggested that while many impacts can be classified as planned outcomes, others are resultant side effects, which can be of a positive or a negative nature. Indeed, negative impacts are quite common, as IT-induced organisational change often results in user resistance and, in extreme cases, possibly even system rejection (Marcus & Robey, 1983; Cooper, 1994). These views are echoed by Martinsons and Chong (1999) who note that *"Even good technology can be sabotaged if it is perceived to interfere with the established social network."*

Historically, information systems development projects have been viewed as exercises in technical change, rather than socio-technical change: *"Most investments in IT are technology-led, reflecting too technical an emphasis"* (Clegg, 2000). As Eason (1988; p 44) has noted, *"Traditional approaches to the development of information systems have concentrated on the delivery of the technology, rather than emphasising the human and organisational changes that are required in order to ensure that the system delivers meaningful benefits."* This is a dangerous strategy, because unforeseen and unresolved negative impacts may increase the likelihood of systems failure. Moreover, beneficial impacts, of both a planned and resultant nature, may not be fully realised without an appropriate programme of organisational change. Systems development projects, therefore, should be primarily considered to be an exercise in organisational change, in which all organisational issues need to be proactively managed.

Previous research has typically used the term '*human and organisational issues*' (Hornby et al., 1992), or more simply '*organisational issues*' (Ahn & Skudlark, 1997; Lederer & Nath, 1991; Doherty & King, 1998a) to describe the full range of organisational impacts of technology that must be managed. While the importance of treating organisational issues is now widely acknowledged (for example: Doherty & King, 1998b; Clegg et al., 1997), little progress has been made in the development of practical treatment approaches that have succeeded in making the transition from research laboratory to widespread commercial usage. One approach to the treatment of organisational issues, with perhaps the greatest practical potential, may well be the '*organisational impact analysis*' (Sauer, 1993), an area which to date has not been widely researched. The primary aim of the research project described in this chapter, was therefore, to develop an innovative organisational impact analysis procedure for the proactive treatment of organisational issues. The following section of the chapter provides a discussion of some of the key contributions to the literature in this domain before an innovative approach to the treatment of organisational issues is presented in the third section. The final two sections provide a detailed discussion of the implications of this research and a summary of its contribution.

ORGANISATIONAL ISSUES DEFINED AND CLASSIFIED

Confidence in the application of information systems has been severely dented, by the litany of high-profile systems failures, such as the London Ambulance System (Beynon-Davis, 1995), the Taurus System (Drummond, 1996) and the Benefits Payment Card System (NAO, 2000) that have afflicted organisations in recent years. Moreover, the information systems literature is very clear on two points; general levels of failure are far too high and the primary cause of this problem is the failure to adequately treat organisational issues (Ewusi-Mensah & Przasnyski, 1994; Lederer & Nath, 1991; Lyytinen & Hirschiem, 1987). However, whilst this has significantly increased levels of interest in the role of '*organisational issues*' (e.g., Clegg et al., 1997; Doherty & King 1998a), there have been few attempts to explicitly define the term. Indeed, even the term 'organisational issue' has not received universal acceptance. For example, Markus and Robey (1983) and Pliskin et al. (1993) follow the example of Schultz and Slevin (1975) and refer to the '*organisational validity*' of systems, while Hornby et al (1992) and Lucas (1975) prefer the term '*human and organisational issues*,' and Clegg et al. (1997) refer to '*human and organisational factors*.' For the purposes of this chapter, however, the generic term '*organisational issues*' (Ahn & Skulark, 1997; Lederer & Nath, 1991; Grundin & Markus, 1997; Doherty & King, 1998a) is preferred because of its common usage, and its simplicity.

Irrespective of the precise terms used, and the lack of explicit definitions, it is clear that all these researchers have been concerned with a similar set of issues. Typically, organisational issues have been defined by providing examples of '*non-technical*' aspects of systems development, which might have an impact on the ultimate success or failure of a project (Eason, 1988; Clegg et al., 1989). A careful analysis of these examples led us to develop a provisional definition for the term '*organisational issue*,' which was presented in an earlier piece of work (Doherty & King, 1997). Over the course of a number of pieces of work (Doherty & King, 1998a, 1998b, 2000), the provisional definition has been refined into the following working definition:

> "*Those issues which need to be treated during the systems development process to ensure that the individual human, wider social and economic impacts of the resultant computer-based information system are likely to be desirable.*"

To fully understand the above definition, it is necessary to articulate what is meant by the term '*treated*.' To treat a specific organisational issue, it is necessary to firstly evaluate the likely organisational impact associated with it, and then if necessary take steps to ensure that the resulting impact is likely to be desirable. For example, if it is found that a proposed system is likely to be poorly suited to an organisation's working practices, then it will be necessary to either modify the system's technical specification, so that the mis-match is avoided, or redesign the working practices so that they are well aligned with the system. In essence, the treatment of organisational issues is the mechanism by which the project team should align the capabilities afforded, and the constraints imposed, by the technical system with the requirements and characteristics of an organisation and its individual employees (see Figure 1).

A literature review was initiated to identify specific issues that conformed to the definition of organisational issues presented earlier. Ultimately, a total of 14 distinct organisational issues were identified that could be segmented into four discrete classes of issue: organisational contribution, human issues, transitional issues and organisational alignment issues. These issues have been used and validated in a number of empirical research studies that have been conducted over the past five years (for example: Doherty & King, 1998a, 1998b, 2000; Al-Mushayt et al., 2001). A full classification of organisational issues is presented in Table 1.

In addition to the four classes of organisational issue highlighted in Table 1, it is also important to make the distinction between those issues that relate to planned impacts, as opposed to those concerning resultant impacts. These two distinct classes of impact can be differentiated, as follows:

- **Planned impacts:** Some organisational issues relate to impacts that are envisaged to be a systems development project's critical outcomes. For example, the system's planned impacts on an organisation's performance will

Figure 1: The role of organisational issues

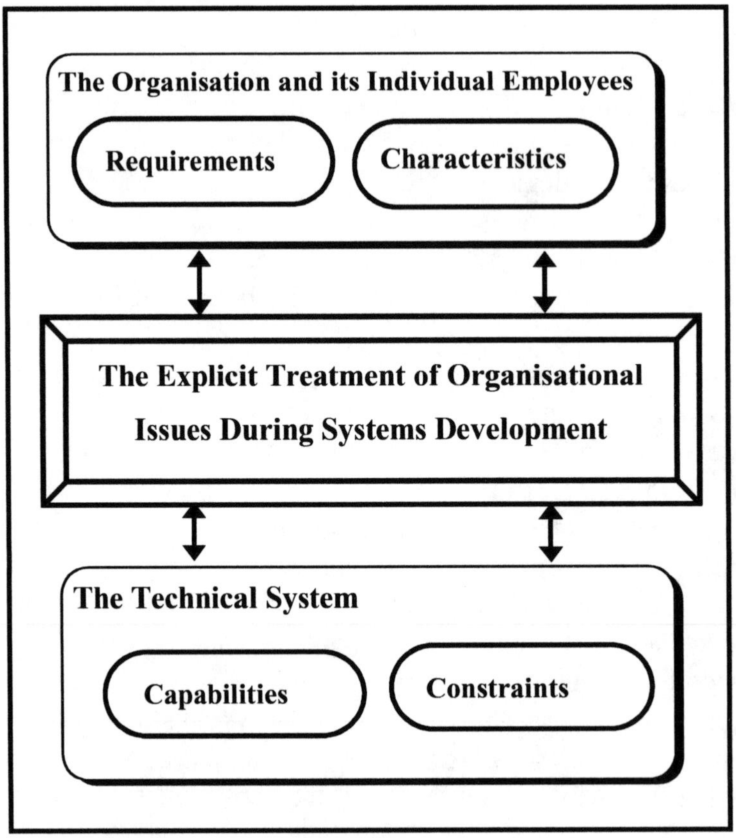

need to be established at a project's outset–how will the system contribute to an organisation's efficiency, effectiveness and competitive positioning? It may also be possible at the project's outset to identify desired organisational impacts relating to an organisation's culture, working practices or business processes.

- **Resultant impacts:** Other impacts can be considered to be by-products of the application of systems. For example, the implementation of a system may impact upon an organisation's power distribution, structure or working practices in ways that had not, or could not have, been envisaged at the project's outset. The concept of '*resultant impacts*' is similar to FitzGerald's (1998) notion of '*second order effects.*' If these effects are explicitly addressed during the system's evaluation/development process, then they can be '*if necessary mitigated, turned to advantage or exploited*' (FitzGerald, 1998).

The distinction between planned and resultant impacts is important, as it has significant implications for how they are evaluated and actioned in the proposed approach to the treatment of organisational issues described in the remainder of this chapter.

Table 1: Organisational issues classified

Category	Specific Issues/Areas of Impact
Organisational Contribution: Issues relating to the extent to which it is envisaged that the financial, operational and strategic performance of an organisation will be enhanced through the introduction of a new system.	Ability to satisfy current needs of organisation
	Capacity to support future needs of organisation
	Prioritisation of tasks, in line with organisational needs
	Degree of alignment with information systems strategy
	Assessment of impact on key business processes
Human-Centred Issues: This category focuses on issues relating to the interface between individual users and the proposed system. These issues can significantly affect the system's usage and ultimately its level of success.	Assessment of health & safety/ergonomic implications
	Evaluation of user motivation/needs
	Assessment of implications of user working styles/IT skills
	Consideration of job redesign implications
Organisational Alignment: This group of issues focuses upon the degree of alignment between a proposed system and its organisational context.	Impact on an organisation's structure
	Implications for organisational culture
	Effect on distribution of power
Transitional Issues: This class is concerned with those practical issues which might affect the successful transition to the new system.	Consideration of timing of implementation
	Assessment of organisational disruption

AN APPROACH TO THE TREATMENT OF ORGANISATIONAL ISSUES

The aims of this section are to establish the rationale for the development of a coherent and proactive approach to the treatment of organisational issues, to describe and review the approach, and then to consider its practical application.

This approach has been formulated from an extensive review of the literature, and the authors' experience working in this domain for the past six years (for example: Doherty & King, 1997, 1998a, 1998b, 2000 and Al-Mushayt et al., 2001).

THE RATIONALE FOR A PROACTIVE APPROACH TO THE TREATMENT OF ORGANISATIONAL ISSUES

Typically approaches to the treatment of organisational issues have been reactive rather than proactive (Lim et al., 1992), and can be characterised as '*too little too late*' and '*marginalised*' (Clegg et al., 1996). System developers have typically employed methods, developed by the IS/IT community, which focus upon the delivery of a technically effective system, on time and within budget (Earl, 1992; Ward & Elvin, 1999). This state of affairs has primarily arisen for the following reasons:

1.   Organisational issues are often intangible, difficult to articulate and touch upon politically sensitive issues (Doherty & King, 1998a).

2.   Typically, the management and execution of information systems projects is delegated to technical specialists, people who do not have the training, skills or indeed the motivation to treat organisational issues (Hornby et al., 1992; Clegg, 2000). Consequently IT professionals often develop ambivalent or even hostile attitudes towards the treatment of organisational issues.

3.   There are relatively few effective socio-technical methods, tools and techniques specifically designed to facilitate the treatment of organisational issues. The wide variety of tools, methods and techniques that have been developed have been conspicuous in their failure to make the transition from research laboratory or university department to widespread acceptance and usage among the systems development community. As Clegg notes (2000), "*In sum socio-technical principles and practices have not had the impact that their proponents might wish.*"

The above barriers are to some extent interdependent. For example, the lack of appropriate tools is probably due, at least in part, to the intangible nature of the issues but also to technical specialists' attitudes, which don't predispose them to trialling tools, when they are made available. Moreover, systems developers' ambivalent attitudes have probably been influenced by the intangible and sensitive nature of the organisational issues. Together, these barriers have contributed an environment where the typical approach to the treatment of organisational issues consists of implementing a system and then reactively dealing with any impacts, as and when they arise. Unfortunately, as was noted in the introduction, this approach is inappropriate for two reasons. Firstly, unforeseen negative impacts may increase the likelihood of systems failure, and secondly planned benefits may not be fully realised without appropriate organisational change. Figure 2 presents an overview of the situation described above. An extra important element of Figure 2 is the notion of the '*reinforcement of attitudes*' feedback loop. The idea being that if IT professionals have experienced problems with respect to the treatment of organisational issues in previous projects, then this might reinforce their negative attitudes towards them. In effect we have a vicious circle: ambivalent or even negative attitudes towards the treatment of organisational issues make systems developers unwilling to experiment with more organisationally oriented tools and approaches, which hinders their development and wider usage. This in turn contributes to the ineffective treatment of organisational issues, which reinforces systems developers' ambivalent attitudes to the treatment of organisational issues.

There is, therefore, a strong incentive for system development teams to find ways to overcome the barriers described above, so that in future organisational

Figure 2: Factors affecting the treatment of organisational issues

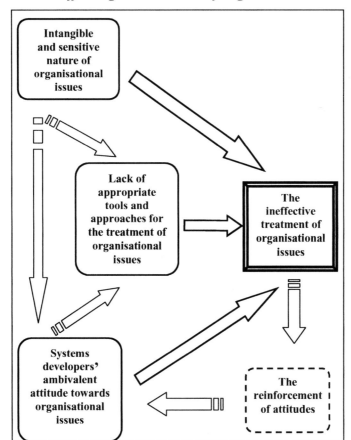

issues are treated in a more proactive and coherent way. While there is little that can be done in terms of changing the intangible and sensitive nature of organisational issues, there is far more scope to improve systems developers' attitudes towards organisational issues, and also improve the availability and usage of tools and approaches to facilitate their treatment.

As this chapter is primarily focused upon the creation of a proactive approach to the treatment of organisational issues, the following discussion concentrates primarily on tools and approaches rather than the attitudes of technical specialists. However, it is demonstrated later that the provision of effective tools and approaches might have a significant, yet indirect effect upon the attitudes of technical specialists.

Many academics and researchers have already taken up the challenge to explore ways in which the processes by which organisational issues are treated can be improved. As a consequence, the academic journals have been exposed to discussions of a wide variety of tools, techniques and methods designed to support the treatment of organisational issues. Such approaches usually fall into one of the following categories:

1. **Socio-technical methods:** Socio-technical methods attempt to produce information systems that are technically efficient and coherent, while also being sensitive to organisational and human needs: "*technical and organisational aspects are considered to be equally important*" (Mumford, 1996; p 9). Specific methods which adopt a more explicit organisational orientation include: ETHICS (Mumford, 1996), Multiview (Avison & Wood-Harper, 1990), Soft Systems Method (Checkland, 1981) and Joint Application Design (Wood & Silver, 1989).

2. **Tools and techniques for the treatment of specific issues:** Many researchers have attempted to develop tools and techniques to aid in the treatment of specific organisational issues. For example, Clegg et al. (1996) have developed a suite of five interdependent tools which have been designed to focus upon organisational scenario analysis, task analysis, task allocation, job design and usability, and can be used in conjunction with more conventional development methods.

3. **An organisational impacts analysis:** Laudon and Laudon (2000, p. 419) have defined an '*organisational impact analysis*' as a study of the way in which a proposed system will affect organisational structure, attitudes, decision-making and operations; however, they also note that in practice this is a much neglected area. Sauer (1993; p 324-325) also makes a strong argument for undertaking an '*assessment of the impact of the information system in the organisational setting,*' but his interest is primarily concerned with its impact upon the distribution of power.

While each of the above contributions has been very useful in increasing our understanding of the nature and treatment of organisational issues, there is little evidence that these contributions have made much of an impact on the practice of systems development. This is probably, at least in part, due to technical specialists' preferences for the more technically oriented tools and techniques, which makes them reluctant to experiment with more organisationally focused offerings. Additional explanations for this are summarised below:

1. **Socio-technical methods:** The socio-technical approaches are not commonly used because systems developers are loath to replace their existing methods, which they are generally happy with from a technical perspective, with a completely new, and often untested approach. As Enid Mumford (1997) notes: *"Management tended to regard these successful (socio-technical) projects as one-offs; there was no great enthusiasm or motivation to spread the approach through their companies."*

2. **Tools and techniques for the treatment of specific issues:** Tools and techniques tend to be very narrow in their focus and therefore limited with respect to the number of organisational issues they can treat. Moreover, most tools have been developed on an experimental basis, rather than with a view to creating a commercially viable product.

3. **An organisational impacts analysis:** Previous descriptions of organisational impact analysis from the literature tend to focus on the concept rather than the practicalities of implementation, and therefore offer little in the way of a workable solution.

The above analysis suggests that one potentially rewarding area for research is through the specification of a coherent and proactive procedure to facilitate the analysis of organisational impacts. The remainder of this section describes such an approach.

A Proactive Approach for the Treatment of Organisational Issues

A schematic representation of the proposed approach for the proactive treatment of organisational issues is presented in Figure 3. Each of the major processes and decision points on this diagram, all of which have been numbered, are discussed below:

1. **Identification of pre-requisite organisational impacts:** While many organisational issues will not be treated until a systems development project is well under way, others will need to be considered right at the outset, if they are to be the planned outputs of the project. For example, while current organisational needs have been classified as an organisational issue, they will need to be addressed at the project's outset, to provide a clear focus for the development effort. As Clegg (2000) notes, *"A system needs to be useful, to meet some articulated purpose, to meet the needs of the business, its users and managers."* Indeed, most of the organisational issues previously categorised as organisational contribution issues will need to be explicitly addressed at the project's outset. It could even be that issues, other than

Figure 3: Proposed approach for proactive treatment of organisational issues

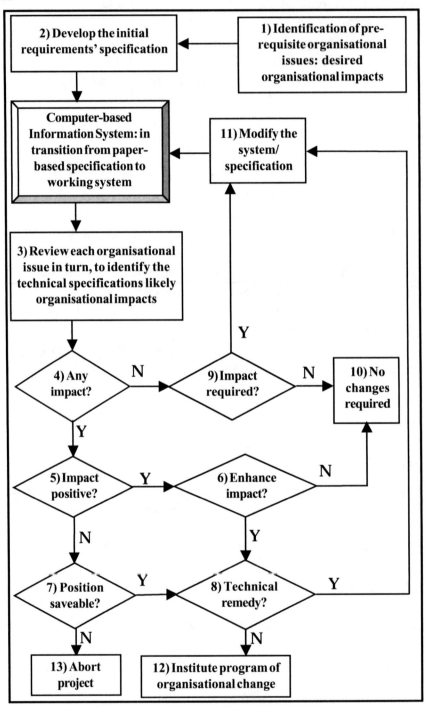

organisational contribution ones, might act as a point of departure for the project. It is possible, for example, to envisage circumstances where an organisation might have cultural objectives, such as facilitating a more empowered workforce, or structural objectives, such as flattening the organisation.

2. **Development of initial requirements specification:** The development of an initial requirement's specification for the delivery of an information system is probably the best understood and certainly the most written about aspect of the proposed approach as it is a fundamental component of all development methods. Indeed, this aspect of the approach can be conducted using the proprietary or in-house method of the developer's choosing.

Having successfully generated an initial requirements' specification, the following multi-phase approach is applied to each organisational issue in turn. This approach assesses the organisational impacts associated with each organisational issue (phase 3), before using the six-phase decision-making process (phases 4-9) to determine the appropriate course of action; namely: no action required, modify the specification, initiate a programme of organisational change or abort the project. The same process is repeated for each organisational issue, in turn, until all 14 organisational issues, as described in Table 1, have been appropriately treated. Each of these steps is described more fully in the following discussion:

3. **Review of organisational issues:** At various stages in the systems development process, as the information system progresses from a paper-based specification through to a working system, the full range of organisational issues, as highlighted in Table 1, should be reviewed. The objective of the review procedure is to assess the likely organisational, economic and human impacts of the information system, once operational. Both Eason (1988; p 82) and Clegg (2000) have emphasised the importance of this process, in which they have commented, respectively, that system designers should "*assess the organisational consequences*" and "*trace the possible impacts*" of all design choices. The review of organisational issues should be conducted at regular intervals, as it helps organisations to take appropriate actions to help facilitate the realisation of positive impacts, while also reducing the likelihood of negative impacts. There are many methods that could be employed for reviewing these impacts. For example, it might be achieved by assembling a team of users, managers and technical specialists, who will thoroughly review the design and seek to identify impacts. In addition to identifying impacts, this process is also likely to be beneficial in terms of increasing user participation and ultimately ownership of the resultant system. Other more structured approaches to the review of impacts might include the application of specific tools and techniques. For example the suite of tools developed by Clegg et al. (1996) might have a role to play in evaluating a range of different organisational

impacts. Another important issue is the timing of the review process, which is fully discussed in the following section of this chapter.

4. **Determine existence of organisational impacts:** The output of the review procedure, described above, will be an assessment of whether there is a significant organisational impact, associated with each organisational issue.

5. **Evaluation of desirability of impacts:** This phase requires that the impact, associated with each organisational issue, is reviewed to assess its desirability. As noted earlier computer-based information systems can have both positive impacts, such as delivery of benefits or increased motivation, and negative impacts, such as user resistance or increases in operating costs.

6. **Assessment of potential for increasing desirability of impacts**: If the previous stage has identified a desirable impact, associated with an organisational issue, it is important to consider whether the impact could be made even more positive if the information system design were to be modified. For example, if it was found that the system is likely to empower the workforce, the question should be asked as to whether the design could be modified to reinforce this positive effect.

7. **Is the situation retrievable?:** In situations where a potentially undesirable impact of the system's operation has been identified, it is necessary to consider whether the situation is retrievable or not. If, for example, it has been found that the system is unlikely to deliver the key benefits or is likely to evoke high levels of user disquiet and resistance, then the option of aborting the system should be considered. Previous studies (e.g., Sauer, 1993; Ewusi-Mensah & Przasnyski, 1994) have recognised the need for organisations to have an abandonment strategy, and the organisational impact analysis might prove to be an effective way of operationalising it.

8. **Is the remedy technical?:** Having identified potentially negative, yet retrievable impacts associated with the system implementation, a decision must be made as to whether the remedy is of a technical or organisational nature. If the appropriate remedy is technical, then a change to the system's specification must be initiated; otherwise, an appropriate programme of organisational change must be drawn up, and ultimately implemented. It should be noted that in some cases the best solution might be to modify the technical specification and, in parallel, initiate organisational change. For example, an analysis of a systems impact on user motivation might identify a negative outcome, such as user resistance or resentment. Potential solutions in such circumstances might include changing the specification so that users have more control over the system's operation, or improving the users' terms and conditions, or making both the technical and organisational changes.

9. **Evaluation of potential for impacts:** If it has been discovered that there is no impact associated with a particular organisational issue, then it is important

to question whether there should be an impact. For example, if it found that the introduction of the system is likely to leave the working practices and business processes unaltered, then questions might be raised. As researchers such as Venkatramann (1991) and Hammer (1990) have noted, simply automating existing processes is unlikely to deliver significant organisational benefits.

10. **No changes required:** In the cases where there is no actual impact or potential for any specific organisational issue, there is no requirement to either change the system's specification or to institute a programme of organisational change.

11. **Modification of specification:** In many situations the organisational issues review process will necessitate changes to the system's specification, in order to correct a negative impact or evoke a more positive impact. In the latter stages of the systems development life-cycle, it is likely that any changes will be made to the system itself, rather than the specification.

12. **Development of programme of organisational change:** In situations where organisational impacts have been identified that have judged to desirable, it is important that a programme of organisational change is planned and implemented to ensure that the impact is realised. If, for example, it has been found that the system is likely to impact on working practices, then it is essential that someone is made responsible for redesigning the working practices and considering related issues, such as job descriptions and performance monitoring. If it is simply assumed that the system can be implemented and the desired changes to working practices will automatically ensue, then problems may well arise. One of the primary criticisms of the formal inquiry into the failure of the CAD system was that the management of the London Ambulance Service (Beynon-Davies, 1995) had envisaged that the implementation of the system would automatically bring about changes to the working practices of staff, rather than explicitly reviewing and planning for its organisational impact.

13. **Abort project:** In situations where it has been found that the introduction of an information system is likely to result in significant organisational impacts of a negative nature, the project should be aborted.

THE APPLICATION OF THE TREATMENT APPROACH

As noted during the previous discussion of the approach, organisational issues are treated both at the outset of the development process and at regular intervals once the development project is underway. At the initiation of the project, it is necessary to establish desired outcomes associated with respect to specific organisational issues. This exercise is likely to highlight specific benefits or perhaps cultural or process-oriented changes that will act as a focal point for the establishment of the requirements specification. Once the project is underway, the big questions are when and how often should organisational issues be treated? If organisational issues are treated infrequently, there is a danger that important impacts will be ignored or that expensive rework, once the system has been implemented, will have to be undertaken to take account of them. If they are considered too frequently, then the process itself becomes very time consuming and costly.

It is likely that organisational issues should be treated at least two or three times during the development process. For example, natural points for their treatment might be after the completion of the requirements specification, then again at the end of the design exercise and lastly when the working system has been delivered, but prior to implementation. It should also be remembered that many organisational issues are interdependent, and consequently changes made with respect to one specific issue might engender impacts in other areas. For example, if changes are made to the specification in order to provide further benefits, then it will be necessary to go through the treatment procedure again to determine whether this has a knock on effect for any other issues. One of the obvious benefits of adopting a two- or three-phase iterative approach is that it allows changing requirements to be monitored and accommodated on an on-going basis.

A Critique of the Proposed Approach

Many respected information systems researchers have recognised the need for more effective socio-technical tools and methods to be developed. For example, Clegg et al. (1997) have identified the pressing need for "*the development of new standards, methods and tools to incorporate human and organisational factors along with technical concern.*" While the work described in this chapter is not trying to develop a highly specific tool or technique, it does propose a more generic framework to ensure that organisational issues are treated in a systematic and coherent way. Having proposed a framework for the proactive analysis of organisational impacts, the critical question is why might this socio-technical approach be successful in gaining wider usage when other approaches have failed? The chief benefits of this approach are that it presents systems developers with a systematic framework which obliges them to confront organisational issues and provides them with the means to effectively navigate their way through a very complex decision-making process. Moreover, a comparison of this approach with some of its predecessors allows the following distinctions to be made:

- **Complementary:** The proposed approach complements, rather than re-places, existing development tools and methods, and there is no requirement for systems developers to abandon their tried and tested practices. For example, this approach could be used in unison with most systems develop-ment methods, even very formal ones such as SSADM.
- **Straightforward:** The approach adopts a common-sense perspective, and it should therefore be relatively easy to learn and apply.

- **Proactive:** By using this approach organisations will ensure that potential problems are recognised and negated, and opportunities are identified and exploited in a timely and effective manner.
- **Comprehensive:** In many ways the work presented in this chapter has strong associations with previous work focused upon benefits realisation management: *"the process of organising and managing, such that the potential benefits arising from the use of IT are actually realised"* (Ward & Elvin, 1999). However, while benefits realisation management typically focuses upon the management of planned positive outcomes, the organisational impact analysis addresses a wider variety of impacts: planned and resultant, positive and negative. Moreover, the decision-making procedure clearly articulates the full range of strategies for treating organisational issues, namely *"modify the requirements specification," "initiate a programme of organisational change," "no action required"* or in extreme cases *"abort the project."*
- **Flexible:** The approach is highly flexible and can be adapted to suit the requirements of a wide variety of information systems projects. For example, it is equally applicable when acquiring a package, as it is when adopting a *"tailor-made"* approach, although in the former case, the degree to which the technical specification can be modified might be quite limited, so initiating programmes of organisational change might be more common.

It has been recognised (Mumford, 1997) that if the socio-technical approach is to be widely used in the organisational context then its supporters *"must be able to demonstrate that its use leads to efficiency, profitability and a high-morale labour force."* It is suggested that the complementary, straightforward, proactive, comprehensive and flexible orientation of the proposed approach may make its use acceptable to the IT practitioner. If this were to be the case, then the reinforcement of negative attitudes highlighted in Figure 1 might just be transformed into a positive feedback loop. In terms of the limitations of the proposed approach, the key deficiency, at present, is a lack of detail with respect to how each of the organisational impacts might best be evaluated. However, work is currently being undertaken to provide more explicit guidance on evaluation techniques which can be integrated into the framework.

CONCLUSIONS

Information technology is now a ubiquitous and increasingly critical part of the fabric of the modern organisation, supporting its day-to-day operations and all aspects of the decision-making process, as well as its strategic positioning. It is therefore not perhaps surprising that the implementation of a new technology or information system is likely to result in a wide array of impacts to the organisation, as well as the working lives of individual employees. It is argued that while many impacts can be classified as planned outcomes, others are resultant side effects, which can be of a positive or a negative nature. Moreover it is suggested that all such impacts must be explicitly and proactively treated to ensure that any potential negative impacts are identified and resolved prior to implementation and to ensure that all beneficial impacts, of both the planned or the resultant variety, are fully realised. The major contribution of the work presented in this chapter is that it proposes a systematic, multi-phase decision-making process, to ensure that all organisational issues are treated in a timely and effective manner.

From the practitioner perspective, the primary contribution of this work may well be that it presents systems developers with a framework for effectively navigating their way through a very complex decision-making process. Moreover, should this approach gain wider usage, it should facilitate the effective treatment of organisational issues, and in so doing may very well reduce levels of systems failure. The chapter should also be of interest to the researcher, as it presents a new and innovative way of viewing the management of socio-technical change that can act as a springboard for further research. It also provides a comprehensive review of an increasingly important body of literature. Immediate priorities, in terms of follow-up research, must focus upon seeking opportunities to apply and validate the approach in a live information systems project, as well as using practical experiences and theoretical insights to add further layers of definition to the framework.

REFERENCES

Ahn, J. and Skudlark, A. (1997). Resolving conflict of interests in the process of an information system implementation for advanced telecommunication services. *Journal of Information Technology, 12*, 3-13.

Al-Mushayt, O., Doherty, N. F. and King, M. (2001). An investigation into the relative success of alternative approaches to the treatment of organizational issues in systems development projects. *Organization Development Journal, 19*(1), 31-48.

Avison, D. and Wood-Harper, A. T. (1990). *Multiview: An Exploration in Information Systems Development*. Maidenhead: McGraw-Hill.

Benyon-Davies, P. (1995). Information systems failure: The case of the London Ambulance Service's computer-aided dispatch project. *European Journal of Information Systems, 4*, 71-184.

Checkland, P. B. (1981). *Systems Thinking, Systems Practice*. Chichester: John Wiley & Sons.

Clegg, C. W., Warr, P., Green, T., Monk, A., Allison, G. and Landsdale, M. (1989). *People and Computers: How to Evaluate Your Company's New Technology*. Chichester: Ellis Horwood.

Clegg, C. W., Coleman, P., Hornby, P., McClaren, R., Robson, J., Carey, N. and Symon, G. (1996). Tools to incorporate some psychological and organisational issues during the development of computer-based systems. *Ergonomics*, *39*(3), 482-511.

Clegg, C. W., Axtell, C., Damadoran, L., Farbey, B., Hull, R., Lloyd-Jones, R., Nicholls, J., Sell, R. and Tomlinson, C. (1997). Information technology: A study of performance and the role of human and organizational factors. *Ergonomics*, *40*(9), 851-871.

Clegg, C. W. (2000). Socio-technical principles for system design. *Applied Ergonomics*, *31*, 463-477.

Cooper, R. B. (1994). The inertial impact of culture on IT implementation. *Information & Management*, *27*, 17-31.

Doherty, N. F. and King, M. (1997). The treatment of organisational issues in IS development projects. In Aviston, D. (Ed.), *Key Issues in Information Systems*, 363-375. *UKAIS Conference*. Southampton: McGraw-Hill.

Doherty, N. F. and King, M. (1998a). The consideration of organizational issues during the systems development process: An empirical analysis. *Behaviour & Information Technology*, *17*(1), 41-51.

Doherty, N. F. and King, M. (1998b). The importance of organisational issues in systems development. *Information Technology & People*, *11*(2), 104-123.

Doherty, N. F. and King, M. (2000). The treatment of organisational issues in systems development projects: The implications for the evaluation of IT investments. In Brown, A. and Remenyi, D. (Eds.), *Proceedings of the Seventh European Conference on Information Technology Evaluation*, 49-58. *ECITE 2000*, Trinity College, Dublin.

Drummond, H. (1996). The politics of risk: Trials and tribulations of the Taurus project. *Journal of Information Technology*, *11*(4), 347-358.

Earl, M. (1992). Putting IT in its place: A polemic for the nineties. *Journal of Information Technology*, *7*(2), 100-108.

Eason, K. (1988). *Information Technology and Organizational Change*. London: Taylor & Francis.

Ewusi-Mensah, K. and Przasnyski, Z. (1994). Factors contributing to the abandonment of information systems development projects. *Journal of Information Technology*, *9*, 185-201.

Fitzgerald, G. (1998). Evaluating information systems projects: A multidimensional approach. *Journal of Information Technology*, *13*, 15-27.

Grundin, J. and Markus, M. L. (1997). Organizational issues in the development and implementation of interactive systems. In Helander, M., Landauer, T. K. and Prabhu, P. (Eds.), *Handbook of Human-Computer Interaction*. New York: Elsevier Science.

Hammer, M. (1990). Re-engineering work: Don't automate, obliterate. *Harvard Business Review*, (July-August), 104-112.

Hornby, C., Clegg, C., Robson, J., McClaren, C., Richardson, S. and O'Brien, P. (1992). Human and organizational issues in information systems development. *Behaviour & Information Technology, 11*(3), 160-174.

Laudon, K. C. and Laudon, J. P. (2000). *Management Information Systems.* Upper Saddle River, NJ: Prentice Hall.

Lederer, A. L. and Nath R. (1991). Managing organizational issues in systems development. *Journal of Systems Management, 24*(11), 23-27.

Lim, K., Long, J. and Silcock, N. (1992). Integrating human factors with the Jackson system development method: An illustrated overview. *Ergonomics, 35*(10), 1135-1161.

Lucas, H. C. (1975). *Why Information Systems Fail.* New York: Columbia University Press.

Lyytinen, K. and Hirschheim, R. (1987). Information systems failures: A survey and classification of the empirical literature. *Oxford Surveys in Information Technology, 4*, 257-309.

Markus, M. and Robey, D. (1983). The organisational validity of management information systems. *Human Relations, 36*(3), 203-226.

Martinsons, M. and Chong, P. (1999). The influence of human factors and specialist involvement on informations systems success. *Human Relations, 52*(1), 123-152.

Mumford, E. (1996). *Systems Design: Ethical Tools for Ethical Change.* Basingstoke: MacMillan.

Mumford, E. (1997). The reality of participative systems design: Contributing to stability in a rocking boat. *Information Systems Journal, 7*(4), 309-321.

National Audit Office. (2000). *The Cancellation of the Benefits Card Project.* London: The Stationary Office.

Pliskin N., Romm T., Lee, A. and Weber Y. (1993). Presumed versus actual organisational culture: Managerial implications for implementation of information systems. *The Computer Journal, 36*, 143-152.

Sauer, C. (1993). *Why Information Systems Fail: A Case Study Approach.* Henley: Alfred Waller.

Schultz, R. and Slevin, D. (1975). A program of research on implementation. In Schultz, R. and Slevin, D. (Eds.), *Implementing Operations Research/ Management Science.* American Elsevier.

Venkatraman, N. (1991). IT-induced business re-configuration. In Scott-Morton, M. (Ed.), *The Corporation of the 1990s.* Oxford: Oxford University Press.

Ward, J. and Elvin, R. (1999). A new framework for managing IT-enabled business change. *Information Systems Journal, 9*(3), 197-222.

Wood, J. and Silver, D. (1989). *Joint Application Design.* New York: John Wiley & Sons.

Chapter III

The Social Responsibility of Information Systems Developers

N. F. du Plooy
University of Pretoria, South Africa

ABSTRACT

Information systems professionals have often been accused of ignoring issues such as ethics, human factors, social consequences, etc., during the development of an information system. This chapter aims to put into perspective that this attitude or 'fact' could be a result of a somewhat outdated mechanistic view of information systems and their role in organizations. Organizations adopt and use information systems for a variety of reasons, of which some of the most influential on the outcome or success of the systems often are neither planned nor anticipated. It is these reasons and their consequences that are the main point of discussion in this chapter. The importance of viewing information systems as social systems is stressed and it is pointed out that the 'social side' of information systems is the 'other side of the coin' of technical development methodologies. In the modern organization all work is so intertwined with the use of information technology that the one side cannot be considered, planned or developed, without considering the other. It is furthermore argued that it is the social responsibility of information systems professional to ensure that the human environment within which systems are being developed is cultivated and nurtured.

INTRODUCTION

Information systems are increasingly one of the most essential components of modern business organizations. Their use has become so integrated with the fabric of organizations that most organizations cannot function without one. They can be regarded as the 'core' of the organization. But what is an information system?

In the literature the term 'information system' is not used consistently. It is not a precise concept and is known by a variety of names, including management information systems, computer-based information systems, information systems and, increasingly, information technology (Markus, 1999). As will be seen later when the author offers a definition of information systems, in this chapter the term is used more or less in the sense proposed by Lee (1999), namely that information systems is an 'instantiation' of information technology. We take 'information system' as a concept that includes, *inter alia*, management policies and procedures, system developers, users, and communication and information systems (CIS).

The role that information systems play in organizations has changed over the years. Initially it was viewed as a somewhat *passive* one, namely 'supporting the functions' of the organization. Currently, this view has expanded to a much more *active* one often called 'determining the future' of the organization and, indeed, of society.

However, information systems adoption and use in organizations have many consequences and raise interesting questions. The quest of many information systems researchers is to try and make sense of this interplay between technology and people, in order to develop more successful approaches to information systems development.

The main thrust of this chapter is that this 'determining' role of information systems is not a deterministic one in the sense that it mechanistically determines the 'future' of organizations. Instead, this role is a softer, socially constituted one that embraces the many social forces that also play a part in determining that 'future,' so that the 'futures' of different organizations may be completely different even if similar technology is being used.

One result of this view is that the developer of information systems has, apart from a technical role, also the role of introducing information systems in a manner that takes cognisance of the notion of the social context of information systems. We wish to investigate how an appreciation and understanding of the social context of information systems changes the traditional role of systems developers. Especially, we wish to concentrate on the social responsibility that these new roles expect from systems developers.

Information systems cannot change the future of an organization without being *used*. However, the process of adoption and integrating this technology in organizations has not been of primary interest in the history of the information systems discipline. Much more emphasis has been placed on the *design and development* of information systems (Truex, Baskerville & Travis, 2000), since the earlier belief was that all these systems were supposed to do was to support the organization in its basic functions.

We have come to understand, however, that *using* information systems also *changes* the organization, since information systems are not value-neutral, and adoption and use do not occur in a vacuum. Adopting and using this technology leaves us with a different organization, unable to return to its former way of doing things.

The chapter proceeds as follows. The first section contains a general discussion of the adoption and use of information systems in organizations. Thereafter, in order to set the scene for the rest of the chapter, we consider the true nature of information systems, concentrating on its so-called 'softer' or 'social' attributes. This is followed by a discussion on the impact of information systems on organizations, again focusing on the human aspects of such impacts. In the next section we ask why organizations adopt information systems, and discuss the resultant mutual interaction between organization and technology that is an inevitable result of adoption and use. This leads to an explanation of the human environment within which information systems are adopted, and to the subsequent social responsibilities systems developers need to cultivate in order to nurture adoption of their technology in an essentially social environment.

Information Systems in Organizations

The interplay or mutual interaction and influence of information systems on organizational structures, as well as the systems developers and workers in the organizations where the systems have been adopted and used (and vice versa), have been researched in depth over the last decade (see, for instance, the work of Orlikowski, 1992, 1993, 1996; Orlikowski and Gash, 1994; Kling, 2000). They conclude that this interplay is an ongoing process that shapes both the technology and the people who design and work with it, thus also influencing the organization at large. For instance, information systems often institutionalise a certain way of work, enforce standardized procedures and suppress individual efforts of 'bypassing the system.'

The high rate of so-called information systems 'failures' (e.g., systems abandoned before completion, completed but never used, very large budget and time overruns) has been a concern since the earliest days of computer-based information systems. It is generally agreed that most, if not all, of these failures could be attributed not to a lack of tools and techniques, but to the neglect of 'human factors' in the dominant systems analysis and design practices (Wastell & Newman, 1996). From a social perspective, Serida-Nishimura (1994) suggests that the fit between the fundamental assumptions and beliefs (the culture, if you wish) of the proposed information systems (often expressed by the specific technology and development approaches used) and that of the organization determines the success of adoption and use of information systems. Organizational culture is intimately linked to organizational leadership, since managers often impose their beliefs on how things should be done in organizations. System developers also have their own view of technology, shaped by their own understanding, assumptions and beliefs about the role of information systems in organizations. These assumptions, values and norms of the systems developers may be and often are at odds with those of the organization.

Information systems are often introduced into organizations with completely disparate goals in mind. These goals could be:

- Automation to achieve increased productivity (Strassmann, 1990).
- To secure a strategic or competitive advantage (King, Grover & Hufnagel, 1989.
- To achieve redesign of business processes (Hammer & Champy, 1993).
- To accomplish disintermediation (Davenport & Short, 1990) or globalization (Ives & Jarvenpaa, 1991).
- To establish interorganizational information systems (Barrett & Konsynski, 1983).
- To provide empowerment and emancipation of workers (Clement, 1994).
- To keep up with the industry (Cash, Eccles, Nohria & Nolan, 1994).

Most, if not all, of these goals have both a deterministic and a non-deterministic side to it. Automation to increase productivity means that workers may lose jobs; empowerment of workers is clearly loaded with organizational political (social) overtones. In order to highlight the softer or human side of information systems, we now consider the various components of such systems, with the emphasis on describing information systems as social systems.

Figure 1: An information system

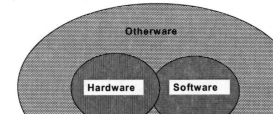

Information Systems as Social Systems

In the context of the discussion in this chapter, we see an information system as consisting of three main subsystems, namely the hardware and software (the 'computing' subsystems) of the information system, and the 'otherware,' often also called 'peopleware' (De Marco & Lister, 1987).

There is an important difference between the three subsystems. The first two are designed to be deterministic and (hopefully) reliable. However, in the 'peopleware' subsystem one finds owners, users and support personnel, etc., with unpredictable behaviour patterns, human failures and shortcomings. This is not a 'designed' subsystem in the same sense that the computing subsystem is designed. People may have agendas and goals that differ vastly from those of the organization (Myers & Young, 1997). This subsystem will, therefore, be non-deterministic–a typical attribute of *open, social systems.*

The consequence of this is that the total system, the information system, is also to a greater or lesser extent non-deterministic. It becomes a technical system with a major social component, so much so that in some cases, the social component dominates. However, most conventional systems development approaches do not equip the developer with tools or knowledge for dealing with the social processes intrinsic to information systems development (Hirschheim & Newman, 1991). The classic example of the 'failure' of the London Ambulance Service is another case in point (Beynon-Davies, 1995).

The Impact of Information Systems on Organizations

Social systems, such as organizations and information systems, display a property typical of all open systems, namely *emergence* (Truex, Baskerville & Klein, 1999). This means, *inter alia,* that the structure of social systems is not predetermined or inherent, but evolves over time as these systems adapt to and interact with their environment.

We see emergence in information systems in the unexpected and unintentional ways in which users use information systems (Orlikowski, 1996). The changes brought about by information systems adoption and use are often a result of emergent change rather than planned change. Emergent change is thus by its very nature unexpected, but no less significant than planned change. This suggests that the transformation occurs through the ongoing, gradual and reciprocal adjustments, accommodations and improvisations enacted by the members of the organization, and to which the information systems must respond.

The use of information systems often interferes in a very autocratic manner with the work of an individual. As this technology is increasingly being used to manage and control work, it affects aspects that most workers like to participate in, namely the planning and shaping of their work. One should bear in mind that work is fundamentally social, involving extensive cooperation and communication. Information systems therefore not only interfere with the individual, but also with the work of the group of which that individual is part, since very few work tasks are completed in isolation. An example of this is when information systems are used as social control systems, e.g., time sheet reporting, controlling the use of email, etc.

The question may be asked if systems developers really understand the work of others sufficiently to be *allowed* to interfere with and change that work (Suchman, 1995). In practice, assumptions are easily made about how tasks are performed rather than unearthing the underlying work practices. Problems may arise, however, when perceptions of what the work entails:

"… are generated at a distance from the sites at which the work they represent goes on or taken away from those sites and used in place of working knowledge" (Suchman, p. 61).

Currently information systems and their designers have possibly the greatest influence on the way work is done in organizations. The next sections will investigate the social and institutional context of information systems to find out what it is that systems developers need to understand in order to become more responsible advocates and implementers of their technology.

Why Organizations Adopt Information Systems

Information systems are adopted for a number of reasons. These are:

Explicitly Stated Reasons
(a)   Perceived benefit (Davis, 1986).
(b)   Increased productivity (Brynjolfsson, 1993).
(c)   Empowerment or increased industrial democracy (Clement, 1994)
(d)   Technology strategy (Orlikowski, 1993).
(e)   Pressure from outside agencies (King et al., 1994; Ruppel & Harrington, 1995).

Implicit Reasons
Some reasons can be termed '*implicit*' or '*after-the-fact,*' not as a planned result or consequence of adopting information systems, but rather as an undeclared reason, which was not clearly stated before the introduction of the technology. These could be:
(a)   Individual and organizational growth (Duursema, 1996).
(b)   Changing the culture of the organization (Orlikowski & Gash, 1994).
(c)   Aiding and abetting political goals in an organization (Myers & Young, 1997).
(d)   Providing a basis for organizational memory (Stein & Zwass, 1995).
(e)   Creating a learning organization (Pentland, 1995).

The 'classic' view of the information systems function in an organization is that its *raison d'être* is to support the organization in its operations, management and decision making. However, judging from some of the *explicit* reasons, but especially from all the *implicit* reasons shown above, it seems that, over the years, information systems in organizations have assumed new roles in the organization, guiding it towards a different future.

The following diagram is a proposition that aims to explain the relationship between information systems and organizations. This diagram shows what happens during the *process* of information systems adoption and use. The diagram is based on the work of Orlikowski (1992). Note how the diagram explains the continuous and reciprocal influence of information systems and organizations.

This proposition states that, apart from the well-known *support* offered to organizations by information systems, its adoption and use also have four other elements, namely that information systems can:

- *Lead* an organization into new markets and new ways of learning.
- Act as a *steering mechanism* to move an organization in a direction dictated by the life worlds of its management or of an external agency such as the government.
- *Guide* an organization's way of doing business as well as its social epistemology.
- *Change* the organization in many ways, structurally as well as socially.

Information systems adoption and use should therefore be understood as an organizational intervention. Often information systems, *in an organizational context*, are not used to solve problems, but to cause organizational change (Dahlbom & Mathiassen, 1993).

Figure 2: The relationship between information systems and the organization during adoption and use (du Plooy, 1998)

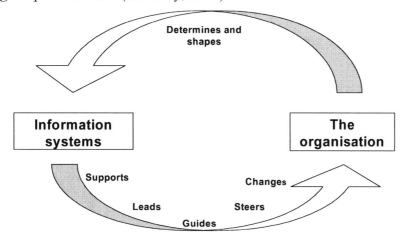

As we have explained, since the information systems are developed according to the dictates of management or systems analysts, the technology will, recursively, have an influence on the organization as a whole. This is because adoption and use of information systems do not occur in a vacuum, but within the social and structural context of the organization. This context we will call the 'human environment' wherein such adoption takes place.

The Human Environment of Information Systems Adoption and Use
Langdon Winner (1986) argued that in respect of introducing new technology, the important task becomes not that of studying the "effects" and "impacts" of technical change, but one of evaluating the material and social infrastructures (ethics, balance of power, social justice, etc.) specific technologies create. Since information systems are socially constructed, these social changes take place within the human environment in which the systems are adopted and used.

In order to cultivate and nurture a human environment, one obviously has to understand how people view information systems and how they understand the meaning of the technology. Furthermore, in order to understand the latter, the technical, social and political aspects of the systems have to be investigated.

What does this human environment consist of? The following is a partial list that will suffice for our discussion here.

(a)   The social context of individuals
  • The *world views* of the agent of change and the intended user
  • The *technological frames of reference* of agents of change
  • *Power bases* of individuals
  • *Partnership*
(b)   The social context of groups
  • *Power bases* of groups
  • The *relevance* of interaction with systems in a group
  • The *shared understanding* by a group of the solution offered by the systems (closure)
  • *Making sense* of information systems
(c)   The social context of information systems
  • The *determining* capability of this technology
  • The *duality* of technology
  • *Empowerment/disempowerment* of workers through information systems
  • The *non-deterministic* aspects of information systems
(d)   The social context of organizations
  • Organizational and ethnic *cultures*
  • Organizational *learning* and *emergence*

- The influence of this technology on the *values and judgment* of an organization
- *Information politics*
- The *influence* of organizations on information systems
- Organizational *norms and values*
- *Emergence* of the organization
- The *adaptation* of the organization to the technology
- Organizational *politics*

(e) The social context of tasks
- The application of technology in different work situations, e.g., *managerial, individual office work, group work*
- The influence of this technology on *business processes, organizational learning* and *internal communication*

(f) The social context of the environment
- The influence of *unions*
- *Disintermediation*
- Pressure from *competitors*
- *Industry* innovations
- *Institutions* influencing IT innovation

We can regard this list with its six characteristic social contexts as a framework describing the 'human environment' (the full social context) affecting information systems adoption and use (Du Plooy, 1998).

These are complex social factors that should be understood in order to appraise their vital role in the process of adoption and use of information systems. These factors are grouped in the list of various social contexts that influence the adoption and use process. The six characteristics of this model should be viewed as an integrated whole that is not divisible into parts. If we do that, we may miss an important context that may have an influence on the success of the adoption process. We need to understand the whole, if we wish to understand the full social context of information systems adoption and use. The 'binding factor' or 'integrating agent' between the various characteristics is their social contexts. Thus, although each of the six characteristics expresses a different dimension of the social context of information systems adoption and use, these dimensions cannot be isolated and considered on their own. The human environment only makes sense when considered in its totality, as a single environment, which interacts recursively with information systems during its adoption and during its use.

The following diagram (Figure 3) shows how the human environment encompasses the relationship between organizations and information systems adoption and use. Note that each side of the cube represents a different characteristic, and

Figure 3: The human environment encapsulating information systems adoption and use (du Plooy, 1998)

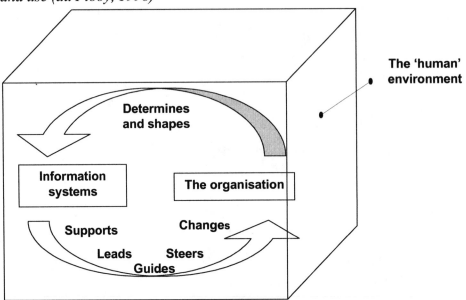

that the cube itself represents the human environment. Showing all the different social contexts as an integrated whole more accurately reflects how the social context of information systems adoption and use should be understood. Note particularly that the human environment is an integration or mix of social contexts of people, organizations, groups, tasks, environments and technology. A mix therefore of 'people' and 'things' or 'structures' that are different in their natures, but that must be viewed as a collective, even a network, that is tied together by the notion of a human environment. Therefore, when considering this human environment, we do not distinguish in the ordinary way between humans and their artefacts or between humans and their structures, but rather view them as 'two sides of the same coin.'

Information systems, due to their close interaction with human actors in organizations, have truly become the artefacts of modernity, of the *hybridisation* that Latour (1993) writes about. Work cannot be performed in the modern organization without this technology, yet at the same time our organizations and ourselves are changed in an ecological sense.

We now need to discuss these results in terms of the social responsibility of information systems professionals.

The Social Responsibility of Information Systems Professionals

With information systems man has created a technology that affects organizations possibly in as profound a way as the invention of printing did many centuries ago. The information systems are no longer the tool of the modern organization; it *is* modern organization.

However, there is still conflict in many organizations about who should assume responsibility for the new roles of information systems, as typified by the following two statements from a user group and a systems developer respectively:

"It (*the idea of a new system*) came; it essentially came from within IT. The reason being is that our IT shop definitely is the change agent when it comes to information systems here at the (organization)..." (Du Plooy, 1998, p 249).

And:

"Typically we do not want to decide this system is the one that we now must develop. Someone from the business side must make that decision, not us...." (Du Plooy, 1998, p 249).

Therefore, although the new roles of information systems are clearly emergent and, in some organizations, very visible, it is still not natural for all managers to regard information systems in this light. There could be a very simple explanation for this. In some organizations information systems are not regarded as part of the mainstream (productive) activities, and are only seen in an administrative support role. However, all indications are that globalization has changed this situation, simply because the business environment is rapidly becoming a full-fledged part of the 'information society,' and organizations with this conservative viewpoint will probably struggle increasingly to survive in a more globally competitive environment.

These new roles of information systems should be played out in a receptive human environment, an environment that is *cultivated* and *nurtured*. Cultivation is used here in a very specific sense. According to Ciborra (1997) the notion of 'cultivation' is a way of shaping technology that is fundamentally different from planning for and constructing a technical system. 'Planning' and 'constructing' are typical mechanistic terms implying rationalism and determinism. 'Cultivation' is about interference with and support of a material or process that is in itself dynamic and able to grow according to its own logic. It is a notion akin to 'bricolage' or 'tinkering' that Dahlbom and Mathiassen (1993) use to describe the continuous small changes that information systems require. We therefore use it to indicate that the process of cultivation is in itself a 'soft' issue, not amenable to mechanistic direction, yet able to be nurtured by human actors within the environment of an organization. How can this be accomplished in the context of information systems?

In the first place, by *recognising the need* for such an environment. Information systems that are dumped or pushed unthinkingly on users encounter resistance that is both unnecessary and counter-productive. The investment in the technology and people is simply too huge to allow this to happen. All actors in the organization must come to some kind of shared (or at least a negotiated) understanding of this need. Basic to recognising the need for the environment is an understanding of the role of information systems.

Additionally, one cultivates a human environment by *really understanding* what it entails. In simple terms, the human environment is the full social context of information systems, the organizational, social, political and ethical concerns that govern and influence information systems adoption and use. It requires an understanding, in both a philosophical and business sense, of the new roles of information systems and how these roles can be contextualised in their particular organization. This understanding must be 'shared' by the different actors involved in information systems adoption and use.

We also need to *prepare* all the actors involved in information systems development and use for the need, the reality and the understanding of this environment. This is quite a task because it requires, *inter alia*, education and training aimed at closing the 'culture gap' between information systems professionals and management (or users) in any organization. It also, more specifically, requires the educating of information technologists on the social and business aspects of their task. They may resist this because it causes uneasiness in that they may over time lose their technical skills and thus become less 'marketable.' Preparing the environment may include relatively simple, but in terms of the typical systems development life cycle, quite uncommon tasks such as preparing the users of new systems for the changes that await them. This may require skills such as change management and organizational development psychology.

Cultivating and nurturing a receptive human environment means that information systems must be perceived by all actors to be a means of achieving empowerment and partnership, both functionally and democratically. Employees should not only *be* empowered, but also *feel* empowered. However, information systems can only live up to their empowering capability if the objectives of the system shift from control to empowerment. The way individuals and groups think about technology and how they make sense of it in their everyday tasks have a direct influence on the type of information systems that will best benefit them.

We also need to *recognise* that organizations and users differ, and that information systems development has to take this fact into account. Maintenance, the old bugbear of the information systems developers, should be recognised for what it is: continual 'tinkering' with the system to accommodate emergence in ways of working and in the organization and its environment. In a living organization it is well nigh impossible to establish the full information requirements of a manager or other user with complete accuracy owing to the non-deterministic aspects of information systems. The 'difference' between different users and organizations in the final analysis is due to their different views of technology, their different worldviews, cultures and technological frames of reference. These all form part of the human environment under discussion here.

We also need to understand the *richness* of the social context within which the technology will be adopted and used. This means understanding organizational culture, politics, attitudes and beliefs. It could also mean responding to the fears and misunderstandings of people regarding the role of the technology.

Finally, we need to *search for the real user* and for understanding of that user's requirements (Markus & Keil, 1994). This has always been and still is the most difficult task in software development. This requires immersing oneself in understanding the business of the user and the requirements of the business processes and, especially, work tasks that the user (or user group) perform. The user must be treated as the *owner of the system* and a partner in the adoption and use of the technology. As the owner, the user has the final say on how the technology should 'look and feel' so that it fits the intended environment philosophically as well as ergonomically. As a partner, the user (in the very broadest sense) needs to determine the business direction and understand the type of information system required to move in that direction. User relationships in the information systems field are about understanding people and their work. These relationships need to be managed. They are clearly best built over time, and success hinges on the ability of analyst and user to work together in the first instance as partners rather than as providers of technology and clients. The essence of good relationships lies in cultivating the human environment, and nurturing it by maintaining good communication between the technologists and the users so that the culture gap can be crossed or eliminated.

A shared understanding of the role of information systems in the organization can facilitate the closing or bridging of the culture gap. This requires much greater involvement of users in the cultivation and nurturing of the human environment. The question now is how prepared are they for this responsibility, and how much do they understand of this environment? It is not merely a question of understanding technology and understanding business, and if you understand both then the problem is solved. To understand the need for a human environment, one needs to understand the full social context of information systems and its implications for the process of information systems adoption and use. The lack of understanding of this human environment is not peculiar to technologists–it is as common among their business counterparts.

Cultivating and nurturing the human environment has a number of implications for information systems development. For instance, systems developers should recognise the existence of information politics as an element of the human environment. Information politics is a result of organizational defences and the 'games' an organization's members play to maintain their power bases and sometimes even their very jobs. This is a real issue in the human environment of information systems, because nothing much can be done to make politics go away. In order for it to change, actors in the organization will have to modify their behaviour. Attempting to do that is not a simple undertaking. In terms of the terminology we now use, we can say that behavioural change may only be achieved in a cultivated and nurtured human environment where at least an attempt at a shared understanding of the use of information and the role of the technology has been made.

The much-neglected fact that information systems are often used as political weapons in organizational infighting to achieve a position of greater power and influence has to be understood. Systems development often becomes a power game between different managers from the user group. The most difficult part in coming to terms with organizational politics is the realisation that the politics of persons and groups differ according to their worldviews, their assumptions and beliefs, and their 'sense-making' of the role of information systems. Thus, in cultivating and nurturing the human environment, the organization recognises the fact of politics and educates the actors involved in adopting and using information systems in coming to terms with these organizational games.

It is clear that information systems development that continues along the old rationalistic or mechanistic lines, cannot deal with the human environment. Priority therefore needs to be given to other approaches that do take this into account. These are participatory design, soft systems methodology and other approaches (ETHICS, SSM, Multiview, etc.) derived from them (Mumford, 1983; Avison & Fitzgerald, 1995; Brooke & Maguire, 1998; Checkland & Howell, 1998). However, these approaches need a worldview different from the older engineering type of methodologies. Changes of worldview are not simple to achieve, and are best realised through continuous education and training, and the nurturing of democratic ideals in organizations.

Preparing the user community for change means more than simply 'training the users.' It means that the users need to be informed of the changes to their job, how they will work differently in the future, what the impact of the system on the whole user community is likely to be, how their new systems link up with other systems, etc. This is an involved task that requires a lot of organizational knowledge and 'people skills.' Often it is best left to organizational sociologists to prepare the community for the forthcoming change.

Typically, IS professionals do not understand this 'social' responsibility of cultivating and nurturing the human environment, even if they have become aware over the years that there is more to information systems development than meets the technical eye.

CONCLUSION

We have introduced the concept of a human environment in which we gathered all the ethical, philosophical, social, political and organizational issues that relate to information systems adoption and use. We submit that these are the human factors referred to in earlier literature, and the social responsibility of information systems professionals is to play their role in cultivating and nurturing this human environment. They are not solely responsible for this task–obviously it is also the responsibility of management and users to engage in this task. But, first and foremost, it is the responsibility of information systems professionals to *recognise and understand the consequences of the adoption and use of information systems.* Being technologists, they are in a better position than most others to appreciate the role of information systems in organizations. Being socially responsible, they need to be aware of the human environment of information systems adoption and use that they must help cultivate and nurture. Thus they may be able to avoid rather than overcome the resistance to their technology and other barriers to its successful introduction. They may find that fewer plans need to be diverted, fewer surprises will occur, fewer opportunistic adjustments need to be carried out on the spur of the moment and better planning could be achieved.

Failure to cultivate and nurture the human environment will constrain information systems adoption and use. The effect of hidden agendas and power politics, the ethical dilemmas and organizational disturbances that typically follow the introduction of information systems may play havoc with the adoption and use process.

Socially responsible information system professionals are also a legitimate one–legitimate in the sense that they are accepted into the organization as responsible partners, abandoning their banners of 'technological high priests' and losing their incomprehensible technical jargon. Being socially responsible they can become partners in establishing the 'best practices' for information systems adoption and use which, to this day, have eluded the profession.

Viewing the interaction between information systems and organizations as embedded within the human environment as shown in Figure 3 puts the role of the technology and its social constitution into proper perspective. This interaction cannot be viewed deterministically, as is so often done. The interaction is encapsulated in the human environment, not separate from it, and, in order to understand the whole, we need to understand both the interaction as well as the social contexts of the interaction.

However, as we have also seen, information systems are no longer a technology that can be kept at arm's length, but have turned into something with which we interact constantly. Since information systems are created by people for the use of other people, they influence the organizational activities of those people in many ways. These influences are not always predictable, and may have many intended and unintended consequences. If we wish to attain a more knowledgeable organization in the end, our efforts should be directed towards understanding our technology in its technological as well as its human environment.

Information systems adoption is a complex phenomenon, because it is embedded within and emerges from a human environment which is a curious hybrid of technology and people that influences the process in many subtle ways. We can no longer conceptualise information systems without thinking about its adoption and use.

Hence, the questions that any information systems professional should ask him/herself are:

- How can I analyse this proposed system in a socially responsible manner? (Who is my real user? Do I talk to the right people? Where does the real power reside?)
- How can I design this system in a socially responsible manner? (How will the quality of work life be influenced? Can jobs be enriched rather than eliminated? Will organizational culture be changed, and if so, is the change acceptable to workers and management?)
- How can I implement this system in a socially responsible manner? (Who owns the system, IT or the user? How is the user corps prepared for the changes that await them? Is the new system one that the users *want* to use?)

Such questions, we maintain, can only be asked if the full social context of information systems is understood, *in other words*, if the importance of cultivating and nurturing a human environment is regarded as an essential characteristic of the socially responsible information systems developer.

REFERENCES

Avison, D. E. and Fitzgerald, G. (1995). *Information Systems Development: Methodologies, Techniques and Tools* (second edition). London: McGraw Hill.

Barrett, S. and Konsynski, B. (1982). Inter-organisational information sharing systems. *MIS Quarterly (Special Issue)*, 93-105.

Beynon-Davies, P. (1995). Information systems 'failure': The case of the London Ambulance Service's computer-aided dispatch systems. *European Journal of Information Systems*, *4*, 171-184.

Brooke, C. and Maguire, S. (1998). Systems development: A restrictive practice? *International Journal of Information Management*, *18*, 165-180.

Brynjolfsson, E. (1993). The productivity paradox of information systems. *Communications of the ACM*, *36*, 67-77.

Cash, J. I., Eccles, R. G., Nohria, N. and Nolan, R. L. (1994). *Building the Information-Age Organization: Structure, Control, and Information Technologies*. Homewood, IL: Irwin.

Checkland, P. and Howell, S. (1998). *Information, Systems and Information Systems: Making Sense of the Field*. Chicester: John Wiley & Sons.

Ciborra, C. U. (1997). Crisis and foundations: An inquiry into the nature and limits of models and methods in the IS discipline. In Galliers, R. (1997). *Proceedings of the 5th European Conference on Information Systems*, June 19-21, 1549-1560. Cork, Ireland.

Clement, A. (1994). Computing at work: Empowering action by 'low-level' users. *Communications of the ACM, 37*, 53-63.

Dahlbom, B. and Mathiassen, L. (1993). *Computers in Context: The Philosophy and Practice of Systems Design*. Oxford: NCC Blackwell.

Davenport, T. H. and Short, J. E. (1990). The new industrial engineering: Information technology and business process redesign. *Sloan Management Review*, (Summer), 11-27.

Davis, F. D. (1986). A technology acceptance model for empirically testing end-user information systems: Theory and results. *Doctoral Dissertation*, Sloan School of Management, MIT.

De Marco, T. and Lister, T. (1987). *Peopleware: Productivity Projects and Teams*. New York: Dorset House.

du Plooy, N. F. (1998). An analysis of the human environment for the adoption and use of information technology. *Unpublished Doctoral Dissertation*, Department of Informatics, University of Pretoria, South Africa.

Duursema, W. C. (1996). The implications of human values and judgment for information management. *Unpublished DCom Dissertation*, Department of Informatics, University of Pretoria, South Africa.

Hammer, M. and Champy, L. (1993). *Reengineering the Corporation: A Manifesto for Business Revolution*. London: Nicholas Brealy.

Hirschheim, R. A. and Newman, M. (1991). Symbolism and information system development: Myth, metaphor and magic. *Information Systems Research, 2*, 29-62.

Ives, B. and Jarvenpaa, S. L. (1991). Applications of global information systems: Key issues for management. *MIS Quarterly*, (May), 33-49.

King, W. R., Grover, V. and Hufnagel, E. H. (1989). Using information and information systems for sustainable competitive advantage: Some empirical evidence. *Information and Management, 17*.

Kling, R. (2000). Learning about information technologies and social change: The contribution of social informatics. *The Information Society, 16*, 217-232.

Latour, B. (1993). *We Have Never Been Modern*. New York: Harverster Wheatsheaf.

Lee, A. S. (1999). Researching MIS. In Currie, W. L. and Galliers, B. (Eds.), *Rethinking Management Information Systems*. Oxford: Oxford University Press.

Markus, M. L. and Keil, M. (1994). If we build it, they will come: Designing information systems that people want to use. *Sloan Management Review*, Summer, 11-25.

Markus, M. L. (1999). Thinking the unthinkable: What happens if the IS field as we know it goes away? In Currie, W. L. and Galliers, B. (Eds.), *Rethinking Management Information Systems*. Oxford: Oxford University Press.

Mumford, E. (1983). *Designing Human Systems for New Technology: The ETHICS Method*. Manchester: Manchester Business School.

Myers, M. D. and Young, L. W. (1997). Hidden agendas, power and managerial assumptions in information systems development: An ethnographic study. *Information Systems & People*, *10*, 224-240.

Orlikowski, W. J. (1992). The duality of technology: Rethinking the concept of technology in organizations. *Organization Science*, *3*, 398-427.

Orlikowski, W. J. (1993). CASE tools as organizational change: Investigating incremental and radical changes in systems development. *MIS Quarterly*, (September), 309-340.

Orlikowski, W. J. (1996). Improvising organizational transformation over time: A situated change perspective. *Information Systems Research*, *7*, 63-92.

Orlikowski, W. J. and Gash, D. C. (1994). Technology frames: Making sense of information systems in organizations. *ACM Transactions in Information Systems*, *1*, 174-207.

Pentland, B. T. (1995). Information systems and organizational learning: The social epistemology of organizational knowledge systems. *Accounting, Management & Information Systems*, *5*, 1-21.

Ruppel, C. P. and Harrington, S. J. (1995). Telework: An innovation where nobody is getting on the bandwagon? *DATA BASE Advances*, *26*, 87-104.

Serida-Nishimura, J. F. (1994). An organizational culture perspective for the study of group support systems. In DeGross, J. I., Huff, S. L. and Munro, M. C. (Eds.), *Proceedings of the 15th International Conference on Information Systems*, December 14-17, Vancouver, Canada.

Stein, E. W. and Zwass, V. (1995). Actualizing organizational memory with information systems. *Information Systems Research*, *6*, 85-117.

Strassmann, P. A. (1990). *Business Value of Computers*. New Canaan, CT: Information Economic Press.

Suchman, L. (1995). Making work visible. *Communications of the ACM*, *38*, 56-64.

Truex, D. P., Baskerville, R. and Travis, T. (2000). A methodological systems development: The deferred meaning of systems development methods. *Accounting, Management and Information Systems*, *10*, 53-70.

Truex, D. P., Baskerville, R. and Klein, H. (1999). Growing systems in emergent organizations. *Communications of the ACM*, *42*(8), 117-123.

Wastell, D. and Newman, M. (1996). Information systems design, stress and organizational change in the ambulance services: A tale of two cities. *Accounting, Management and Information Systems*, *6*, 283-300.

Winner, L. (1986). *The Whale and the Reactor: A Search for Limits in an Age of High Technology*. Chicago, IL: University of Chicago Press.

Chapter IV

Information Technology in Construction: How to Realise the Benefits?

Lauri Koskela and Abdul Samad Kazi
VTT Technical Research Centre of Finland, Finland

ABSTRACT

Advancement in the utilisation of computers has, in recent years, become a major, even dominating research and development target in the architecture, engineering and construction industry. However, in empirical investigations, no major benefits accruing from construction IT have been found. Why do the many IT applications, which when separately analysed seem so well justified, fail to produce positive impacts when the totality of the construction project is analysed? The objective of this chapter is to find the explanation for this paradox and to provide initial guidelines as to what should be done to correct the situation.

INTRODUCTION

Advancement in the utilisation of computers in construction has in recent years become a major, even dominating research and development target. This is clearly reflected in the number of related research undertakings, published scientific papers and in educational curricula. There are numerous conferences specifically addressing construction computing and integration issues. This *Zeitgeist* may well be illustrated with the following quote from an editorial of the *ASCE Journal on Construction Engineering and Management* (Farid, 1993, p.195):"The productivity and competitiveness of the construction industry can only be improved with the transfer and implementation of computing and other advanced technologies."

Although the ground for this optimism is seldom explicitly stated, it is easy to understand it. We all are using software, for word-processing, spreadsheet calculation or drawing, that clearly makes us more productive. Sending a letter by e-mail is speedier and less costly than using conventional mail. Indeed, there are countless information technology (IT) applications which, when the task it supports is only considered, seem to be perfectly efficient and to promise a major productivity increase.

On the other hand, investigations into the actual impacts of IT in construction reveal a not very flattering picture. Especially regarding site construction, the use of information technology has not brought any major benefits–on the contrary, it is claimed that the impacts may have been negative. Thus, the rhetoric and visions associated with construction IT have turned out to be alarmingly distant from the reality of construction IT usage. Why do the many IT applications, which when separately analysed seem so well justified, fail to produce positive impacts when the totality of the project, firm or industry is analysed? The objective of this chapter is to find the explanation for this paradox and to provide initial guidelines as to what should be done to correct the situation.

BACKGROUND

The Baseline

It is interesting that communication in the construction industry has been analysed from a socio-technical angle before the wide introduction of computers into this industry. In a pioneering study carried out by the Tavistock Institute (1966), characteristics of the structure and functions of the industry were empirically analysed. The overall approach was to consider building from a communications point of view. Interdependence and uncertainty were found to be the two important characteristics of construction. It was found that the building industry depends to a large extent on the application of an informal system of behaviours and management to work adequately. As the root cause of problems, the disparity of the characteristics of the formal and informal systems in relation to the needs of the real task with which they are concerned is put forward. The formal system (contracts, plans, etc.) does not recognize the uncertainty of and interdependence between the operations of the building process. On the other hand, the informal system of management is geared towards handling uncertainty and interdependence, but it produces a climate of endemic crisis, which becomes self-perpetuating. Further research on designing organizational forms with less uncertainty and on tools for coping with interdependency, especially in design, was suggested (Tavistock, 1966). It is unfortunate that this research was not continued.

Use of Information Technology in Construction

Mechanization of intellectual work by means of computers started in the 1960s (Grierson, 1998). Computers are now widely used for automating and supporting various tasks in construction. Increasingly, computers are also used for supporting and automating the information flows that integrate these tasks. However, as yet no real computer-integrated construction has evolved (Laitinen, 1998). This stems from the reality that the construction business in general involves the temporary convergence of core competencies from different players to deliver a unique product, the building. Each individual player uses his/her specific IT tools to facilitate his/her specific work objective. Consequently information sharing through IT between different players is in essence a nightmare (Kazi et al., 2001).

Impacts of Information Technology in Construction

What, then, have been the impacts of IT in construction? A number of studies have been carried out recently in order to answer this question. Howard et al. (1998) found high levels of benefit from construction IT in design and administration in Scandinavia, while management applications have resulted in little change. Especially, contractors reported little change in productivity resulting from materials or site management. Similarly, in their study on construction IT in Finland, Enkovaara et al. (1998) found that for contractors, IT had not produced any benefits, whereas in subcontracting and client procurement activities, IT benefits were negative, i.e., the benefits accrued have not offset the costs. A similar study in Canada (Rivard, 2000) comes to largely similar results. According to it, most benefits have been in the areas of general administration, design and project management. These benefits accrue to the fact that the number of mistakes in documentation have decreased, and the quality of documents and the speed of work have both increased. On the other hand, the complexity of work, the administrative needs and the costs of doing business have increased. It is concluded that the benefits of information technology come at a cost. Also Gann (2000) observed that in many firms, IT-related investment and training costs had been higher than the expected benefits.

Perhaps the most systematic study into the benefits of IT in construction is that of Thomas (2000), where outcomes of 297 projects (primarily heavy industrial) were studied. The outcome variables addressed cost growth, duration, schedule growth, safety, field rework, changes and other issues. Project data originating from owners and contractors were analysed separately. Projects were divided into four classes according to the level of use of information technology, where the first represented the highest use and the fourth the lowest. It is concluded that both owners and contractors can expect overall project and construction cost savings. Let us consider in more detail the results for owners, who represented the largest category in the sample. For owners, the project cost savings due to moving from the fourth class to the first class are 0.8% and the construction cost savings correspondingly 3.9%. However, the results indicate a cost increase of 7.3% when proceeding from the fourth class to the third class. Also many other variables showed deterioration when the third class is compared to the fourth class. In fact, from the total 20 variables considered, 11 were worse after the introduction of information technology, while one remained the same (Figure 1). Thomas interpreted this as that the question is about performance penalty for the learning curve effect–cost and schedules are impacted when project team members experiment with new technologies.

Factually, Figure 1 reveals that a transition towards more use of information technology regularly leads to deterioration in a considerable number of variables, while remaining variables show improvement or no change. These results provide more evidence to the finding that information technology, while providing benefits, also has *detrimental impacts*. However, in contrast to Thomas' view, we contend that such detrimental impacts are not only related to the initial introduction of information technology. When variable values for the second and the first classes are compared, it turns out that only 11 variables improve, whereas 10 variables get worse when use of information technology increases. Thus, it must be added that a learning curve effect seems to operate also when advanced information technology is introduced, that is, in the opposite end of the IT usage scale. There seems to be a trough-shaped occurrence of IT penalties.

A troubling finding in Thomas' (2000) study is that increased use of IT by contractors is associated with a clear decrease of safety. Also, increased IT use seems not to help contractors to speed up projects; in contrary, a minor slowing down can be perceived. For owners, change costs and field rework cost were negatively impacted when IT use increased. On the other hand, owners could achieve schedule compression through increased IT use.

The lack of impact of information technology on capital projects is also illuminated by a recent study of the Business Roundtable (1997), which defines the universal characteristics of best capital project systems, based on benchmarking a great number of projects. Whether these characteristics are used or not has a definite impact on the profitability of the project. The best company transforms a 15% return on investment (ROI) project, based on average performance, into a 22.5% ROI project, while the poorest performers corre-

Figure 1: The number of improving, deteriorating and unchanged variables when the use of information technology is increased in construction projects

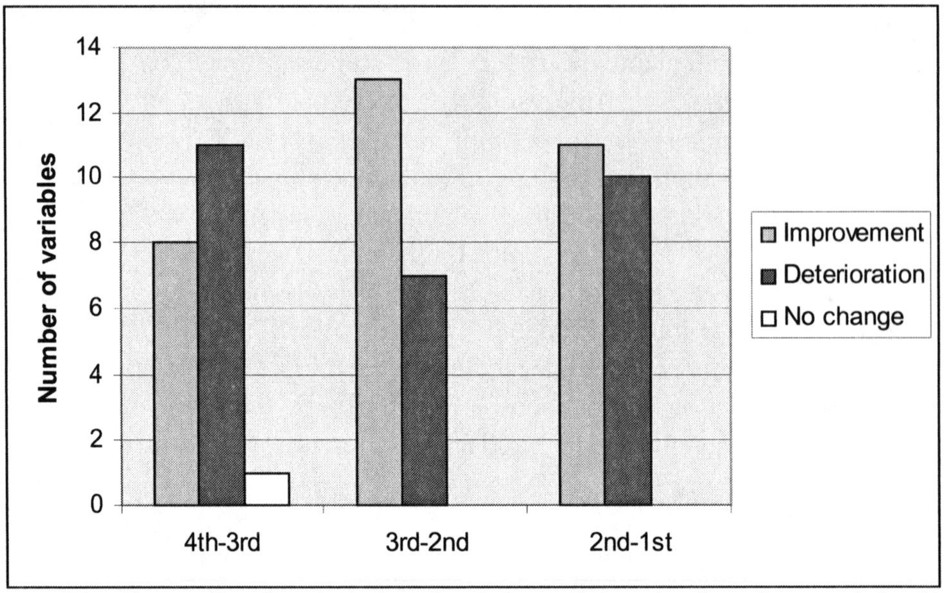

The 4th quartile of projects is using information technology least and the 1st quartile most. The column title, say "4th-3rd", refers to the differences in variable values when one quartile (the 4th) is compared to another quartile (the 3rd). The impacts were assessed by means of 21 variables. Original data, originating from owners, is from Thomas (2000).

spondingly end up at a 9% ROI. The characteristics were organisational or managerial; information technology was not among them. In other words, it seems that it has not been possible to create competitive advantages through IT utilization alone.

All in all, the empirical investigations give a confusing picture. Surely it is disappointing to find that considerable investments into the use of information technology have rendered only a cost reduction of 0.8%, especially when it is well known that the same impact–and actually considerably bigger–could be achieved through other, apparently less expensive means (as pinpointed in the study of the Business Roundtable, mentioned above). However, it has to be noted that the studies into IT impact in construction are still scarce, and there are considerable methodological problems related to them. Thus the results should be treated with caution. All told, there is yet no empirical justification that information technology would contribute to breakthrough changes in the performance of the AEC[1] sector, as has been suggested by the mainstream thinking.

Why Is the Impact of Information Technology so Lacking?

Various reasons have been offered as an explanation for these disappointing results. Commonly presented reasons include the low maturity of organisations in construction regarding IT use (Enkovaara et al., 1998) and barriers provided by the peculiarities of construction, especially fragmentation (Brandon et al., 1998). However, we contend that there are deeper reasons for this lack of intended impact of information technology in construction. These reasons will be best presented when embedded in the historical development of the modes of thinking about computing in construction.

The Conventional View on Computing

At the risk of oversimplification, it can be argued that the underlying conceptual framework (or mental model) of construction computing has been as shown in Figure 2. Information technology implementation leads directly to benefits and improvement in construction. This corresponds to the general approach to the use of information technology, largely prevalent still at the beginning of the 1990s. As formulated by Schrage (1997), the rationale of this thinking may be briefly crystallized as follows: if organizations only had greater quantities of cheaper, faster and more useful information, they could increase their profitability and enhance their competitive position. The underlying logic is that IT makes certain activities more cost effective, and–according to the logic of conventional accounting–the total costs are consequently reduced.

Unfortunately, it has been found that there is a productivity dilemma generally regarding IT investments: it has been difficult to find evidence for major productivity impacts contributed by the information technology (Gibbs, 1997). A new study by the McKinsey Global Institute (2001) gives further support to the belief that investments into information technology have not significantly contributed to productivity increase at the level of the national economy. There have been several explanations to this lack of economy-wide impact.

Firstly, Strassmann (1997) has provided extensive justification for the argument that IT investments have simply been poorly managed. Decisions on IT investments have factually been delegated to technical experts, and the level of scrutiny applied to other investments has not been applied.

Secondly, Davenport (1994) has argued that, in simple terms, the underlying view on information technology, as presented above, has developed to a bottleneck

Figure 2: Underlying conceptual framework of construction information technology (inspired by Davenport, 1993)

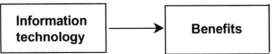

in itself due to its excessive focus on technology, rather than the context of its application. What is needed is better understanding of the organizations that use technology, rather than the understanding of information technology and its potential. Of course, this is the basic argument of the socio-technical approach: technical and social systems should be jointly optimised (Munkvold, 2000).

A third explanation is related to the situation, typical in the sphere of production, where the majority of costs have their origin in physical processes, rather than information processes. By improving information processes, we hope to improve the physical processes. Unfortunately the impact on physical processes is indirect only, and strong causal mechanisms leading to benefits are not necessarily present. If the physical process is in a constant chaos, information technology as such rarely helps. In fact, in the context of manufacturing, it has been observed that Computer Integrated Manufacturing acts as a magnifying glass: it makes the good production system much better and it makes the poor system much worse (Melnyk & Narasimhan, 1992).

A fourth explanation is related to the way we have been thinking about costs. As Johnson and Kaplan (1987) have shown, the traditional way of thinking has been that costs are caused by direct work. Thus, by providing IT that helps employees to carry out their work activities, we can reduce costs. However, as activity-based cost accounting has shown, overhead costs especially are caused also by many other cost drivers than direct work, and if information technology is not addressing the cost drivers in question, the impact of IT at least cost-wise will fall short.

Let us investigate whether it is possible to find indications about the occurrence of these explanative mechanisms in construction. Firstly, like in general business, construction IT investments have not been based on careful calculations. In a study on American AEC firms, it turned out that 75% of the firms had never tried to figure out the return on investment for information technology spending (Engineering News Record, 1997). Similarly, a British study concluded that formal cost benefit analyses are not widely used to assess possible investments in information technology (Churcher et al., 1996). The findings of Enkovaara et al. (1998), that in many cases the level of personnel competence or the degree of structured data have not corresponded to those required by an IT application, also pinpoint to managerial problems.

Secondly, Gann (2000) lists a number of reasons that are related to the arguments provided by Davenport. In most cases, systems were introduced into traditional organizational structures that hindered the ability to achieve widespread benefits. Incomplete and inconsistent datasets and a lack of explicit, codified knowledge hampered the development of IT systems. Often, the low level of trust between organizations prevented the use of inter-organizational IT networks.

Thirdly, the fact that benefits have been very modest in contracting, whereas more substantial benefits have been achieved in such information-related areas as design and administration, point to the explanation that it is not necessarily easy to influence physical processes, such as work flows or material flows, by means of information processes. Applebaum (1982) provides an interesting analysis of the introduction of up-to-date computer methods and a large, bureaucratically organised management team to the construction project. He describes the resulting situation as follows: "...we have virtually two separate organizations; one for the management function and one for getting the work done. The two organizations do not coordinate their work, and they are characterized by different goals and view-points" (p. 229). Pietroforte (1997) also finds that the demands of fast-tracking further increases the dislocation between the pattern of roles and rules predicted by standard contracts and the one that emerges from practice. In other words, the observations made by the researchers of the Tavistock Institute, referred above, have not lost their validity. It is easy to conclude that the use of computers in formal management is bound to be of little value for informal management, which actually gets the work done.

Fourthly, it is widely known that a substantial share of costs and time in construction are contributed by non-value-adding activities (Koskela, 2000), caused primarily by poor coordination of tasks. Information technology that has been primarily addressing individual tasks cannot influence these costs substantially. In contrary, information technology may even increase non-value adding activities. Indeed, giving us a rare glimpse on what actually is happening in design, Sverlinger (1996) observed that half of the disturbances in design are due to design organizations themselves, rather than the design process in question. Furthermore, he found that design tools are the most frequent cause of internal disturbances in design firms. Most design tools were computer-based.

Thus, the generic mechanisms that have diminished the impact of the use of information technology in general seem to have operated also in construction. The conceptual model of IT implementation has simply been too shallow and insufficient, leading to several kinds of misplaced conduct.

Re-Engineering View on Computing

Next, it is necessary to discuss re-engineering, which has been proposed as a solution to at least some of the problems of the use of information technology, as treated above. The idea of business process re-engineering (or redesign) was developed during the study of the impact of IT on organizations by MIT. Business process redesign was defined as one of five levels of IT-induced reconfiguration of organizations (Venkatraman, 1991). It was stated that our current principles of organization are geared towards exploiting the capabilities offered by the Industrial Revolution. It was argued that the IT revolution could alter some of these principles. Another article by participants in the study mentioned (Davenport & Short, 1990) illuminates which kind of new principles were thinkable. However, it was only the article of Hammer (1990) and the subsequent book (Hammer & Champy, 1993) that sparked the interest in reengineering. Business process reengineering (BPR) was developed into a consulting package and became a buzzword. The first examples of BPR were from administration and services, and this focus prevailed, but also manufacturing companies started their re-engineering initiatives. However, towards the end of the 1990s, the fashionability of re-engineering waned, and it was increasingly discussed critically (Mumford & Hendricks, 1997).

In re-engineering, it is acknowledged that information technology applications do not directly contribute to benefits, but through the intermediation of information processes (Figure 3). Information (or material) processes may restrain or amplify the effect of information technology. In re-engineering, the interest is especially focused on the cases where information technology enables a new, widely superior process design (for example Hammer, 1990; Davenport & Short, 1990; Rockart & Short, 1989). According to Hammer, recognizing and breaking away from outdated rules and fundamental assumptions is the key issue in re-engineering.

The approach of re-engineering solves at least part of the shortcomings of the conventional view on information technology, as discussed in the previous section. The focus is turned from information technology as such, to changing information processes. However, one cannot be fully satisfied with re-engineering as a foundation: it is rather a management recipe (Earl, 1994), lacking an explicit theory. One critical shortcoming is that the concept of process, central in the reengineering rhetoric, has not been precisely defined. Koskela (2000) has argued that the term of process has been interpreted in three different ways, each leading to a different set of principles and practices. Historically, the first interpretation was that the question is of a *transformation* process. Actually, this has been the definition of the term process in reengineering literature (Garvin, 1998). However, the prescription of reengineering has been more focused on a second interpretation, where one holds process as a *flow*. Indeed, close reading of the seminal re-engineering articles and books reveals that what were considered as problems to be addressed were dysfunctionalities caused by the transformation concept, like excessive buffers, fragmentation and inadequate feedback along chains. What was recommended as a solution were process design principles or solutions emanating from the flow concept, augmented with IT capabilities. The third interpretation views a process

Figure 3: Underlying framework of re-engineering (Davenport, 1993)

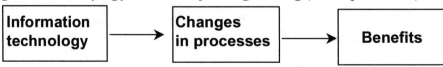

as *value generation*. Although not systematically applied, even this interpretation is frequently mentioned in the rhetoric of re-engineering.

The other critical shortcoming of re-engineering is that it addresses only the *design* of processes. Instead, how the re-engineered process should be *controlled* and *improved* is largely left outside the focus. If the improvement potential lies in the ways control and improvement is carried out, it will remain untapped in a re-engineering initiative.

Interest in re-engineering has rapidly increased in construction research and practice (Betts & Wood-Harper, 1994; Ibbs, 1994). Indeed, re-engineering has to some extent shown the way towards a more effective approach to information technology. However, the interest in construction reengineering waned towards the end of the 1990s, as it did in other industries. On the other hand, similar initiatives are being carried out, but under different banners.

One of the most popular ways of re-engineering construction has been the design-build (DB) mode of realizing a construction project. Even if information technology does not necessarily play any prominent role in the execution of a DB project, it is interesting to consider this initiative for the sake of comparison. In a DB project, the client gives, in a single contract, the execution of both design and construction to one company (usually contractor) that has the freedom to integrate design and construction in a suitable way. The performance of the design-build delivery system in comparison to other major delivery systems has been studied in two recent studies in the U.S. and UK (Konchar & Sanvido, 1998; Bennett, Pothecary & Robinson, 1996). The results indicate that statistically, the design-build process outperforms the traditional design-bid-build (DBB) process in several respects; however, the differences are not great. The U.S. study finds DB to be 6% less costly than DBB, whereas the UK study estimates that DB is 13-32% less costly than DBB (however, these figures have been calculated in incompatible ways and it is difficult to draw general conclusions from them). It can be noted that such an impact of an organizational solution outweighs the impacts of the use of information technology, discussed above.

A Suggested View on Construction Computing

With which conceptual framework, then, should we equip ourselves when wanting to use IT in construction? An interesting direction is given by Fenves (1996). He calls for a science base of application of information technologies in civil and structural engineering. According to Fenves, one component of this science base would deal with the understanding of the processes of planning, design, management, etc., that engineers use:

"... we need to agree on an intellectual framework, in order to create a scientific understanding or abstraction of engineering processes in practice." (p. 5)

This can be interpreted as follows: the bottleneck in construction computing is not due to a deficiency in information technology in general or its specific applications, but to a deficient understanding of construction. Thus, what Fenves wants to add to construction computing research is an understanding of operations in general and of construction specifically. Information technology solely cannot cure the fundamental problems of construction–only better theories and concepts can, and support can be given by information technology. It is proposed to structure this issue as illustrated in Figure 4.

Here it is explicitly acknowledged that all three factors–(emerging) generic operations management principles, understanding of construction peculiarities (and their implications, such as decentralized organization and informal decision-making)–and information technology–may bring about changes in information and material processes. These three approaches interact with each other, and they may amplify or restrain each other's influences to information and material processes. In other words, the introduction of computers to construction does not qualitatively provide anything new from the point of view of the theoretical analysis of production systems: computing is worthwhile only as far as it can contribute–better than alternative means–to the realization of the principles of production.

The way changes and benefits emerge in construction is dependent on the fit between interventions emanating from these three fields as depicted in Figure 4. Let us illustrate this through examples.

There are three channels through which information technology can contribute to changes in information and material processes in construction. Firstly, information technology may directly change processes, by mechanising or supporting tasks carried out by people. Secondly, information technology may contribute to the

Figure 4: The interrelationships between operations management, understanding of construction and information technology

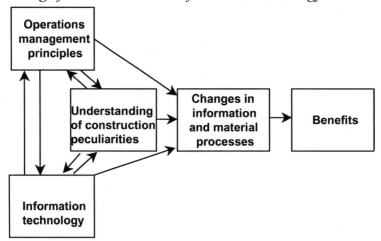

realization of a certain operations management principle. A central theme in modern operations management is that variability should be reduced in production (Hopp & Spearman, 1996). Excessive variability is a chronic problem of construction. Thus, it is required to search for computer-based means for the reduction of variability. One example is provided by three-dimensional CAD design, where possible geometric interference of components designed by different designers–a problem stemming from construction peculiarities–is automatically avoided. Thirdly, information technology may be used for eliminating the problems associated with construction peculiarities. One such problem is the scarcity of learning based on repetition in construction–practically all buildings are one-of-a-kind. However, this problem can at least partially be remedied through computer simulation and visualization of the product and process of construction.

On the other hand, the principles of operations management and the construction peculiarities provide a constraint for information technology. Firstly, information technology should not deteriorate the realization of operations management principles. For example, variability should not be increased by the introduction of information technology. Unfortunately, evidence shows that the various IT problems, like machine, software and communications breakdowns, and deficient skills, are a considerable source of variability. Thus, the background variability of the IT infrastructure should be reduced. Secondly, the peculiarities of construction, such as one-of-a-kind product, site production and temporary organization, and their implications, provide a challenging environment for information technology, and solutions fit to this environment should be aimed for. This means, among other things, that IT applications should support the communication of uncertain and qualitative information that characterises the design process (Pietroforte, 1997).

It follows that understanding and utilization of the interactions among the generic operations management theory, construction peculiarities and capabilities of computing are most important in the successful advancement of IT in construction.

CONCLUSIONS

Unfortunately, the analyses made indicate that there are no quick fixes regarding the possibilities for increasing the benefits accruing from the use of information technology in construction. Increased understanding leads to the conclusion that the use of information technology is an extremely complicated issue that we have only started to grasp. However, five areas of improvement become apparent. Firstly, we, both as practitioners and researchers, have to reject the deeply ingrained notion that information technology in itself brings about benefits in construction. Rather, the effects of information technology are intermediated through information and material process, which can–and should–be improved also by other means. Secondly, the firms in the AEC sector should try to get their IT investments into control. Sound managerial principles should be used along all life cycle phases of an IT project. Especially the implementation phase has to be emphasized, for avoiding detrimental impacts. Joint consideration of the technical and human part of an information system is one important precondition for success. Thirdly, in the development of new information systems for construction, more emphasis should be placed on how organizational and managerial changes can effectively be supported by information technology, rather than only holding IT as the major driving force that necessitates organizational changes. Fourthly, regarding scientific research, there is a need for a reintegration of research addressing construction computing with advanced construction management research focusing on new organizational and managerial solutions. Recently, the research on construction computing has increasingly emerged as a discipline in its own–somewhat untimely, as integration to related fields would rather be needed. Fifthly, construction computing research, addressing up till now mostly the development of new concepts, methods and tools, should adopt empirical research into its methodical arsenal. How are information systems developed and implemented in practice? What actually happens when people are using information technology in construction?

ENDNOTES

1   Architecture, Engineering and Construction

REFERENCES

Applebaum, H. A. (1982). Construction management: Traditional versus bureaucratic methods. *Anthropological Quarterly*, *55*(4), 224-234.

Bennett, J., Pothecary, E. and Robinson, G. (1996). *Designing and Building a World-Class Industry*, 91. Reading, MA: University of Reading.

Betts, M. and Wood-Harper, T. (1994). Reengineering construction: A new management research agenda. *Journal of Construction Management and Economics*, *12*, 551-556.

Brandon, P., Betts, M. and Wamelink, H. (1998). Information technology support to construction design and production. *Computers in Industry*, *35*, 1-12.

Churcher, D. W., Johnson, S. T., Howard, R. W. and Wager, D. M. (1996). IT in construction–Quantifying the benefits. *CIRIA Report 160*.

Davenport, T. (1993). *Process Innovation–Re-Engineering Work Through Information Technology*, 336. Boston, MA: Harvard Business School Press.

Davenport, T. (1994). Saving IT's soul: Human-centered information management. *Harvard Business Review*, (March-April), 119-131.

Davenport, T. H. and Short, J. E. (1990). The new industrial engineering: Information technology and business process redesign. *Sloan Management Review*, (Summer), 11-27.

Earl, M. J. (1994). The new and the old of business process redesign. *Journal of Strategic Information Systems*, 3(1), 5-22.

Engineering News Record. (1997). Design firms spend 3% of revenue on technology. October 6, 7.

Enkovaara, E., Heikkonen, A. and Taiponen, T. (1998). *Rakennusalan Informaatioteknologian Kypsyys- Ja Hyötytason Mittaus* (In Finnish: *Measurement of Maturity and Benefits of Construction Information Technology*). Mimeo, Finland.

Farid, F. (1993). Editorial for special issue: Applications of microcomputers and workstations in construction. *Journal of Construction Engineering and Management*, *119*(2), 193-195.

Fenves, S. J. (1996). The penetration of information technologies into civil and structural engineering design: State-of-the-art and directions toward the future. In Kumar, B. and Retik, A. (Eds.), *Information Representation and Delivery in Civil and Structural Engineering Design*, 1-5. Edinburgh: Civil Comp Press.

Gann, D. (2000). *Building Innovation: Complex Constructs in a Changing World*. London: Thomas Telford.

Garvin, D. A. (1998). The processes of organization and management. *Sloan Management Review*, 39(4), 33-50.

Gibbs, W. W. (1997). Taking computers to task. *Scientific American*, (July), 64-71.

Grierson, D. E. (1998). Information technology in civil and structural engineering design in the twentieth century. *Computers and Structures*, 67, 291-298.

Hammer, M. (1990). Reengineering work: Don't automate, obliterate. *Harvard Business Review*, (July-August), 104.

Hammer, M. and Champy, J. (1993). *Reengineering the Corporation*, 223. London: Nicholas Brealey.

Hopp, W. and Spearman, M. (1996). *Factory Physics: Foundations of Manufacturing Management*, 668. Boston, MA: Irwin/McGraw-Hill.

Howard, R., Kiviniemi, A. and Samuelson, O. (1998). Surveys of IT in the construction industry and experience of the IT barometer in Scandinavia. *Itcon*, 3, 45-56.

Ibbs, C. W. (1994). Reengineering construction work processes. *The International Journal of Construction Information Technology*, 2(4), 27-47.

Johnson, H. T. and Kaplan, R. S. (1987). *Relevance Lost–The Rise and Fall of Management Accounting*, 269. Boston, MA: Harvard Business School Press.

Kazi, A. S., Hannus, M. and Laitinen, J. (2001). ICT support for distributed engineering in construction. In Stanford-Smith, B. and Chiozza, E. (Eds.), *E-Work and E-Commerce: Novel Solutions and Practices for a Global Networked Economy*, 909-915. Amsterdam: IOS Press.

Konchar, M. and Sanvido, V. (1998). Comparison of U.S. project delivery systems. *Journal of Construction Engineering and Management, 124*(6), 435-444.

Koskela, L. (2000). An exploration towards a production theory and its application to construction. *Espoo, VTT Building Technology*, 296. VTT Publications; 408. ISBN 951-38-5565-1; 951-38-5566-X. WWW: http://www.inf.vtt.fi/pdf/publications/2000/P408.pdf.

Laitinen, J. (1998). *Model Based Construction Process Management,* 136. Stockholm: Royal Institute of Technology, Construction Management and Economics.

McKinsey Global Institute. (2001). *US Productivity Growth, 1995-2000.*

Melnyk, S. A. and Narasimhan, R. (1992). *Computer Integrated Manufacturing.* Homewood, IL: Business One Irwin.

Mumford, E. and Hendricks, R. (1997). *Reengineering Rhetoric and Reality: The Rise and Fall of a Management Fashion.* http://bprc.warwick.ac.uk/rc-repb-6.html.

Munkvold, B. E. (2000). Tracing the roots: The influence of socio-technical principles on modern organisational change practices. In Coakes, E., Willis, D. and Lloyd-Jones, R. (Eds.), *The New SocioTech: Graffiti on the Long Wall*, 13-25. London: Springer.

Pietroforte, R. (1997). Communication and governance in the building process. *Construction Management and Economics, 15*, 71-82.

Rivard, H. (2000). A survey on the impact of information technology on the Canadian architecture, engineering and construction industry. *ITCon,5*,37-56.

Rockart, J. F. and Short, J. E. (1989). IT in the 1990s: Managing organizational interdependence. *Sloan Management Review*, (Winter), 7-17.

Schrage, M. (1997). The real problem with computers. *Harvard Business Review*, (September-October), 178, 183-188.

Strassmann, P. A. (1997). *The Squandered Computer*, 426. New Canaan, CT: The Information Economics Press.

Sverlinger, P.-O. (1996). Organisatorisk samordning vid projektering. *Report 44*. Institutionen för byggnadsekonomi och byggnadsorganisation. Chalmers tekniska högskola. 118 p. (Organizational Coordination in the Design Phase.)

Tavistock Institute. (1966). *Interdependence and Uncertainty*, 83. London: Tavistock Publications.

The Business Roundtable. (1997). *The Business Stake in Effective Project Systems*. Washington, DC.

Thomas, S. R. (2000). *Impacts of Design/Information Technology on Project Outcomes*, 39. National Institute of Standards and Technology.

Venkatraman, N. (1991). IT-induced business reconfiguration. In Scott Morton, M. (Ed.), *The Corporation of the 1990s*, 122-158. New York: Oxford University Press.

Section II

The Individual and Information Resource Management

The Individual and Information Resource Management

M. Gordon Hunter
University of Lethbridge, UK

The first section of this book presents an introduction and discussion of the socio-technical paradigm. The third section discusses how users may configure information systems. Paradoxically, as Wenn suggests, perhaps the users are configured by the information systems.

This section, then, presents a bridge between the comprehensive discussion of the socio-technical paradigm and the configuration of users/systems. Issues are discussed surrounding individuals through an exploration of their experiences within the social environment of the information technology profession. This discussion is focused upon the individual through the lens of the socio-technical paradigm.

Our sojourn across the bridge from paradigm to configuration will include three stops. Each one will allow us to gaze out upon the vista of human cognition and information systems and across the vast domain of socio-technical systems. Also, each stop will provide a different perspective on the subject as interpreted by the chapter authors. I am sure you will take joy in the journey.

In the first chapter, Jeffrey Stanton presents a discussion of the facilitation and regulation of personal information flows. He suggests that stakeholders in the systems development process should be cognizant of the issues surrounding individual privacy and performance within the overall organizational context. Stanton presents a framework of information boundary theory within the perspective of boundary management. The framework is a response to attempting to deal with personal information flows and may be employed to address information systems design issues.

The second chapter, by Leoni Warne, discusses the challenges created by information systems failures. She investigated how conflict among the stakeholders of the information system development process affects project success/failure. Warne concludes that human factors play a large part in information systems failures, especially as a result of the conflict which inevitably arises. "Managing the power, politics and organizational conflict inherent in information systems is increasingly recognized as being of critical importance to successful information systems development" (Warne, this volume).

In the final chapter, Mike Metclafe outlines an approach for systems developers to take in order to respond to the conflicting demands of stakeholders. He begins by describing the three aspects of information systems development problems. These aspects include technical, personal and organizational considerations. Metcalfe then takes the reader from the perspective of investigating problems to that of addressing concerns. As Metcalfe suggests, "… 'problem solving' … should be relabeled 'concern solving', as it [is] so much about dealing with stakeholders' concerns rather than objective problems" (Metcalfe, this volume). This is not merely a semantic shift, but one of responding to a different contextual perspective of stakeholder involvement in information systems development.

These three chapters present different perspectives of the individual within the socio-technical systems paradigm. I know you will thoroughly enjoy reading them as they lead you from paradigm to configuration. After this brief journey you may be justified in finding yourself a spot in the coffee shop of reflection.

Chapter V

Information Technology and Privacy: A Boundary Management Perspective

Jeffrey M. Stanton
Syracuse University, USA

ABSTRACT

With the rising popularity of the Internet and some widely publicized occurrences of privacy loss due to information technology, many individuals have recently become more concerned with the privacy and security of sensitive information. These concerns have special relevance within work organizations because of the substantial amounts of data that organizations typically collect about the work and non-work activities of their employees. This chapter presents a new theoretical perspective called Information Boundary Theory, that describes whether, when, and why employees care about the privacy and security of sensitive information at work. Analysis of interview data from N=25 non-managerial U.S. workers provided preliminary support for four of the new theory's research propositions. The chapter describes implications of the theory and the research findings for the design and deployment of information technology systems within organizations and maps a research agenda for future uses of the theory.

INTRODUCTION

The deployment of information technology into organizations has continued to accelerate over recent years. Information technology systems that leverage networks, databases, and telecommunications channels carry, distribute, display, and store an increasing amount of data that has personal relevance to individual workers. Thus, designers, administrators, and users of such systems may have a strong interest in facilitating and assuring proper regulation of personal information flows. From a technical standpoint such matters are handled through a variety of mechanisms such as encryption and access control, but from a social standpoint, it is important to understand what information must be protected, when, and why. In this chapter I synthesize a framework for understanding the regulation of personal information flows based on three component theories relevant to the privacy of personal and performance information in organizational settings. This framework, called information boundary theory, uses a guiding metaphor from psychologically grounded research on communications boundary management. In support of the viability of the framework, I discuss qualitative data from an interview study that provided a preliminary assessment of the framework. Finally, I discuss applications of the framework to future research and to the practice of information systems design.

INFORMATION TECHNOLOGY AND PRIVACY: A BOUNDARY MANAGEMENT PERSPECTIVE

Commercial, non-profit, and governmental organizations use information technology in a variety of ways to obtain and communicate data about their employees, clients, customers, and other relevant individuals. While this observation has been true for many years, key issues such as privacy have become particularly salient with the widespread availability of new data collection, transmission, and storage strategies facilitated by the Internet, intranets, databases, and related information technologies (see, for example, Agre, 1997; Kahin & Nesson, 1997, p. x; U.S. Congress, 2000). In parallel to these developments, increased use of telecommunications media to support the quotidian communications needs of organizations has resulted in a consequent increase in the transmission of sensitive personal information through such channels as email, voicemail, and instant messaging. Investigations of these issues have clearly shown that organizations and their members must take special care in regulating the flow of personal information through the wide variety of information technology systems available now and in the future (Eddy, Stone & Stone-Romero, 1999; Pincus and Trotter, 1995; Sipior, Ward, & Rainone, 1998; Stanton & Weiss, 2000).

From a purely technical standpoint, specific remedies to ensure the security of data (e.g., authentication, access control, encryption, etc.) have long been available, and researchers continue to expand and enhance the repertoire of available techniques. From a socio-technical point of view, however, these techniques comprise a toolbox; the difficult work lies in knowing when a particular tool is needed and why. Thus, in designing or administering an information system that handles personal information, it is important to understand the perspectives and needs of those individuals whose privacy is at stake–workers, managers, clients, customers, and others whose personal information is collected, transmitted, and stored by information technology.

To this end, this chapter describes a theoretical framework for information privacy that I have synthesized from three relevant component theories. The new framework provides predictions about how information collection, storage, and dissemination strategies affect people's attitudes, beliefs, and behaviors toward the institutions that seek to obtain the data. The framework may have particular relevance for information system design that has as its goal the development, implementation, and administration of digital government systems, e-commerce, customer relations management systems, human resource information systems, collaboration software, cooperative work systems, and other information technologies that handle sensitive personal information.

The information boundary theory that I describe below developed out of research investigating uses of monitoring and surveillance technologies within organizations. Analysis of two waves of interview and survey data (Stanton, 2000; Stanton & Weiss, 2000) suggested the viability of synthesizing communications boundary management theory (Petronio, 1991), justice theory (Alder, 1998; Alder & Tompkins, 1997), and a general expectancy-valence framework for privacy protection (Stone and Stone, 1990). In general terms, the framework predicts that individuals' reactions to uses of information technology to collect information about them should follow rules for "boundary opening" and "boundary closure." Boundary opening and closure are dynamic, psychological processes of regulation by which people attempt to control the flow of "intimate" information. In the remainder of this chapter, I introduce the component theories, develop the framework, outline the results from a recent interview study that was designed to provide a preliminary assessment of the framework, and discuss the implications of the framework for future research and practice.

SYNTHESIS OF INFORMATION BOUNDARY THEORY

Researchers have investigated workplace privacy from a variety of perspectives. For example, studies have focused on privacy invasions of physical space (e.g., Cangelosi & Lemoine, 1988; Duvallearly & Benedict, 1992) and of social space (e.g., LePoire, Burgoon, & Parrott, 1992). Organizational researchers have investigated privacy in personnel selection (Connerly, Mael, & Morath, 1999; Fusilier & Hoyer, 1980; Jones & Joy, 1991; Kirchner, 1966 Stone & Stone,

1987), in the storage and use of human resources data (Eddy, Stone, & Stone-Romero, 1999; Stone, Gueutal, Gardner, & McClure, 1983; Woodman et al., 1982), and in the monitoring of employee communications and performance (Sipior, Ward, & Rainone, 1998; Stanton & Barnes-Farrell, 1996; Stanton & Weiss, 2000).

Although workplace privacy has provided fertile ground for research, no predominant theoretical perspective has emerged to account for the psychological mechanisms guiding employee attitudes and behaviors about workplace privacy. Stone and Stone (1990) provided a general expectancy-value framework that helped to classify and organize a variety of motivations for privacy protection behaviors. Later, Stone and Stone-Romero (1999) widened the focus of their model to account for balance and conflict among different constituencies concerning organizational privacy issues. In neither case, however, did their work explicate the psychological antecedents, processes, and outcomes that shape workers' reactions to privacy-related issues in the workplace. For additional insights into these mechanisms, it is necessary to incorporate theoretical developments from other areas of social science. Specifically, Petronio (1991), in the field of communications, proposed and tested a "communication boundary management" (CBM) model built on the work of Altman (1975, 1976) and others to explain privacy regulation in marital, family, and other interpersonal contexts. In complementary developments, Alder (1998; Alder & Tompkins, 1997) argued for the utility of organizational justice as an explanatory factor in understanding employees' reactions to workplace monitoring and surveillance. Together, these three theories provide a lens through which the privacy implications of organizational communications and data management practices can be examined.

COMMUNICATION BOUNDARY MANAGEMENT APPLIED TO ORGANIZATIONS

In describing her theory of communications boundary management, Petronio (1991) argued that all human relationships contain an intrinsic tension between intimacy and autonomy. Intimacy, on the one hand, comprises revelatory processes through which one individual becomes known to another. Autonomy, conversely, is promulgated by communicative and other behaviors that protect and separate the self from others. Applications of these ideas to marital relationships, parent-child relationships, and so forth are straightforward, but Petronio has argued (Petronio & Chayer, 1988) that the tension between intimacy and autonomy is intrinsic in workplace relationships as well. These concepts map onto workplace privacy concerns with the assertion that employees view monitoring, surveillance, personal data collection, and technology-mediated organizational communications as potentially revelatory of themselves. Here are some illustrative examples: Having one's task performance or computer activities monitored provides a communication conduit through which a supervisor or manager can receive detailed information about one's productive (or unproductive) activities. Likewise, working in an environment with video surveillance cameras makes one's conscious and unconscious behaviors available for scrutiny while on company premises. Collection of personal data (e.g., lifestyle information for insurance purposes) also reveals intimate aspects of the self to others within the work environment. Finally, communication of opinions or ideas over email, voicemail, or other messaging technologies can publicize one's point of view about people and other important matters. I do not mean to imply that these forms of revelation are inappropriate or undesirable, but rather that they all constitute communicative activities in the workplace by which the self (e.g., an employee) becomes known to the other (e.g., coworkers, supervisors, managers, or human resources professionals). I do hypothesize, however, that stakeholders such as employees have a strong interest in or feel the need to "regulate" these forms of communication.

Regulating communication in order to influence whether and how others learn about the self provides the opposing force to revelation in Petronio's (1991) CBM theory. Thus, in tension with the conduits for revelation described above are individuals' well-documented needs for autonomy and control (cf. Deci & Ryan, 1991; Greenberger & Strasser, 1986; Spector, 1981). For example, after allowing for idiosyncratic individual differences, most employees appear to have at least some motivation to control their immediate work environment, their choice of tasks, their rate of working, and the impressions that other individuals have of them (particularly powerful others such as managers). With reference to this latter motivation, large bodies of literature on impression management (Giacalone & Rosenfeld, 1991; Morrison & Bies, 1991) and socially desirable responding (Moorman & Podsakoff, 1992) attest that individuals have consistent and sometimes strong motivations to control how others see them.

CBM theory (Petronio, 1991) asserts that people balance the tension between intimacy and autonomy by negotiating psychological boundaries between themselves and others. A boundary in this context is thus defined as a (usually tacit) "psychological contract" between oneself and another concerning the amount, nature, and circumstances of requesting, sending, and receiving personal information. Boundaries become open for sending and receiving information and closed for restricting the flow of information to and from the self. Open boundaries encourage requests for more information and closed boundaries discourage them. The details of CBM theory explicate a set of rules by which psychological needs within a dyadic relationship and the type and context of the personal information interact to determine boundary opening and closure (see Petronio, 1991). Of particular interest for applications to the workplace, "senders" open their boundaries when there is interdependence in the dyad, when the sender does not perceive an undesirable level of vulnerability to negative reactions by the "receiver," and when potential exists for an expressive or instrumental benefit of transmitting information across the boundary. Not coincidentally, these are elements that conceptually overlap with social psychologists' definitions of trust (Boon & Holmes, 1991; Lewicki, McAllister, & Bies, 1998). For example Boon and Holmes (1991) defined trust as, "a state involving confident positive expectations about another's motives with respect to oneself in situations entailing risk" (p. 194). In brief then, I have translated CBM for workplace applications by suggesting that individuals open their communication boundaries—and are therefore amenable to revealing personal information through performance monitoring, mediated communication, and other organizational data collection methods—when they perceive trust in their relationship with the organizational "other." The other is personified by the information receiver, for example, a manager, supervisor, or human resources professional. Individuals also may realize, however, that this receiver is usually not simply the other member in a dyadic relationship but may also play the role of an official organizational representative with the intention and means of using the revealed personal information to serve the organization's purposes. The implication is that the receiver's role as an organizational member or representative may be as important a consideration in negotiating boundaries as the employee's personal relationship with the specific individual.

At this point it is possible to intermix additional implications pertaining to the use of information technology as a medium for the transmission of personal information in organizations. Petronio's (1991) research focused primarily on how boundary regulation occurs in face-to-face interactions. To support her propositions she drew on a rich tradition of social psychological and anthropological research on verbal and non-verbal behavior. For example, in a face-to-face situation, an individual can open a communications boundary beyond the dyad by raising her voice so that others can hear the message. Closing a boundary in a face-to-face situation could entail physically withdrawing from a conversation or using "verbal judo" to divert an inquiry to another topic. Mapped into the domain of mediated communication and technology-facilitated personal data collection, individuals have a larger repertoire of techniques for regulating disclosure, but are also subject to a broader range of situations where a catastrophic loss of control over personal data is possible. Taking email as just one of many possible examples, boundary opening to transmit a message beyond the dyad can be accomplished actively through "carbon copy" and "blind carbon copy" mechanisms, while, analogously to the face-to-face situation, boundary closure can be accomplished simply by withdrawing from the dialog (i.e., refusing to reply). On the other hand, an email message, once transmitted, is more vulnerable to loss of regulatory control even than gossip (the face-to-face equivalent of forwarding an email), because the message is seen by in a form directly authored by the self, and because the amplifying power of the technology makes possible wider (and quicker) rebroadcast as well as semi-permanent storage of the message.

These insights form a central concern of the final section of this chapter: information technology amplifies both opportunities for boundary regulation and possibilities of loss of boundary control. Information systems designs that attempt to successfully incorporate the regulation of personal information can do so by providing tools for boundary regulation and barriers or firewalls to prevent catastrophic loss of control. Before examining these tools and firewalls, however, it is important to understand the circumstances under which individuals desire to open and close their information boundaries. The organizational justice and expectancy-valence theories described below can help to pinpoint these circumstances.

ORGANIZATIONAL JUSTICE APPLIED TO BOUNDARY NEGOTIATION

Alder (1998; Alder & Tompkins, 1997) provided a literature review of monitoring and surveillance methods in the workplace highlighting both negative and positive effects of monitoring documented by various researchers. Alder then argued that an organizational justice perspective could provide insights into how employees would react to organizational performance monitoring procedures. Stanton (2000) provided empirical evidence from several diverse samples confirming that organizational justice served as a useful explanatory model for understanding how the characteristics of electronic and traditional performance monitoring affected employees' reactions to monitoring. Although the theory and the findings were framed specifically to explain reactions to performance monitoring, these ideas arguably extend to a more general consideration of personal information flows in organizations as they relate to monitoring, surveillance, communication, and other forms of personal data flow that are managed by organizations and their information technology.

One successful theoretical perspective attributes individuals' preference for fair procedures and treatment to their need for affirmation of identity with a valued group. Termed the "group-value" model of organizational justice (Lind & Tyler, 1988), the theory proposes that people value their membership and status in certain groups, and that fair treatment by group members and in group practices affirms their membership and status. For example, when a person is the target of gossip from another group member, this treatment is seen as unfair because it reflects badly upon the target's status as a group member. Thibaut and Walker (1975), Leventhal (1980), Bies (1987; Bies & Moag, 1986), Greenberg (1993), and others have discussed the conditions and factors that may lead to evaluations of fairness and unfairness, but Alder (1998; Alder & Tompkins, 1997), using the group-value model as a guide, distilled these down to four basic propositions. First, Alder asserted that personal data collection practices have sufficient impact on the work lives of employees to be seen by them as playing an important role in organizational justice. Second, Alder indicated that the personal data content collected and transmitted by information systems must have the highest possible "mission relevance" in order to be seen as fair (e.g., a performance evaluation system could capture work history but not race). Third, Alder commented that personal data collection policies and practices that encourage or at least allow a value expressive function (i.e., "voice" in Thibaut and Walker's terms) will be seen as most fair. Examples of such value expression would be the opportunity for employees to give feedback on the design and implementation of an information system that will process their personal data, or mechanisms built into the procedures of data processing that allow employees to address or appeal problems recorded in these systems. Finally, drawing on previous justice research, Alder described a zone of acceptance in which employees would not scrutinize the fairness of organizational monitoring practices. Routine requests for performance information fall within this zone, and such requests, too ordinary to arouse employee concerns about their status in the group, would not trigger an evaluation of the criteria for fairness described above.

SYNTHESIS OF CBM AND JUSTICE WITH STONE AND STONE'S EXPECTANCY-VALUE THEORY

Stone and Stone (1990) provided a general framework for predicting privacy protection behaviors based on an expectancy-value (EV) framework. EV frameworks have been applied to choice behavior and other motivated behavior in many work situations (Pinder, 1998). Vroom's (1964) valence-instrumentality-expectancy theory and Porter and Lawler's (1968) rework of this are widely known organizational applications, but these and other EV frameworks all hearken back to seminal work by Lewin (1938) and Tolman (1959). Recent work on EV (e.g., Feather, 1995) is reflected in this simple formulation, "…a person's values, once engaged, induce valences (or positive and negative subjective values) on actions and their possible outcomes and future consequences. Actions are assumed to occur in relation to these induced valences and the person's expectations about the likelihood of achieving the outcomes and future consequences" (Feather, 1988, p. 105). Stone and Stone's (1990) application of EV to privacy protection reflects the same underlying assumptions: "In the process of engaging in certain behaviors, including those designed to protect OP [organizational privacy], individuals are assumed to behave in ways that they believe will result in the most favorable net level of outcomes... Consistent with expectancy models of motivation, cognitions about outcome levels are assumed to be a function of expectancies, valences, and instrumentalities" (Stone & Stone, 1990, p. 363).

In short, Stone and Stone (1990) considered motivation to protect privacy as a rational process of maximizing instrumental outcomes (e.g., by hiding information that might adversely affect a personnel action such as promotion). Instrumental outcomes, in this context, refer primarily to material or financial gains and losses and are thus distinct from the expressive outcomes intrinsic in theories of justice. By first adding the perspectives associated with CBM theory (Petronio, 1991), we can expand the repertoire of behaviors subject to explanation: Stone and Stone's privacy protection behaviors are akin to the closing of boundaries to achieve positive or avoid negative outcomes, whereas CBM additionally accounts for the opening of boundaries, strategies for negotiating the conditions of opening and closing, contextual factors governing the conditions under which senders transmit particular types of personally significant information to receivers, and the information requesting behavior of receivers. For example, CBM would explicate a conversation (i.e., the boundary negotiation) between a job applicant and an HR professional, in which the applicant hears a justification of the intended use of some information (i.e., the contextual factor) and decides to provide the information (i.e., boundary opening).

Next, by incorporating the organizational justice perspective, we can enhance understanding of the instrumental goals that boundary opening and closing can serve: employees' concerns about the job-relatedness of monitoring and surveillance suggest a desire to shape how others view their on-the-job behavior (including non-prescribed activities such as organizational citizenship behaviors). Additionally, however, both CBM and the organizational justice perspective indicate that individuals wish to regulate the flow of personal information on bases other than purely instrumental ones. In particular, the organizational justice perspective suggests that revelation of personal information may serve expressive goals that test and affirm an individual's status as a group member.

Together, then, these theories suggest a set of related general research propositions. First, if monitoring, surveillance, communication, and other organizational forms of personal data flow are parallel to dyadic communication as described by CBM, then individuals should frame their conceptions of these practices in terms of the flow of personal information within human relationships (e.g., "telling about me," "knowing what I'm doing," "becoming known," or perhaps "becoming visible to others"). Individuals should be capable of articulating the calculus of boundary negotiation, i.e., the conditions under which permitting information flow about them is acceptable or unacceptable. The negotiation of boundaries should be highly dependent on the status of the relationship between the employee/sender and the organization/receiver. I have offered a shorthand term for the relationship status most conducive to the opening of boundaries: trust. If trust exists between the sender and the receiver, boundaries should open to the flow of more and more "intimate" types of information content. Incorporating the justice perspective, intimate, in this context, refers to information that is personally relevant but not "mission relevant." To the extent that trust does not exist or has faltered in the relationship, senders may attempt to close boundaries to all but the most directly mission relevant types of information. Senders will evaluate receiver requests for information in light of the trust in the dyad and organizational justice concerns about the information. Senders will most likely open boundaries to information that serves their instrumental or expressive ends. Finally, a zone of acceptance may exist in which the sender transmits routine forms of information across the boundary without explicit consideration of instrumental or value expressive goals.

I have intentionally framed these ideas as a complex of related, general research propositions because the merger of these component theories, while promising, is not at this time mature enough to offer hypotheses of sufficient specificity to warrant quantitative measurement and statistical inference testing. In recognition of the preliminary status of this framework, I have sought early evidence by conducting a series of semi-structured interviews. This research explored whether these hypothesized communication boundaries exist in workplace situations and, if so, how employees negotiate the opening and closing of these boundaries in reference to contextual factors such as the type of information requested by the organization. The research was reported in detail in Sarkar, Stanton, and Line (2001) and is summarized briefly below.

METHOD

My research team conducted interviews with n=25 non-managerial employees (40% males) from a variety of industries in the continental U.S. Participants' job responsibilities included emergency medical technician, construction worker, cashier, secretary, data processing analyst, child support investigator, customer service representative, welder, and a variety of other types of work. Half of the respondents had been on their present job at least two years. We used a semi-structured interview protocol that was designed to elicit descriptions of the conditions under which respondents would or would not reveal various kinds of performance and non-performance information to their organizations. The interview contained seven questions about monitoring, surveillance, and the organizational collection of personal information based on earlier interview work conducted by Stanton and Weiss (2000). Each question described a hypothetical company policy concerning a certain type of personal information and asked the respondent to indicate whether he or she would share that information and the rationale behind that decision. We transcribed the interviews verbatim (including interviewer queries), coded the resulting transcriptions, and conducted frequency analysis of code assignments to identify major thematic content (see Charmaz, 1995; MacQueen, McLellan, Kay, & Milstein, 1998; Strauss & Corbin, 1990). We used the procedures described in Carey, Morgan, and Oxtoby (1996) to improve intercoder agreement. We iterated through these procedures until we obtained 80% agreement across all respondents and questions. We triangulated on the themes by examining combinations of codes. In particular, we examined coding patterns that emerged in conjunction with material indicating the acceptability or unacceptability of information requests. Within these patterns we related codes back to respondent verbatims to ensure that our findings accurately represented the ideas of the respondents.

RESULTS

Descriptive Information

A total of 953 code assignments was made across all questions and respondents for an average of about 38 codes per respondent. That is, interviewees on average stated about 38 distinctly recognizable ideas during the course of their interview. Table 1 lists the set of thematic code descriptions and their frequency of occurrence. The most frequently occurring code (n=355) captured the idea that the respondent felt that the monitoring, surveillance, or data collection technique under discussion was acceptable to them: they would not hesitate to share the information requested. Conversely, the next most frequently occurring code (n=120) captured the idea that the respondent felt that they would not feel comfortable sharing the information requested. The frequent occurrence of these two opposing ideas reflects the primary orientation of the interview, which was to seek the boundary between acceptable and unacceptable information in order to explore the respondent's detailed reasoning concerning the negotiation of this boundary. The remainder of this analysis comprises one section describing conditions for sharing of information–boundary opening–and another section for withholding or protection of information–boundary closing. The analyses described below all reflect an examination of the co-occurrence of at least two thematic codes and thus do not always match the overall frequencies reported in Table 1.

Conditions for Opening Boundaries

Zone of Acceptance. Three themes emerged pertaining to the typicality of organizational information requests. A theme describing a policy as common practice in most organizations was assigned nine times in conjunction with the code for acceptable transmission. This theme captured the idea that some personal information was typically requested and therefore, by custom, not sensitive. Another theme indicating prior experience with the technique appeared 13 times in conjunction with the theme for acceptable transmission. Finally, a theme indicating generic availability of requested information appeared four times with the theme for acceptable transmission. These themes all appear to capture Alder's (1998; Alder & Tompkins, 1997) idea of a zone of acceptance. Senders may often respond to information requests perceived as routine and ordinary by transmitting the information without thoughtful scrutiny.

Job Relatedness/Justice. Five themes emerged pertaining to the job-relatedness of the requested information. One theme, capturing the idea of the "employer's right to know," was used 13 times. Verbatims for this theme supported the employers' right to certain information because of their ownership of the underlying resource. Two additional themes, which appeared a total of 10 times, further emphasized the importance of business-related use of the underlying resource. Another thematic code, assigned twice, pertained to transmitting information to individuals outside of human resources as long as the information was performance related. The final theme in this area coded the importance of observing employee behavior only in work-related spaces. These codes all appear to capture Alder's (1998; Alder & Tompkins, 1997) ideas about the perceived fairness of monitoring job-related behaviors. In these responses, senders were willing to provide the requested information about their whereabouts, who they called on the phone and what they said, and other aspects of their job behavior, just as long as the information collected had a business-related purpose. Another justice theme concerning the acceptability of data collection pertained to the importance of preset company policies governing the procedures (coded five times). As above, the notion of established rules that decision makers must follow is a hallmark of some theories of procedural justice (e.g., Leventhal, 1980).

Instrumental Goals. Several themes emerged pertaining to instrumental goals that would be served if the employee/sender transmitted the requested information. The most frequently occurring theme, emerging in 16 verbatims, pertained to abuse of company resources. In these verbatims respondents believed that certain types of information collection were justified because they prevented

Table 1: Thematic code descriptions and occurrence frequencies

Frequency	Thematic Code Description
355	Monitoring/information request is acceptable
120	Monitoring/information request is unacceptable
49	Question not asked in this interview
41	This monitoring/information request invades privacy
36	Monitoring/information request is unacceptable but will comply
30	This monitoring/information request prevents abuse of company resources
28	I am concerned about security of the system
22	I like my job
22	The monitoring/information requested is not job related
20	Employer does not have the right to know this
20	This technology helps improve organizational efficiency
17	If this policy/practice discriminates among employees
15	I have experienced this technology before
14	The requested information may reach someone who is not authorized to have it
14	This policy/practice shows that the company does not trust employees
13	There must be guidelines about monitoring, storage, and how information is used
10	Computers are unreliable guardians of data
8	This is a common, acceptable practice in most organizations
8	Employer has the right to know this
8	This technology can provide protection when in danger
8	The monitoring/information requested is job related
7	I have not experienced this technology before
7	Access to this personal data should be restricted
7	Only if monitoring personal spaces
6	Only if tracking personal e-messages
6	It is difficult to cope with constant up-grades
6	If knowledge of this data collection is shared with me
5	Knowing the character of employees important to avoid making bad hiring decisions
5	Only if monitoring public places
5	One should obtain this employee data from supervisors not electronic databases
4	Only if tracking business related messages
4	Historical information about this is irrelevant to future decisions
4	If gathered information is used to make employment decisions
3	This monitoring can inhibit performance
3	This information can be learned by face-to-face contact with the person
3	Only if monitoring is non-secretive
2	This monitoring helps provide accurate feedback
2	This monitoring helps improve performance
2	This practice can cause physical ailments
2	This practice has made us dependent on technology
2	My job meets my needs
2	Only if monitoring is secretive
2	One cannot trust the guardians of the data
1	Do not wish to respond to this question
1	This monitoring leads to fair performance evaluations
1	This practice is equivalent to guilty without trial
1	More authorities should have access to personal data
1	I do not like my job
1	This information is irrelevant if I can physically do the job

"cheaters"–coworkers who might try to beat the system–from receiving more than their share of organizational resources. Two themes, each coded three times, reflected the importance that people place on having compatible coworkers, and concerns about workplace security and their concomitant willingness to appear on video cameras. Two different themes, each coded twice, related to job performance.

Each of these themes provides a basis on which the respondent reasoned an advantage of providing the information requested. As such these themes fit Stone and Stone's (1990) predictions about the importance of instrumental motivations. Importantly, however, the themes all suggest motivations for revelatory behavior–opening of boundaries–rather than privacy protection. Themes about disclosure of surveillance (coded four times) and sharing information from testing (coded three times) also emerged as relevant to the acceptance of these policies. Some respondents expressed a belief that if organizations kept surveillance secret, it implied a lack of trust of the employees. Other verbatims pertaining to the results of genetic testing suggested that employees wanted to access their information so that they would be able to "appeal" any adverse results. The notion of an appeal process is central to many formulations of procedural justice. Thibaut and Walker (1975) have also indicated that appeals serve a value expressive function.

Conditions for Closing Boundaries

In an interesting contrast to Stanton and Weiss (2000), the most frequently mentioned general rationale (coded 38 times) for boundary closure was a concern for personal privacy. In general, respondents initially mentioned privacy and then, with follow-up questions from the interviewer, made their rationale known for considering a particular information inquiry a privacy issue. In 10 of these cases, respondents mentioned an intimacy theme (e.g., not wanting an organizational representative to know about bathroom habits). The next most frequently mentioned general rationale (coded 24 times) was an expression that the employer did not "have a right to" the information requested. Indicating that some types of information and requests were "none of the organization's business" was the typical mode of expressing this idea. As with privacy, this theme provides little insight into the motivations or conditions for boundary closure, so one must look to the associated themes to understand these issues.

Job Relatedness/Justice. Five different themes emerged suggesting that individuals close their communication boundaries when requested information is not job related. First, in general terms, respondents indicated that the information requested was not relevant to performance on the job in 16 different statements. On a related note, seven respondents mentioned that certain types of information should remain within the employee-manager dyad rather than becoming available to a wider audience of managers. Two additional reasons for boundary closure were coded separately but shared a common theme. First, six employees described as unacceptable any policies that might permit access to employees' personal communications. These verbatims also suggested a belief that organizations should provide employees with access to resources for private communications while at work. On four occasions, respondents extended this right to include the communications with customers, clients, or vendors. Note that although most of these verbatims pertained to telephone monitoring, one respondent mentioned the desire to control access to personal email communications and another respondent wished to control access to job-irrelevant medical information.

On four occasions, respondents described a "water under the bridge" theme: an indication that employers should not have the opportunity to use evidence of past problems against an employee in decisions such as hiring. Another justice theme that emerged (12 instances) was a concern for the release of information that might result in unfair discrimination against an incumbent employee or applicant. Although these verbatims reflected some well-known types of employment discrimination (e.g., racial bias), other verbatims indicated concern for discrimination based on personal habits (e.g., smoking or alcohol usage), family situation (e.g., being a single mother), health status, and financial status. In each case the respondent indicated an unwillingness to provide the requested type of information because of the possibility that the information would be used as the basis of an unfavorable (and unfair) employment decision.

Trust/Security/Access Control. Four themes emerged that related to trust. First, respondents frequently (coded 17 times) expressed mistrust of the underlying technology that was supposed to secure their personal or employment-related information. In clarification of this theme, 15 responses expressed concern that the underlying technology would permit information access to individuals who should not have that permission. On a related note, two responses indicated mistrust for the "guardians" or owners of the data. In a separate theme, 13 responses indicated that the specified information request was unacceptable because it indicated that the organization did not trust you.

Instrumental Motivations. Only one instrumental reason for boundary closure emerged. Two responses indicated a fear that performance monitoring practices might have adverse effects on job performance.

DISCUSSION

To summarize, the interview data appeared to support four of the predictions of the framework. First, as Alder (1998; Alder & Tompkins, 1997) suggested, a zone of acceptance appears to exist within which employees do not scrutinize information requests for acceptability. Second, boundary opening and closure both appear to be partially governed by organizational justice considerations: mission-relatedness of the information, an appeals process, and preset guidelines to govern the use of the requested information. Third, boundary opening is also partially governed by instrumental motivations such as conservation of the organization's resources. In some cases, a concern for equity–also considered an organizational justice concept–may form the basis of such motivations. Interestingly, only one instrumental theme for boundary closure emerged; employees reported more strategies to pursue instrumental goals through revelation of information rather than withholding information. Finally, mistrust appeared to figure prominently into boundary closure considerations. In particular, mistrust of technology and the people who have access to it was a primary motivation for withholding information. In regard to boundary opening, some of the comments hinted at predicted themes of trust and value expression, but these references failed to emerge as strongly as other themes summarized above.

Taken together, the interview evidence supported the idea that monitoring, surveillance, communication, and other organizational forms of personal data flow are analogous to dyadic communication as described by CBM. Interview respondents were apparently capable of articulating the calculus of boundary negotiation. The negotiation of boundaries appeared to be at least somewhat dependent on the status of the relationship between the employee/sender and the organization/receiver: when trust exists between the sender and the receiver, boundaries may open to the flow of more and more "intimate" types of information content. Senders also seem to open boundaries to information that serves their instrumental or expressive ends. Finally, a zone of acceptance seems to exist in which the sender transmits routine forms of information (particularly those that are "mission relevant") across the boundary without invoking the calculus of instrumental or value expressive goals.

Unifying Monitoring, Surveillance, Data Collection, and Communication

By synthesizing communications boundary management and organizational justice with a general expectancy-valence framework, I asserted that seemingly different organizational policies and practices could be examined in a unified way. Specifically, I suggested that performance monitoring (e.g., by computers, video cameras, etc.), surveillance of non-performance behavior (e.g., email and web tracking), collection of personal data (e.g., in applying for insurance), and mediated communications (e.g., by email), could all be viewed as personal information flows governed by organizational policies and the capabilities of the related information technology. The interview data appeared to support this view in that a concise and well-defined set of conditions and motivations appears to govern boundary opening and closing for all four types of personal data collection. In each case, a zone of acceptance exists in which information requests are fulfilled without careful scrutiny. Outside the zone of acceptance, boundary opening or closure depends upon organizational justice considerations (e.g., mission-relatedness), trust, and/or instrumental considerations (e.g., conservation of organizational resources). Some notable asymmetries appeared (e.g., instrumental concerns seemed less relevant for boundary closure), although it is difficult to ascertain whether these occurred as a result of the limitations of our sample and research methods.

On Compliance

In the above discussion of boundary closure, respondents said that they would not comply with the information request in most cases. In 17 different instances, however, respondents mentioned that they found the information request unacceptable but would comply nonetheless. In the breach, such a response seems more probable than outright refusal or other kinds of resistance strategies. When an information request has been honored only under duress, this represents a suspension of the normal dyadic negotiation of communication boundaries. In extreme cases, when an individual has been forced to reveal information that would preferentially be protected, one might say that a privacy violation has taken place. Petronio (1994) discussed such violations in her study of parents and college-age children returning home during break. Specifically, when boundary negotiation between parent and child broke down, or when the parent ignored previously negotiated boundaries, the child often made a behavioral response. Responses to such privacy violations comprise a varied set of privacy restoring behaviors, some of which are relatively benign within the family context (e.g., leaving a warning note) and some which are more severe (e.g., running away from home). It is feasible to hypothesize a parallel set of processes that occur within organizations when employees perceive that their privacy has been violated. Depending upon the severity of the violation, employees could be expected to attempt to restore privacy through a variety of methods. In extreme cases (presumed to be relatively rare), resistance, retaliation, or withdrawal might occur.

On the Dyadic Boundary

We made no predictions concerning different types or levels of boundaries, but Derlega, Metts, Petronio, and Margulis (1993) described a distinction between an interpersonal boundary within the dyad, and the boundary between the dyad and the "outside world." This distinction captures the idea that, for example, a sender may make some revelations to a spouse that the sender expects will not be divulged outside of the marital dyad. The interview data appeared to suggest that an employee might construct such a boundary around the dyad formed with their immediate supervisor or manager. Our data indicated that when employees expected that certain sensitive data (such as formal performance evaluations) might be transmitted outside the dyad, this expectation could lead to boundary closure. This highlights an important complication: the manager, in the role of a receiver, may simultaneously represent him or herself (on a purely personal level) and the department or organization as an official representative. In future development of the theoretical synthesis provided in this chapter, the framework should incorporate the distinction between interpersonal boundaries and the dyadic boundary. Relatedly, it is likely that there are distinct psychological boundaries around an individual's work group and that dyadic and interpersonal boundaries with group members are nested within these larger "community" boundaries.

Limitations of this Evidence

Because of the small sample size used in this study, these results are not representative of the population of U.S. workers or any sub-population thereof. Thus it is possible or even likely that the full range of issues influencing boundary opening and closure has not appeared in this study. In particular, future research that focuses on unique and distinct segments of the workforce (e.g., older workers, temporary workers, or cultural minority members) may find a substantially different mix of motivations and priorities concerning privacy regulation. Although results from this study can safely be interpreted as suggestive of several important and enduring themes that would likely be endorsed by many workers, ascertaining the applicability of any one theme to a representative sample of employees should serve as the focus of future research. For example, exploring the presumptive relationship between mission-relatedness and boundary opening and closure in a large sample of homogeneous individuals (e.g., employees) would have value in substantiating the universality of this theme.

Design and Practice Implications

Even though these recommendations must be tempered by an understanding of the limitations of the preliminary status of this framework, I believe that framework supports several recommendations for positive design and practice. First, every indication from our results indicates that employees do care about privacy in organizational settings. Beyond a "zone of acceptance" for routine information requests, the framework indicates that is imperative for organizations to gauge the impact of any policies and practices that involve collection of personal or performance information about individuals. When such data collection is warranted, favorable relations with employees, customers, and other stakeholders can be maintained by ensuring that information collection practices are perceived as fair and mission-related. Policies should be communicated and practices conducted with the awareness that trust between individuals and the organization can quickly and easily be undermined by requesting or obtaining information that individuals perceive as unfair, potentially discriminatory, or unrelated to the organization's mission.

Understanding the Zone of Acceptance. Certain kinds of information requests and flows can occur without special attention to individuals' boundary regulation. The best method of understanding this zone of acceptance probably lies in conducting a stakeholder survey to ascertain specifically what kinds of personal data are considered unremarkable and under what circumstances, but a few heuristic rules probably suffice for many cases. Information requests that can be fulfilled anonymously probably fall within most people's zone of acceptance. For example, individuals often complete anonymous attitude surveys with little concern about the privacy of their responses. Non-controversial, publicly available data also typically fall within the zone of acceptance. For instance, an individual's gender can typically be determined by a casual observer (even over the telephone), so few individuals resist having this personal data coded into employee or customer databases.

Designing to Facilitate Boundary Regulation. One clear imperative implied by the content of this chapter is that designs of organizational information systems should incorporate tools that help stakeholders regulate their information boundaries. Although the framework eloquently affirms the need for such tools, there is a considerable body of prior writing that has explored the form that such tools might take. For example, three possibilities appeared in the "Code of Fair Information Practices" that appeared several decades ago in a federal government report (U.S. Dept. of Health, Education, & Welfare, 1973). First, the report suggests, "There must be a way for a person to find out what information about the person is in a record and how it is used." More generally, every organizational information system that manages personal information flows should contain a retrieval mechanism through which individuals can locate and review prior correspondence and stored records that contain information that originated with them. Second, the report continues, "There must be a way for a person to correct or amend a record of identifiable information about the person." This point closes the loop with the first point: given a method of reviewing one's own personal information, there must also be a method for correcting it if it is wrong or inappropriately incomplete. Finally, the report says, "There must be a way for a person to prevent information about the person that was obtained for one purpose from being used or made available for other purposes without the person's consent." This is by far the most difficult of the three stipulations from a system design point of view, but it also exemplifies the heart of the boundary regulation concept. An information system user must have the tools to designate that a certain information flow belongs to a particular audience, for a particular purpose, and for a particular lifetime or timeframe. Most importantly, the information system must then enforce those designations and limit overrides to the smallest possible community of system administrators. Few if any existing organizational information systems meet the ideals contained in these three stipulations.

Promoting Boundary Opening. Another design imperative implied by the content of this chapter is that an information system whose essential goal is communication or sharing of information should promote boundary opening rather than boundary closure. (Note that this need not be the goal of all information systems: a mental health database containing sensitive personal histories might best be designed to discourage information sharing.) According to the data described in this chapter, boundary opening occurs when organizational justice considerations are appropriately supported. Three specific (and ubiquitous) justice themes emerged. First, in regard to mission-relatedness of the information processed, an information system should include sufficient structure to encourage the request and exchange of only mission-relevant data. Think, for example, of the potential positive impact of designing an email system that prevented people from inadvertently sending highly personal messages to wide distribution lists. Such a system would not prevent people from communicating such information to a trusted confidante, but could provide a friendly warning to help individuals from sharing intimate information beyond the dyadic boundary. Second, information systems that contain or transmit personal data should contain a structure for an appeals process. Double opt-in methods in market research databases exemplify this issue: such systems pose a final question–are you *sure* you want us to use your demographic data for this purpose–before committing the individual's personal data to the database. Finally, information systems should communicate to their clients and carefully enforce specific guidelines governing the use of the information in the system. Privacy policies on e-commerce websites provide one example of such guidelines, although it is not always clear that the enforcement behind the policy is sufficient.

CONCLUSION

Future research on the topic of information boundaries could explore the possibilities and limitations of the theoretical framework presented here. As a first step, the idea of a psychological boundary, presented in this chapter as an instance of a tacit psychological contract, should find expression as a set of behavioral, attitudinal, and affective constructs pertaining to boundary opening and boundary closure. This step would serve the dual purpose of sharpening the definition of boundaries and supporting a structured method of assessing boundary opening and closure in specific situations. Built on this progress, the general research propositions described in this chapter can then become sharper and more specific a priori hypothesis statements. Together, these developments would support subsequent exploration of the information boundary framework.

This exploration can take two distinct and equally important forms. First, one set of research projects should focus on testing whether the basic propositions of the framework that received preliminary support in this chapter can survive a retest using different research methods and contexts. Second, a more applied set of projects could include development of specific artifacts, such as an experimental email interface, that embodied some of the ideas for promoting boundary opening suggested in this chapter. Research could then compare such artifacts to their more traditional predecessors to ascertain whether any benefit was derived from including features that enhance users' trust and perceptions of fairness. With basic and applied evidence concerning the utility of information boundary theory, it will be possible to reassess the promise suggested in the present chapter of understanding individuals' motivations to regulate the flow of personal information through the wide variety of information technology systems available now and in the future.

ACKNOWLEDGEMENT

This research was supported in part by National Science Foundation award SBR9810137 and in part by award SES9984111. The National Science Foundation does not necessarily endorse the findings or conclusions of this study.

REFERENCES

Agre, P. E. (1997). Introduction. In Agre, P. E. and Rotenberg, M. (Eds.), *Technology and Privacy, the New Landscape*, 1-28. Cambridge, MA: MIT Press.

Alder, G. S. (1998). Ethical issues in electronic performance monitoring: A consideration of deontological and teleological perspectives. *Journal of Business Ethics, 17,* 729-743.

Alder, G. S. and Tompkins, P. K. (1997). Electronic performance monitoring: An organizational justice and concertive control perspective. *Management Communication Quarterly, 10,* 259-288.

Altman, I. (1975). *The Environment and Social Behavior*. Monterey, CA: Brooks/Cole.

Altman, I. (1976). Privacy: A conceptual analysis. *Environment and Behavior, 8,* 7-29.

Bies, R. J. (1987). The predicament of injustice: The management of moral outrage. In Cummings, L. L. and Staw, B. M. (Eds.), *Research in Organizational Behavior, 9,* 289-319. Greenwich, CT: JAI Press.

Bies, R. J. and Moag, J. S. (1986). Interactional justice: Communication criteria of fairness. In Lewicki, R. J., Sheppard, B. H. and Baxerman, M. (Eds.), *Research on Negotiation in Organizations, 1*, 43-55. Greenwich, CT: JAI Press.

Boon, S. D. and Holmes, J. G. (1991). The dynamics of interpersonal trust: Resolving uncertainty in the face of risk. In Hinde, R. A. and Groebel, J. (Eds.), *Cooperation and Prosocial Behavior*, 190-211. Cambridge, UK: Cambridge University Press.

Cangelosi, V. E. and Lemoine, L. F. (1988). Effects of open versus closed physical environment on employee perception and attitude. *Social Behavior and Personality, 16*, 71-77.

Connerly, M. L., Mael, F. A. and Morath, R. A. (1999). Don't ask-please tell: Selection privacy from two perspectives. *Journal of Occupational and Organizational Psychology, 72*, 405-422.

Dallas v. England, 846 S.W.2d 957, 1993 Tex.App. LEXIS 643 (Tx.Ct.App 1992), rev'd, 849 S.W.2d 941, 1994 Tex. LEXIS 17 (Tex. 1994).

Deci, E. L. and Ryan, R. M. (1991). Intrinsic motivation and self-determination in human behavior. In Steers, R. M. and Porter, L. W. (Eds.), *Work Motivation*. New York: McGraw-Hill.

Derlega, V. J., Metts, S., Petronio, S. and Margulis, S. T. (1993). *Self-Disclosure*. Newbury Park, CA: Sage.

Duvallearly K. and Benedict, J. O. (1992). The relationships between privacy and different components of job-satisfaction. *Environment and Behavior, 24*, 670-679.

Eddy, E. R., Stone, D. L. and Stone-Romero, E. F. (1999). The effects of information management policies on reactions to human resource information systems: An integration of privacy and procedural justice perspectives. *Personnel Psychology, 52*, 335-358.

Feather, N. T. (1988). From values to actions: Recent applications of the expectancy-value model. *Australian Journal of Psychology, 40*, 105-124.

Feather, N. T. (1995). Values, valences, and choice: The influence of values on the perceived attractiveness and choice of alternatives. *Journal of Personality and Social Psychology, 68*, 1135-1151.

Fusilier, M. R. and Hoyer, W. D. (1980). Variables affecting perceptions of invasions of privacy in a personnel selection situation. *Journal of Applied Psychology, 65*, 623-626.

Giacalone, R. A. and Rosenfeld, P. (Eds.). (1991). *Applied Impression Management: How Image-Making Affects Managerial Decisions*. Thousand Oaks, CA: Sage.

Greenberg, J. (1993). The social side of fairness: Interpersonal and informational classes of organizational justice. In Cropanzano, R. (Ed.), *Justice in the*

Workplace: Approaching Fairness in Human Resource Management. Hillsdale, NJ: Erlbaum.

Greenberger, D. B. and Strasser, S. (1986). The development and application of a model of personal control in organizations. *Academy of Management Review, 11*, 164-177.

Jones, J. W. and Joy, D. S. (1991). Empirical investigation of job applicants' reactions to taking a preemployment honesty test. In Jones, J. W. (Ed.), *Preemployment Honest Testing: Current Research and Future Directions*, 121-131. New York: Quorum.

Kahin, B. and Nesson, C. R. (1997). *Borders in Cyberspace: Information Policy and the Global Information Infrastructure.* Cambridge, MA: MIT Press.

Kirchner, W. K. (1966). A note on the effect of privacy in taking typing tests. *Journal of Applied Psychology, 50*, 373-374.

LePoire, B. A, Burgoon, J. K. and Parrott, R. (1992). Status and privacy restoring communication in the workplace. *Journal of Applied Communication Research, 20*, 419-436.

Leventhal, G. S. (1980). What should be done with equity theory? New approaches to the study of fairness in social relationships. In Gergen, K., Greenberg, M. and Willis, R. (Eds.), *Social Exchange: Advances in Theory and Research.* New York: Plenum.

Lewicki, R. J., McAllister, D. J. and Bies, R. J. (1998). Trust and distrust: New relationships and realities. *Academy of Management Review, 23*, 438-458.

Moorman, R. H. and Podsakoff, P. M. (1992). A meta-analytic review and empirical test of the potential confounding effects of social desirability response sets in organizational behaviour research. *Journal of Occupational & Organizational Psychology, 65*, 131-149.

Morrison, E. W. and Bies, R. J. (1991). Impression management in the feedback-seeking process: A literature review and research agenda. *Academy of Management Review, 16*, 522-541.

Petronio, S. (1991). Communication boundary management: A theoretical model of managing disclosure of private information between marital couples. *Communication Theory, 1*, 311-335.

Petronio, S. (1994). Privacy binds in family interactions: The case of parental privacy invasion. In Cupach, W. R. and Spitzberg, B. H. (Eds.), *The Dark Side of Interpersonal Communication*, 241-257. Hillsdale, NJ: Lawrence Erlbaum.

Petronio, S. and Chayer, J. (1988). Communicating privacy norms in a corporation: A case study. Paper presented at the *International Communication Association*, New Orleans, LA.

Pincus, L. B. and Trotter, C. (1995). The disparity between public and private sector employee privacy protections: A call for legitimate privacy rights for private sector workers. *American Business Law Journal, 33,* 51-89.

Sarkar-Barney, S., Stanton, J. M. and Line, K. (2001). Crossing the line: When do organizations ask for too much personal data about workers? In Alge, B. J. (Ed.), *Design Considerations in Electronic Workplace Surveillance Systems.* Symposium presented at the *16th Annual Conference of the Society for Industrial and Organizational Psychology,* April, San Diego, CA.

Shahar v. Bowers, 836 F. Supp. 859, 1993 U.S.Dist. LEXIS 14206 (N.D.Ga., 1993).

Sipior, J. C., Ward, B. T. and Rainone, S. M. (1998). Ethical management of employee e-mail privacy. *Information Systems Management, 15,* 41-47.

Soroka v. Dayton Hudson Corp., I Cal.Rptr.2d 77, 1991 Cal.App. LEXIS 1241 (Cal.Ct.App. 1st Dist. 1991).

Spector, P. E. (1982). Behavior in organizations as a function of employee's locus of control. *Psychological Bulletin, 91,* 482-497.

Stanton, J. M. and Barnes-Farrell, J. L. (1996). Effects of computer monitoring on personal control, satisfaction and performance. *Journal of Applied Psychology, 81,* 738-745.

Stanton, J. M. (2000). Traditional and electronic monitoring from an organizational justice perspective. *Journal of Business and Psychology, 15,* 129-147.

Stanton, J. M. and Weiss, E. M. (2000). Electronic monitoring in their own words: An exploratory study of employees' experiences with new types of surveillance. *Computers in Human Behavior, 16,* 423-440.

Stone, D. L. and Stone E. F. (1987). Effects of missing application blank information on personnel selection decisions: Do privacy protection strategies bias the outcome? *Journal of Applied Psychology, 72,* 452-456.

Stone, D. L. and Stone-Romero, E. F. (1998). A multiple stakeholder model of privacy in organizations. In Schminke, M. (Ed.), *Managerial Ethics: Moral Management of People and Processes,* 35-59. Mahwah, NJ: Erlbaum.

Stone, E. F. and Stone, D. L. (1990). Privacy in organizations: Theoretical issues, research findings and protection mechanisms. *Research in Personnel and Human Resources Management, 8,* 349-411.

Stone, E. F., Gueutal, H. G., Gardner, D. G. and McClure, S. (1983). A field experiment comparing information privacy values, beliefs, and attitudes across several types of organizations. *Journal of Applied Psychology, 68,* 459-468.

Thorne v. El Segundo, 726 F.2d 456 (9th Cir. 1983), cert. denied, 469 U.S. 979 (1984).

U.S. Congress, House Committee on the Judiciary, Subcommittee on Courts and Intellectual Property. (2000). Electronic communication privacy policy disclosure: hearing before 106th Congress, 1st session, May 27, 1999. Washington, DC: U.S. G.P.O.

U.S. Dep't. of Health, Education and Welfare. (1973). Secretary's Advisory Committee on Automated Personal Data Systems, Records, Computers, and the Rights of Citizens viii., Washington, DC: Government Printing Office.

Woodman, R. W., Ganster, D. C., McCuddy, M. K., Tolchinsky, P. D. and Fromkin, H. (1982). A survey of the perceptions of information privacy in organizations. *Academy of Management Journal, 25*, 647-663.

Chapter VI

Conflict and Politics and Information Systems Failure: A Challenge for Information Systems Professionals and Researchers

Leoni Warne
Defence Science and Technology Organisation, Australia

ABSTRACT

Managing the power, politics and organizational conflict inherent in information systems is increasingly recognized as being of critical importance to successful information systems development. The focus of this chapter is the extent to which conflict among participants in an information systems development may be said to contribute to project failure. The chapter describes a research study that explores the nature of conflict in an information systems development and the extent to which conflict may be perceived to impact on the successful progress of a project. In particular, the study was designed to determine which type of conflict (i.e., conflict between which type of stakeholders) may pose the most risk to an information systems development and to determine to what extent conflict can be said to be a contributing factor to information systems failure.

The study was structured into three distinct stages. The first stage was a major case study conducted to explore the nature of conflict in a prematurely terminated information systems development and to probe the extent to which conflict was perceived to pose a risk to information systems projects.

The second stage involved surveying IT Managers to test the wider applicability of the case study findings. The third and final stage involved developing a predictive model of conflict showing the relative weighting of each of the variables investigated, using logistic regression. The most significant outcome of the study was that information systems developments can be detrimentally affected by the impact of conflict among users who have commissioned or will use the system. Managing and resolving conflict in an information systems environment is clearly a difficult, challenging and time-consuming exercise, but the findings of this research study suggest that the rewards, in terms of higher success rates, should be worth the commitment.

INTRODUCTION

As the new millennium unfolds, it brings with it certain axioms about organizations and the information systems that support them. These axioms, although spawned in the last millennium, are likely to be founding tenets of the next. This chapter discusses the nexus of two such truisms: organizations are political systems, and information systems are a vital and integral part of them.

Information systems researchers and practitioners have long been concerned about the high failure rates of information systems projects. There are no studies that have yet provided the information systems community with the 'silver bullet' by isolating a single factor that will guarantee project success, but there are many studies that have identified parts of the problem. In fact, there has been a growing realisation that no single factor, methodology or tool can ensure success in every situation.

Managing the power, politics and organizational conflict inherent in information systems is increasingly recognized as being of critical importance to successful information systems development. Furthermore, the need for improvements in the success rate for information systems development demands that researchers and practitioners give greater attention to the cultural and human factors involved in business process redesign and information management. Yet, there still does not appear to be a clear understanding of how these issues may impact on a project.

The extent to which conflict among participants in an information systems development may be said to contribute to project failure was the focus of the study described in this chapter. In the absence of any definitive models on the degree of risk posed by conflict on information systems development in the existing literature, this study was an attempt to build a theory of the impact conflict may have on the successful progress, completion and implementation of an information systems development project, and to discover more about the types of conflict that may pose a risk.   The objective of this chapter, then, is to outline the study, its background and its findings, and to demonstrate the need for further research in this area. It is the author's contention that further research is required to extend our understanding of the interaction between people in organizations and the systems that are developed to support them; to investigate more thoroughly this particular 'socio' aspect of socio-technical development.

THEORETICAL BACKGROUND

As the IT industry evolved in the latter half of the last millennium, the search for the factors influencing success and failure of information systems projects intensified. However, although there may have been incremental improvements, this intensive activity did not result in dramatic changes to the success rate. The 'rate of failure' is itself debatable. Lyytinen and Hirschheim (1987) cite Gladden's 1982 survey finding that 75% of all system developments undertaken are either never completed or the resulting systems are not used. In a later paper, Lyytinen (1988a) states that "many reports show that somewhere between one-third to half of all systems fail and some researchers have reported even higher failure rates"; Laudon and Laudon (1997) estimate about 75% of all large systems are operating failures.

Some of the discrepancies in these figures may lie in the different definitions of failure in use. Ewusi-Mensah and Przasnyski (1991) examine project failure in terms of three levels of project abandonment: *total*, where the project is terminated before full implementation; *substantial*, where major truncation or simplification of the project makes it radically different from the original specification; and *partial abandonment*, where the original scope of the project is reduced without entailing major or significant changes to the project's original specifications.

Keil (1995) investigates escalation failure, a specific type of failure that occurs when a project "takes on a life of its own, continuing to absorb valuable resources without reaching its objective." Lyytinen and Hirschheim (1987) define failure as "expectation failure," which occurs when a project may meet stated or implicit requirements but does not meet a specific stakeholder group's expectations. Lyytinen and Hirschheim also identified the three distinct types of failure used in previous literature on information systems failures as: *correspondence failure*, when the stated objectives of the project are not met; *process failure*, when the project cannot produce a functional system (or, more commonly, cannot produce it within budget); and *interaction failure*, when users reject the system either explicitly or by minimal use. According to Lyytinen and Hirschheim, these three types of failure can be interpreted as special instances of expectation failure.

Sauer (1993) pragmatically defines a project to be a failure "when development or operation ceases, leaving supporters dissatisfied with the extent to which the system has served their interests." Lyytinen (1988b) reports on a study that shows that systems developers' view of failed systems is dependent on their stakes in the development, and accordingly differs from user or management perceptions.

While the definitions and the exact rate of failures may remain debatable issues, no-one in the industry could deny that, whatever the figures are, the failure rates are too high, and the industry is obliged to improve them. Although there may have been a time when IT and the people who managed it, were regarded with awe and left alone to practise their black art (Connors, 1994), this is no longer the case. Today, information systems are an integral part of modern business life and no organization of any size can exist without them (Philipson, 1994). The bigger the organization, the bigger the investment in information systems and the more important return on investment becomes. Many organizations have introduced chargeback arrangements, service level agreements and other procedures to make information systems staff accountable for outcomes and answerable for the resources they consume (Connors, 1994). The ability to effectively identify and manage risks to information systems projects is more important than it ever was.

To this end, much of the literature and research on IT management tends to focus on technical aspects of the development and implementation process, with much emphasis on the technical skills required, hardware reliability, software quality and numerous discussions on the relative merits of different methodologies (including methodologies for optimizing user-involvement in the development process). There is also a considerable emphasis on management issues–the need for rigorous planning, effective cost benefit analysis, realistic estimating, careful resource management and effective project control. However, while there has always been some discussion on the people skills required by IT managers, the IT management literature is still largely technically based. Although technical issues are obviously very relevant and important, in the past decade there has been an increasing emphasis on the social and organizational factors that may contribute to information systems failure.

The portrayal of organizations as political systems is common in the management literature, but less so in the IT literature. This concept suggests that organizations are most usefully understood as sites where participants interact in pursuit of a range of interests (Dunford, 1992; Martin et al., 1991). Some of these interests may be common or complimentary, other interests will differ and conflict. Dunford explains that organizations are political entities because different interests develop on the basis of both vertical and horizontal differentiation: horizontally because of different group and individual interests; and vertically, because interests at different hierarchical levels will often differ. The political process in organizations influences outcomes in terms of the way power is exercised, and this exercise of power may in itself be influenced by actions intended to change the relative power of parties in an organization (Sauer, 1993). Checkland and Scholes (1990) state that politics is ultimately concerned with the disposition of power. Mintzberg

(1983) defines politics as the machinations created in the pursuit of power and the effects the resulting conflicts have on organizations. Power and politics, therefore, are inextricably intertwined (Warne, 1995). This political perspective of organizations highlights the complexity and multiplicity of objectives within organizations, where outcomes are likely to revolve around the ability to get one's preferences accepted; to have the greatest influence on decisions made and directions taken; and where actions can be analyzed in terms of power interests, the management of conflict, and the mobilization of support and negotiation. Pfeffer (1981) defines organizational politics as those actions and activities aimed at acquiring, developing and using power and other resources "to obtain one's preferred outcomes in a situation in which there is uncertainty or dissensus about choices." Power in organizations, therefore, is an integral part of the political model of organizations, and conflict is often the outcome (Warne, 1998).

An information system development is an instrument of change, and the larger the information systems project, the greater the number of people in the organization affected by the development. Therefore, the larger the information systems project, the greater the opportunity for organizational conflicts to occur and the more likely that these conflicts will impact on the success of the project. According to Robey et al. (1989), by introducing an information system and changing the method of processing, the political structure of the organization is inevitably affected. This suggests that any large or integrated systems development project would be fertile ground for the kind of conflict borne of protecting one's interests in an organization (Warne, 1998). According to Hirschheim and Newman (1991), integrated systems offer many advantages, but they are also a source of much conflict within organizations, as they undermine existing power structures. Pichault (1995) hypothesizes that "in organizations where the power distribution is concentrated (centripetal systems), a technologically related organizational change project will tend to be considered as a threat and will probably lead to failure."

Over the past decade, the literature reporting that human and organizational factors are perceived to be a major cause of information systems failure has expanded (Davenport, 1994; Davenport et al., 1992; Hirschheim & Newman, 1991; Markus, 1983; Newman & Robey, 1992; Robey et al., 1989; Sauer, 1993). It appears that the information systems component of the IT industry is becoming increasingly aware that technical and technological problems are not always the sole cause for project failure. According to Newman and Sabherwal (1996), information systems managers should be aware that project-related factors are not the only determinants for continuing project support. Social, psychological and structural factors may also be determinants for sustaining commitment and support.

Information on the impact of conflict on information systems development is scattered throughout the literature. There are some case studies or papers that focus on it, but these are almost exclusively focused on conflict between users and developers. In most cases, conflict is briefly mentioned as another finding in a larger study or an additional factor that should be considered, but conflict itself is rarely explored in any depth. One exception is a model of conflict showing causal relationships among participation, influence, conflict and conflict resolution that was extended by Robey et al. (1993) to include project success as an output variable. This research confirmed that conflict is negatively related to success. However, the model did not explore the impact of different types of conflict and how they were managed (Warne, 1997).

Hirschheim and Newman (1991) characterize conflict as constructive or destructive, but little is known about how destructive conflict may be, and what sort of conflict is the *most* destructive to an information systems project. While existing research appears to concentrate on the antecedents to conflict in terms of power imbalance, resistance to change and organizational politics, little information exists about the nature of conflict in an information systems environment or about which type of conflict may pose the *most* risk. These matters were the focus of the research study described in this chapter.

THE STUDY

The purpose of the research study was to investigate and identify the impact of conflict on the success of information systems development. While hypotheses and research propositions were tested and investigated, the broader objectives of the study were to explore the nature of conflict in an information systems development and the extent to which conflict may be perceived to impact on the successful progress of a project. In particular, the study was designed to determine which type of conflict (i.e., conflict between which type of stakeholders) may pose the most risk to an information systems development; and, furthermore, to determine to what extent conflict can be said to be a contributing factor to information systems failure (Warne, 1997, 1998).

This study was structured into three distinct stages. The first stage was a major case study conducted to explore the nature of conflict in a prematurely terminated information systems development and to probe the extent to which conflict was perceived to pose a risk to information systems projects. The second stage involved surveying IT managers to test the wider applicability of the case study findings. The third and final stage involved developing a predictive model of conflict showing the relative weighting of each of the variables investigated, using logistic regression. The methodology and findings for each stage of the study are comprehensively reported on elsewhere (see Warne, 1995, 1997, 1998). The purpose of this chapter is to give an overview of the study as a whole and to reflect on the need for pursuing further studies in this area.

First Stage of the Study—The Case Study

For the initial exploratory stage, a case study approach was chosen, as this methodology lends itself to a concentrated focus on the subject and accommodates several data-gathering techniques. The initial exploratory stage of the research study was based on the premise that an information systems development project will often change the way information sources are controlled, and that this change may disrupt the power-base in organizations, producing political conflict.

A large, failed information systems project was used as a case study to facilitate the investigation of the key factors influencing development failures. Sauer (1993) suggests that case studies of failure are useful to: raise problems about the phenomenon of failure; stimulate theories on the causes of failure and the cause-effect chains that lead to failure; and stimulate the development of problem-solving mechanisms. Furthermore, a failed project is finite, with limited but complete records which make it possible to perform a comprehensive research study (Warne, 1995).

The primary objective of this stage was to develop a better understanding of the impact of organizational power and politics on information systems development by investigating the extent to which this impact contributed to the failure of a large complex information system project.

Definitions

The following terms were defined for use in this study:
- *End Users* were defined as potential users of a system. This included staff liaising with computing staff about system requirements.
- *Senior Management Users* were senior-level managers who managed staff using the system, or staff expected to use the system, senior staff on the project steering committee or any other committees influencing the information systems development and senior management staff who had some decision-making power in regard to the project.
- *Users* were both end users and senior management users.
- *Developers* were members of the information systems project development team and their supporting and clerical staff, contractors from outside the organization who were employed to work on the development of the project, and members of the organizations information systems department who had some responsibility for the development or ultimate maintenance of the system.
- *Participants* described both users and developers, as defined above.
- *Failure* was defined in terms of the Ewusi-Mensah and Przasnyski (1991) definition of total abandonment, where a project is terminated before full implementation.

This definition was also consistent with Sauer's (1993) definition of failure where development of an information system ceases, leaving supporters' interests unsatisfied. For the purposes of this study, success was limited to "non-failure" as defined above. Although this definition clearly excludes several known categories of failure and success, it meant that failure and success could be objectively declared and was considered to be an acceptable limitation for this study (Warne, 1995).

The Case Study Project Selected

The case study selected for investigation was a Department of Defence Project that was initiated in June 1990 and was to have run for nine years. The Case Study Project (CSP) development was intended to create an infrastructure for integrating common human resource functions (while allowing for necessary differences between the three Armed Services) and to eliminate the inefficiency of many disparate systems performing similar functions. The project was, therefore, involved with a large matrix of geographically distant stakeholders from the top management of each of the Armed Services and the Department of Defence, to the end users in departmental sections throughout the Australian Defence Organization (ADO).

For the CSP a project management methodology involving a large component of user participation was adopted for the development. A High Level Design (HLD) study was conducted to identify a Business Case and strategies for project development, implementation and management. A Joint Application Design (JAD) approach was used in over 45 workshops involving hundreds of representatives to gather comprehensive user requirements and identify functional requirements. The HLD Report, completed in November 1991, identified 49 functions that could be integrated and supported by information systems. Following the acceptance of the HLD by the project Steering Committee and project sponsors, approval was given to proceed and the CSP embarked on the development of 19 sub-systems in five phases, for conclusion in 1999.

The project was terminated, after only two-and-a-half years, in November 1992. The project had attempted to specify, to its client's satisfaction, a level of manpower and operational cost savings that would support the Business Case for the project. However, some of the client groups would no longer agree to the previously identified staffing savings that were used to justify the Business Case. The premature termination of the CSP appeared to be largely due to conflicts between the potential users and the developers of the project and, ultimately, the influence of the user representatives on the Project's Steering Committee. The official reason for the Project's failure was the failure to meet the Business Case. This project seemed to be an ideal candidate for study (Warne, 1995).

Findings of the First Stage of the Study

The case study was supported by a document study, exploratory interviews and a survey.

A thorough document study of project files and reports, Steering Committee Minutes, Project Management methodologies and other relevant project documentation was conducted. The Department allowed full access to unclassified files and documentation relating to the CSP. This was facilitated by the fact that the CSP files were still available at the original site.

Detailed conversations and taped, in-depth interviews were conducted with project participants. The purpose of these discussions and interviews was to capture reactions about the termination of the project. The interviews revealed the perceived organizational issues.

Finally, a detailed questionnaire was prepared, tested and posted to the entire population of 290 identified project participants. The purpose of this survey was to verify perceived perceptions about the factors being studied. The questions were derived from the results of the document study and interviews. The final questionnaire contained four demographic questions to identify the category of respondent, 59 statements with a Likert-scale for agreeing or disagreeing and 10 blank lines for any qualitative comments respondents might want to make (Warne, 1995).

Document Study

The CSP was well documented with regular and comprehensive reports on project status and files containing records of JAD workshops, Project Meetings, Business Reviews and a complete record of project Steering Committee Minutes. It was these minutes that proved of most interest. There were nine Steering Committee Meetings over the two-and-a-half years the CSP was in existence. During this time, there were different people holding several of the Steering Committee positions. The minutes showed a record of continued disagreement and conflict on the Steering Committee that began with the very first meeting.

The first Steering Committee Meeting was deferred pending clarifications of major differences in perception of some key issues regarding the project. These issues were discussed in a series of meetings, but there were still unresolved issues that were addressed in further 'out of session' meetings. Therefore, the first Steering Committee Meeting was not held until four months after the Project had begun.

When the minutes of this first meeting were released, five weeks later, several of the attendees asked for amendments (22 amendments in all), some of which other members of the Steering Committee objected to. The final minutes for the first Steering Committee meeting were released three months after the original draft minutes were issued. The project had been underway for seven months. The project was clearly already in conflict at this early stage, and an analysis of the full set of documentation indicated that the project continued in this vein until it was finally terminated (Warne, 1995).

Interviews

The findings of the preliminary round of interviews and conversations with participants indicated a high degree of emotional reaction to the termination of the CSP. In many instances, the interviews generated more heat than light. Clearly, many of the development staff felt the project was unfairly terminated. The general consensus was that, while it was client unwillingness to commit to infrastructure changes and the subsequent savings that was responsible for the final termination of the project, the underlying causes were more sinister. The developers, and some users, believed that a perceived threat to organizational areas of control and power turned initial senior management support into political maneuvering for its demise.

On the other hand, some users and some former developers (who had left the project before it was terminated) were pleased that the project had ended, although their reasons differed. Reasons cited included: the belief that the project should never have been started because integrating functions across the services would never work; that the project management style was inappropriate; that there was a lack of any real common understanding between users and the development team about the purpose of the project; and, occasionally, the official reason, that the Project simply could not make an adequate Business Case.

Survey

When all responses were tallied, 197 of the original 290 questionnaires sent out had been returned. Discounting the 21 of these that were returned unopened, because the addressees were unknown, the 176 completed returns represented a substantial 61% response rate for the survey instrument.

Surprisingly, a majority of responses (65%) included some degree of qualitative comments–often very lengthy and detailed. Obviously, many of the respondents still had clear memories and definite opinions about the project despite the considerable time lapse since its termination.

It is also interesting to note that while 49% of senior management users and 51% of end users responded, a greater percentage of developers (65%) responded to the questionnaire. This is not surprising given the relative degree of involvement these categories of participant would have had in the day-to-day running of the project. The comparison of results between different categories of respondents (developers, end users and senior management users) produced interesting results. A selection of these follows:

Senior Management Support

Although 69% of users and 81% of developers agreed that "*There was a great deal of support for [the CSP] in the initial stages,*" this support was perceived to have dissipated as the project progressed. This is not surprising, as support from top management is dynamic and likely to fluctuate as a project proceeds. This can be exacerbated in an organization like Defence, where there is often a regular turnover in top management positions.

All categories of respondents (82% of developers, 88% of end users and 86% of senior management) agreed that "*Senior user management used its power to terminate the development of [the CSP].*" Similarly, 90% of developers, 78% of end users and 72% of senior management agreed that, in fact, that power was applied and "*[the CSP] was terminated because it was not supported by some powerful members of senior management.*"

Power and Politics

A large majority of all categories of participants (81% to 97%) agreed that "*[the CSP] attempted to address the needs of several distinct and politically powerful parts of the Defence organization.*" Furthermore, a majority of respondents agreed that "*[the CSP] had to deal with several essentially self-contained sections of the Defence organization that were relatively independent and concerned with their own unique priorities and tasks*" and that "*many potential users had a limited view of [the CSP], looking at it only from their own perspective and not seeing it in broader corporate terms.*"

A majority of all participants (56% of developers, 70% of end users and 53% of senior management users) also agreed that "*the interests and requirements of some users would have been subordinated to those of others more powerful in the Defence organization than themselves, if the project was ever completed.*" While the majority of all categories agreed with this question, it was the end users that had the greatest number of affirmative answers. Clearly, the end user category of participants was the group most likely to be permanently affected by the proposed new system, and, no doubt, this group of respondents also included some of the *least* powerful participants.

In response to the statement, "*Users and [the CSP] developers both respected each other's role and power in the organization,*" 68% of developers agreed, 60% of end users agreed and 37% of senior management users agreed. Interestingly, the largest disparity here was not between the users and the developers, but between senior management and the rest of the respondents. In response to the statement, "*Some potential users were concerned that if [the CSP] was developed their power base in the organization would be eroded,*" 92% of developers agreed, 64% of end users agreed but only 38% of senior management users agreed. Again, the disparity of perceptions between senior management and the rest of the participants for several of these questions suggested that most respondents believed that there were political machinations in play although each category may have believed different people were involved. Certainly, most respondents recognized the fact that numerous conflicting interests abounded and that positions were under attack and being defended (Warne, 1995).

Conflict

The conflict in the CSP was perceived in a number of ways. In response to the statement *"There was a lack of understanding and empathy between users and developers,"* 47% of developers agreed, 55% of end users agreed and 86% of senior management users agreed. There was a significant disparity between the senior management respondents and all others. A definite pattern of different perceptions from different categories of respondents emerged from the answers to these questions. A developer agreeing with the question qualified it by saying "only by those users whose own single-service projects were aborted because of [the CSP]." Some developers gave both positive and negative answers and qualified them with words like "some groups."

In contrast, it was end users that differed from the others when asked if *"Disagreements regarding the project were resolved harmoniously."* In this case, 24% of developers agreed, 52% of end users agreed and 21% of senior management users agreed. A developer, disagreeing with the question, wrote, "Invariably so with those not implacably opposed to the concept and loss of power. Some key players did not wish any change to the status quo."

Furthermore, a clear majority of all respondent categories (60% of developers, 76% of end users and 67% of senior management users) believed there were disagreements and conflict among user groups at JAD workshops. An end user agreeing with the question stated, "Service jealousy of own methodology." Similarly, a majority of respondents (92% of developers, 91% of end users and 73% of senior management users) agreed that *"there was conflict amongst members of [the CSP] Steering Committee."* The project was clearly seen to be subject to various levels and types of conflict by the majority of project participants.

Contributory Factors to Project Failure

Several questions in the survey asked for perceptions about why the CSP was terminated and what conditions may have ensured its survival. Clearly, most respondents did not believe that *"[the CSP] was terminated because the users didn't require the proposed system."* An overall majority (74%) of all respondents, as well as the majority in each category (79% of developers, 79% of end users and 53% of senior management), disagreed with this statement.

Neither the management nor the project management methodology used by the project was perceived to be a significant problem, despite the contention of some of the developers interviewed for the case study. Only a minority in all categories (30% to 33%) agreed that *"[the CSP] was terminated because the project was poorly managed."* Only a small minority of respondents in all categories (27% of developers, 27% of end users and 10% of senior management users) also agreed with the statement that "*[the CSP] would have survived if it had used different project management principles.*"

Officially, the reason the CSP was terminated was the fact that the Project Office failed to come up with an adequate Business Case to support the development, and the majority of all respondents in all categories (80% to 88%) agreed with this question. However, this was the subject of many qualifying explanations and comments from respondents in all categories. The following is a typical comment, from a developer:

"This was the official position. However, several options with viable business cases were proposed: a key Program would not agree with the consequences which would have severely diminished its size and power base. [Some sections] would not acknowledge avoided costs proposed. Costs which were subsequently incurred many times over within only the first year following [the CSP] closure."

By comparison, both developers (75%) and end users (58%) agreed that "*[the CSP] would have survived if senior user management had been willing to commit to proposed manpower savings.*" Only 24% of senior management users agreed to this question.

When it came to the more widespread issues of conflict and disharmony, a majority of the end users (59%) and developers (65%) agreed that "*[the CSP]'s inability to resolve the conflict surrounding it was the basic reason for its termination.*" However, senior management users were evenly split on this question (50% agreeing).

These results support the proposition that the pursuit, and protection, of power and the resultant conflict was seen by a majority of respondents as contributing to the ending of the project. This was a dominant feature of much of the qualitative comment supplied with the questionnaires. The following are typical of the many comments:

"[The CSP] threatened several user areas ... Support was given for [the CSP] by higher levels of user committee in its earlier stages but was later withdrawn ... Many users were reluctant to offer up savings as they perceived that this would infer that they had 'excess' manpower...." [Comment made by a developer.]

"The failure of [the CSP] was due principally to vested interests by some elements within the Department who perceived a loss of influence if [the CSP] were to have proceeded. This was to the detriment of some of the main intended beneficiaries." [Comment made by an end user.]

"I believe the project failed as several services were not willing to offset personnel savings against future savings, many of which were difficult to quantify to the satisfaction of users. I suspect that timing was particularly relevant as, at the time commitment was required, the services were under significant pressure on staffing levels." [Comment made by a senior management user.]

Clearly, the majority of respondents believed that the organizational politics and the protection of power-bases endemic in the CSP were major factors in the termination of the project. The CSP operated in a climate of conflict at a number of levels: conflict among developers; conflict between users and developers; conflict among user groups defending their own divisional procedures; and conflict between end users and their managers. However, the major source of conflict was between senior user management and the rest of the participants, with senior managers lobbying overtly and covertly to gain control for their divisions (Warne, 1995).

Second Stage of the Study—Survey of IT Managers

The most surprising outcome of the case study was that the project was most detrimentally affected by the impact of conflict among users. This level of conflict would be largely invisible to developers, and in any case, would often be dismissed as not being relevant to them. The second stage of the research study was, therefore, designed to test the wider applicability of the case study findings.

Definitions

Conflict was not defined for this study. Conflict can be constructive or destructive (Davis et al., 1992; Hirschheim & Newman, 1991; Marakas & Hornik, 1996) and it was considered to be preferable to allow respondents to interpret the term as they perceived it. However, the *types* of conflict of interest to the second stage of this research were defined to be Developer/Developer conflict, Developer/User conflict and User/User conflict, and the *extent* of each conflict type was scaled as major, significant or minor. Also of interest was the openness of the conflict, with overt conflict defined to be conflict that was openly visible and not concealed. Covert conflict was defined to be conflict that was hidden or secret, often involving an attempt to change decisions by political maneuvring and exploitation, rather than by explicit means.

The research objectives of this stage of the study were determined to be:
- to explore the nature of conflict in information systems development and the extent to which conflict may be perceived to impact on the success of projects;
- to determine which sort of conflict (from Developer/Developer, Developer/User and User/User) may pose the most risk to an information systems development; and

- to determine if conflict was generally detected, managed and resolved in the information systems development environment (Warne, 1997).

The Survey

A questionnaire was prepared to gather data to meet the research objectives. These were to gauge the perceived importance of the *openness* of conflict, the *extent* of conflict observed among developers, between users and developers, and between different users or user groups; and the *degree* to which the different *types* of conflict impeded effective project progress. Information was also sought on the detection and resolution of conflict. A checkbox style was used for much of the survey, with some qualitative questions included. The questionnaire was divided into two parts: the first dealing with overt and then covert conflict in the largest, delivered (successful) project the respondent was involved with, and the second part dealing with overt and then covert conflict in an unfinished or terminated (unsuccessful) project. In each of these four sections, respondents were asked to report on up to 10 different types of conflict, so up to 40 cases of conflict could be identified on each questionnaire.

Senior Information Technology managers were targeted, rather than project managers or end user managers, because they were considered likely to have more comprehensive experience and a more objective view of the issues from both the business and information systems perspectives. The sample was limited to public sector IT managers in the same geographical region as the Defence Headquarters studied in the case study, to eliminate extraneous variables. There was a total of 68 IT managers targeted with the survey.

Findings of the Second Stage of the Study

Twenty-seven valid responses were received and analysed, reflecting a 40% response rate. These 27 respondents reported on 393 instances, or cases, of conflict in projects with which they had been associated. Altogether, the respondents represented more than 329 years of IT experience and more than 187 years of IT management experience.

In regard to the type of information systems projects the respondents had been involved with: all respondents had been involved with information systems projects that had been successfully delivered and utilised by the users (more than 183 projects), and 80% of respondents had been involved with prematurely terminated projects (more than 50 projects). Altogether, the responses represented experiences with more than 250 information systems projects (Warne, 1997).

Part 1: Large, Completed Information Systems Development Projects

Respondents were asked to consider the largest, completed, information systems development project they had been involved with and then answer the questions that followed. The results of this part of the questionnaire were primarily gathered for the purposes of comparison when fitting a predictive statistical model in the third stage of the study, and are not reported on indepth in this chapter. However, it was interesting to observe, during the preliminary statistical analysis of the survey responses, that there were only minor differences between the first (Large Completed Project) and the second (Terminated IS Project) part of the survey. The only significant differences were:

- the percentages of conflict perceived to be major or significant were much higher in terminated projects;
- the percentages of conflict that managers attempted to resolve were much higher in large, successful projects; and
- the percentages of conflicts successfully resolved in large projects, although still very low, were higher than the percentages of conflicts successfully resolved in terminated projects.

The full range of responses for this part of the questionnaire are not presented in this chapter, but can be found elsewhere (see Warne, 1997). However, it may be informative to include the responses to the question: "*Do you believe this conflict impeded the effective progress of this large project?*" When asked this question, 96% of respondents who were aware of overt conflict during the project believed it impeded the progress of the project, and 71% believed that this impediment was significant or major. Similarly, 69% of respondents who identified covert conflict associated with the project believed it was a major or significant impediment to the progress of the project (Warne, 1997).

Clearly, many large projects attempted to continue on despite a considerable amount of unresolved conflict, and despite the fact that the majority of respondents believed that overt and covert conflict impeded the effective progress of the project.

In contrast, a small number of respondents' experience was with conflict in its constructive role, as a useful way to air and resolve differences:

"I saw the conflict as reasonably healthy; it seemed to be resolved amicably on all occasions, as we concentrated on the issues, not the people, when we disagreed"

"The project changed operations so much that conflict was to be expected. Sometimes the conflict led to (heated) discussions which actually helped clarify issues."

Part 2: Terminated Information Systems Development Projects

In the second part of the survey, respondents were asked to consider another project they had been associated with, this time an information systems development project that was terminated before the system was delivered to the client–in other words, a failed information systems project as defined for this study. The questions asked were virtually identical to those asked in the first part of the survey to facilitate comparison. Altogether, 93% of all respondents indicated that they had been involved with a terminated project. In answer to the question "*did this terminated project involve the centralisation or integration of information resources that would change the way these resources would be controlled in the organization?*" 76% of respondents said yes.

Openness of Conflict in Terminated Projects

Sixty-eight percent of respondents said they were aware that conflict "*arose during the development of the terminated project.*" Of these, 100% stated that this conflict was so overt and obvious they were aware of it during the project, and 53% said that there was also some covert conflict within the project. Of those that identified covert conflict, 78% claimed to have become aware of the conflict during the project, and only 22% said they did not become aware of the covert conflict until after the project was over. This is consistent with the data for large, successful projects, with the exception that slightly fewer respondents reported conflict during the development of the terminated project. However, this may simply be a function of the relative length of the projects, with longer projects offering more time and opportunities for conflict.

A number of explanations were offered as to how respondents became aware of covert conflict within the project environment:

- "Attempts to postpone decisions during committee/approval processes"
- "Gossip"
- "You notice subtle resistance where you do not expect it"
- "Feedback from industry representatives or from user representatives"
- "Information not being shared–side projects being organized"
- "Visiting end-users and discovering that what was delivered was not asked for"
- "Rumors–delays by management in decisions and approval requests to alter recommendations"

Conflict Types and Extent

Respondents were asked to identify the type and extent of overt and then covert conflict they were aware of during the project. They were asked to select the type from the list reproduced below, and to indicate whether the degree of conflict was major, significant or minor. Types of conflict were given as:

- Developer/ Developer Conflict:
  * Among members of the development team
  * Between members of the development team and the Project Manager

- Developer/ User Conflict
  * Between potential end users and developers
  * Between end-user management and developers
  * Between corporate management and developers
- User/ User Conflict
  * Among different end-user groups
  * Between potential end users and end-user management
  * Among different groups of user management
  * Between user management and corporate management

Respondents were encouraged to add 'Other' types of conflict they had encountered. Several respondents responded to this invitation, but the conflict situations they described (e.g., developer/database administrator, consultant/client department, financial staff/end users) could all be categorised under one of the three different types defined for this study.

The results suggested that Developer/User conflict (86% of overt and 59% of covert conflict considered to be major or significant) and User/User conflict (77% of overt and 75% of covert considered major or significant) were the most problematical in terminated projects. This result was also consistent with the results for large, successful projects, although, not surprisingly, there was a much greater percentage of user-related conflict that was considered to be major or significant in the terminated projects.

The data for covert conflict indicated that User/User conflict was again much more likely to create problems than Developer/User conflict, and Developer/User conflict was more problematical than Developer/Developer conflict (where only 35% of overt and 40% of covert conflict was considered major or significant). This may be because most Developer/User conflict is likely to be overt, whereas much User/User conflict can be covert or concealed (Ahituv et al., 1994; Marakas & Hornik, 1996).

However, the relativities between the three types were consistent with the data for large, successful projects. In other words, Developer/Developer conflict was considered to be far less of a problem than either User/User or Developer/User conflict.

While only 10% of the overt conflict considered to be of a major or significant extent was attributed to Developer/Developer conflict, 41% was identified as Developer/User conflict and almost half (49%) due to User/User conflict. In regard to covert conflict, 11% of major or significant conflict was Developer/Developer conflict, 29% was Developer/User conflict and 60% was User/User conflict (Warne, 1997).

Some of the qualitative comments returned with the questionnaire gave reasons why some of the destructive conflict recorded had occurred. The following comments were typical:

- On Developer/Developer Conflict
  * "Mainly a difference in professional opinions of the Project Manager and senior team member."

* "From observing the Project Manager taking the advice of the wrong staff instead of managers of functional areas. The Project Team became introverted and two-dimensional."

- On Developer/User Conflict
  * "Conflict also occurs between technology developers and end-users generally concerning different views of user requirements."
  * "Users were not supportive of the project as they did not support the developer selection process."
  * "The system was the vehicle/catalyst for major conflict over organizational change. Eventually I refused to allow any resources to be dedicated until the management issues were resolved."

- On User/User Conflict
  * "Particularly the conflict between end-user groups which was not within the control of the project manager to resolve."
  * "Conflict related primarily to lack of common understanding of system requirements and an inadequate consultation process before the specification was released to the developer. Hence users were in conflict with one another going into test, wanting changes."
  * "Pig-headed senior user who wanted what was best for him, not the organization."

Conflict Management

For each individual description of conflict respondents identified, respondents were asked how that conflict was assessed and managed as a risk to the project. Respondents were asked to indicate "yes," "no" or "don't know" for both overt and covert conflict for each of the risk management responses or outcomes listed below.

Management of Overt and Covert Conflict in Large Projects:

- Formally Assessed
- Detected In Time
- Resolution Attempted By Project Manager
- Conflict Resolved

Obviously, covert conflict can only be managed if it is detected, so while respondents were asked if overt conflict was formally assessed, they were asked if covert conflict was detected in time to have acted on it, if necessary.

The results showed that very little formal risk assessment was conducted to detect conflict in information systems projects and, where it was conducted, it was largely used to assess Developer/User conflict (17%), and, only in one case, User/User conflict. In the terminated projects the respondents were involved with, no formal risk assessment was conducted on Developer/Developer conflict. As for large projects, the project manager appeared to attempt resolution of the overt conflict for approximately half of the User/User and Developer/User conflicts and for a little more than one-third of Developer/Developer conflict. However, when it came to covert data, the project manager attempted to resolve an even smaller percentage of the detected conflict.

The data suggested that the success rate of conflict resolution in the information systems project domain was extraordinarily low. These findings were consistent with those for large projects, differing more in magnitude than in relativities. Some of these results are listed below.

- Resolution of Overt Conflict Attempted by Project Manager:
  * 35% of Developer/ Developer Conflict
  * 51% of Developer/ User Conflict
  * 49% of User/ User Conflict
- Resolution of Covert Conflict Attempted by Project Manager:
  * 0% of Developer/ Developer Conflict
  * 24% of Developer/ User Conflict
  * 32% of User/ User Conflict
- Overt Conflict Resolved
  * 15% of Developer/ Developer Conflict
  * 3% of Developer/ User Conflict
  * 0% of User/ User Conflict
- Covert Conflict Resolved
  * 0% of Developer/ Developer Conflict
  * 18% of Developer/ User Conflict
  * 18% of User/ User Conflict

Relationship to Termination

The majority of respondents felt that conflict (both overt and covert) was, to some extent, responsible for the termination of the project. In response to the question, *"Do you believe this conflict impeded the effective progress of this terminated project?"* 53% of respondents stated that they believed that overt conflict was a significant or major impediment, and 33% stated that covert conflict was a major impediment.

Furthermore, 35% of respondents stated that they believed *overt* conflict to be the prime reason for the projects' termination while an extraordinary 44% stated they believed *covert* conflict to be the prime reason for termination. Clearly, conflict is an issue that should not be ignored by project managers and system developers.

It is interesting to note that the most frequently reported form of major or significant *overt* conflict was between corporate managers and developers. This is consistent with the literature on the need for maintaining top management support (Ahituv et al., 1994; Ewusi-Mensah & Przasnyski, 1991; Sauer, 1993) and suggests that this dynamic can involve considerable conflict. The three most frequently reported forms of major or significant *covert* conflict were:

- conflict among different groups of user management;
- conflict between user management and corporate management; and
- conflict among different end user groups (Warne, 1997).

This is consistent with the literature on power and information politics in organizations (Davenport et al., 1992; Hirschheim & Newman, 1991; Marakas & Hornik, 1996; Robey et al., 1993) suggesting that a primary cause of conflict is the politically charged ownership and control of information resources in organizations. The implementation of an information system, which may change and devolve ownership, can be viewed as a threat and result in covert and overt machinations to subvert or change the course of the information systems development.

Third Stage of the Study—The Predictive Model

The primary objective of the third and final stage of this research study was to fit a model of conflict factors impacting on project success based on the findings of the second stage of the study and the five independent variables that were derived from that research. There were a number of hypotheses tested in this stage of the study and a series of statistical analyses conducted to derive a predictive model (Warne, 1998).

Logistic regression was used for the analysis. Where a response to a regression analysis is binary, the researcher wishes to determine the role of a set of regressor variables on the binary response, and there is a need to predict or estimate the probability of one of the two possible responses for a combination of regressor variables, then Logistic Regression is an appropriate approach (Myers, 1996). The data gathered for this stage of the research study was treated as a number of exploratory, independent variables, and a binary response (success or failure). As such, this procedure was considered to be the most appropriate for the analysis of the gathered data and the formulation of a model of conflict.

Findings of the Third Stage of the Study

The SAS statistical package was used for this analysis, and the Logistic Procedure is explained in detail in Chapter 27 of the SAS manual (SAS, 1989). For each instance of conflict identified by a respondent, the following associated responses were recorded:

- the perceived Extent of the conflict (minor, significant, or major);
- the Degree of Perceived Impediment (none or little, significant or major, prime reason for termination);
- Conflict Assessment and Management (none, conflict not detected (for covert conflict), conflict detected but ignored, conflict formally assessed as part of the project risk management procedures, conflict resolution attempted, and conflict resolved)
- Openness of Conflict (whether covert or overt),

- Type of Conflict (Developer/ Developer; Developer/User or User/User); and
- whether the project in question was a Failure (terminated) or a Success (large, completed) project.

The resulting table contained 393 rows of data, or cases. Each of the independent variables examined in this study consisted of values, or categories, arranged into numbered nominal or ordinal scales. For the initial procedure, the values on the scales were presented in a hypothesized, increasing order of magnitude (Warne, 1998).

Regression Results

The data was loaded into the SAS Logistic Regression Procedure to screen out variables and fit the model. Each variable was removed one by one to see which variables had the biggest effect on the model. A manual stepwise and backward procedure was used to screen out variables. T-values were calculated separately for each run of the Procedure. All other things being constant, if one value of a variable was found to be significant, then associated values of that variable were also considered significant.

It was found, in the first series, that the openness of the conflict did not contribute significantly to the probability of project success. On the basis of the data collected for this study, whether the conflict was conducted overtly or covertly appeared to be irrelevant. This variable was removed from the model for subsequent fittings.

The Logistic Procedure produced best-fit estimates for the model. The outcome of the regression analysis was a predictive algorithm or model of conflict in information systems development, in which all other variables were found to be significant. From tables produced in the logistic regression procedures, it was also possible to assess the relative importance of the variables in the model by using the chance probability figures. In this way, it could be seen that the importance of the variables in the model were in the following order, with the first listed having the most negative impact on project success:

- Extent of the Conflict;
- Perceived Degree of Impediment that conflict causes a Project; then the
- Form of Conflict Assessment and Management used; and finally,
- the Type of Conflict.

To determine the relative importance of the values within the variables, further analysis was necessary (Warne, 1998).

Independent Variables in the Model Algorithm

The raw data in the table used for regression analysis was used to determine the observed probabilities of success, examining one independent variable at a time.

Chi-squared analysis for each of the tests was well within the 10% limit set for this study, except in the case of the Type of Conflict variable.

Extent of Conflict

The probability of success derived from the observations showed that a project with Minor conflict had a 0.746 (75%) probability of succeeding, with Significant conflict a 0.596 (60%) probability of succeeding, and with Major conflict a 0.586 (59%) chance of succeeding. Although the difference between Significant and Major extent of conflict was minimal, there was clearly an increasing probability of failure as the extent of conflict increased.

Perceived Degree of Impediment

The observations for Degree of Impediment that conflict causes a project showed that in projects with None or Little perceived impediment, the probability of success was 0.888 (89%); with Significant or Major impediment, this fell to 0.729 (73%) and obviously, when the impediment caused by conflict was seen to be the Prime Reason for Termination of the project, then the probability of success was 0.

Assessment and Management of Conflict

With six different values or categories in this variable, there were more fluctuations in the probabilities. In projects where some conflict was successfully resolved, there was a 0.871 (87%) probability of success. This was an interesting outcome given the very small rates of resolution reported by respondents (for example, in large, successful projects, only 24% of identified Developer/Developer conflict, 13% of Developer/User conflict and 8% of User/User conflict was successfully resolved). Where resolution of conflict had been Attempted, probability of success was 0.652 (65%). Where conflict was Formally Assessed as part of the project risk management procedures, probability of success was 0.611 (61%). If conflict was Detected, but Ignored (in successful projects), the probability of success was 0.651 (65%) which was slightly larger than the 0.615 (62%) probability of success when conflict was Not Detected in time to act on it (where conflict was covert). When No Action at all was taken in regard to conflict in a project, the probability of success fell to 0.444 (44%). Despite the slight fluctuations, it was clear that, on the basis of the observed data, the probability of success increased as more was done to attempt to manage and resolve the conflict.

Type of Conflict

The observed data showed that in projects where Developer/Developer conflict existed, there was a 0.704 (70%) probability of success; where Developer/

User conflict existed a 0.634 (63%) probability of success; and where User/User conflict existed a 0.610 (61%) probability of success, suggesting that the probability of failure increased if conflict involved users, and in particular among user groups. However, a chi-squared analysis showed a chance probability of 0.299–well *outside* the 10% limit set for this study. This suggested that, for the data gathered, the differences in probability of success among the three different types were not significant. Nevertheless, it seemed clear that there was, in fact, an important difference between the probability of success where conflict was among developers, and the probability of success where conflict involved users or user groups. To test the validity of this statement, the data was collapsed into two categories: conflict among developers and conflict that involved users, and a one-tailed hypothesis test applied.

The one-tailed test produced a z value of 1.4975, which gave a chance probability of 0.0668 which allowed the researcher to reject the null hypothesis and accept the directional hypothesis with a significance value well within the 10% limit set for the study (Warne, 1998).

Predictive Algorithm

Based on the information derived from the observed probabilities, and the better understanding it provided about the independent variables in the model, it was possible to postulate a final, enriched algorithm for a Model of Conflict, such that:

Where the combination of variables exists within an information systems project development such that there is a:

- Perceived Conflict;
- Degree of Perceived Impediment caused by the conflict;
- the Expectation of some Assessment and Management of Conflict; and finally, where
- the Type of Conflict is characterized by conflict involving users and conflict among developers),

then it is possible to predict that the probability of Project success will decrease.

This negative impact on project success is increased where:

- Extent of Conflicts is perceived to be significant or major;
- Perceived Impediment to the Project is perceived to be significant or major,
- there is little or no successful action taken in terms of resolving the conflict, and
- where the conflict involves users, either among themselves or between users and developers.

Further Analyses

Further statistical analysis, both descriptive and inferential, revealed some interesting links and associations between the variables (Warne, 1998). Some of these findings included:

Figure 1: Model of conflict factors negatively impacting on project success

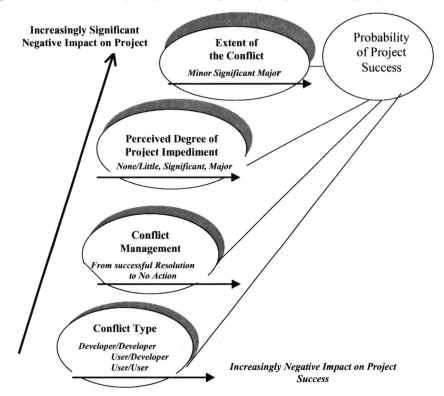

- Developer/User conflict was most frequently formally assessed as part of a project's risk assessment procedures. User/User conflict was *more* frequently formally assessed than Developer/Developer conflict (although not as frequently as Developer/User conflict).
- Developer/Developer conflict was more frequently detected than conflict involving users. User/User conflict was less frequently detected than conflict involving developers.
- Project Managers attempted to resolve conflict involving users more frequently than they attempted to resolve Developer/Developer conflict.
- Developer/Developer conflict was more frequently resolved than conflict involving users. User/User conflict was less frequently resolved than conflict involving developers.
- User/User conflict of a major or significant extent has the most detrimental effect on perceived degree of impediment to successful project progress.
- User/User conflict was the most potentially damaging type of conflict in an information systems development environment (greatest extent and least resolved).

- Developer/Developer conflict was the least potentially damaging type of conflict in an information systems development environment (smallest extent and most resolved).
- Information systems projects involving the centralization or integration of information resources that would change the way these resources would be controlled in the organization were more frequently associated with conflict than other types of information systems projects.

IMPLICATIONS FOR THE FUTURE

The findings of this study suggest that information systems researchers, practitioners and computing professionals involved in information systems development must recognize that internal organizational conflict could put a systems development at risk. To ensure project success, this risk must be assessed and managed.

While there is an increasing acknowledgement of this phenomenon in the literature, it is still largely embryonic. In a recent paper on risk management, Smith et al., (2001) affirm that senior executives are beginning to realize that serious human and organizational risks are associated with information systems projects. They acknowledge that while risks associated with the people in the project environment may be less obvious, they should still be managed, as "the influence of corporate power politics cannot be ignored in business decision-making around information technology, as many IS managers found to their dismay" (Smith et al., 2001).

The research described in this chapter clearly showed that conflict among users over control of information resources can be just as destructive to an information systems project as conflict between users and developers, and that in projects where conflict is perceived to significantly impede the progress of the project, this conflict can also impact on the success of the project. Furthermore, this study has shown that the more effectively conflict is managed and the more conflict resolution is attempted in an information systems development, the more probability of project success increases.

Implications for Practitioners

The results of the study suggest that, to facilitate a successful outcome to an information systems development, at the very least, IT managers should incorporate conflict assessment and management procedures as part of their formal risk assessment and control procedures. Furthermore, this risk management must include resolution of conflict among different user groups where this conflict may impact on the successful progress of the project.

While past and current trends are for Developer/User conflict to be recognized as a risk to information systems projects, User/User conflict should increasingly becoming the focus of future risk assessment procedures and conflict management.

The results of this study could be applied to set priorities for conflict resolution. However, further research is clearly necessary to fully understand the full implications of this particular 'socio' influence on information systems.

Implications for Researchers

While there has been a resurgence in interest in the social aspects of information systems development, there is clearly a need for more research in the area of conflict.

The most important recommendation for further research is to reinforce the validity of the findings of this research study by replicating the research with a much larger sample and extending it into the private sector. However, in addition to this important but predictable recommendation, the research study has highlighted the need for some less obvious areas for further research.

The data gathered in the Stage 2 Survey indicated that project managers only attempted to resolve detected conflict in about half of the instances of perceived conflict. Further research is needed to understand why project managers decide *not* to attempt to resolve so many conflicts and the criteria they apply in making those decisions.

While the research study described in this chapter may have provided IT managers with a new set of criteria for identifying potentially damaging conflict situations, further research is required to know when the optimal time to apply these criteria is, and what priority these decisions on conflict should have in the context of total project requirements.

Finally, given the extraordinary low rate of conflict resolution where resolution *is* attempted, further research is mandatory to discover what forms of conflict resolution are the most successful in the information systems development environment, and when and how they should be applied in order to maximize the probability of project success.

CONCLUSION

The research described in this chapter had some obvious limitations, including very narrow definitions of failure and success. However, this is likely to result in the impact of conflict being minimized in this study, with the true impact of conflict in information systems development being much greater than the results presented here. However, the results of the research study certainly support the common premise that the success of an information system project is dependent on effective cooperation and collaboration of all parties involved, and clearly identifies conflict as a potential threat to the viability of an information systems development. The study has produced a set of criteria for determining the type of conflict that may be most destructive to an information systems development, and therefore most in need of resolution. The most significant outcome of the study was that information systems developments can be detrimentally affected not only by the lack of visible top management support and conflict between and users and the developer, but also by the impact of conflict *among* users who have commissioned or will use the system.

Conflict among the users participating in an information systems development and the role this plays in project failure is not as well documented as conflict between users and developers and, therefore, not always recognized as being part of an IT manager's domain. Many developers still believe that organizational politics is not their concern. According to the study results, project managers attempted to resolve less than half of the detected conflict in an information systems project, and the success rate for resolving conflict of all types was woefully small. Unfortunately, many project managers still do not accept that there is a need to involve themselves in this aspect of organizational dynamics and many still consider this to be a "management" problem, and not of particular concern to systems staff. Similarly, IT Managers have tended to dismiss the issue as the Business Manager's responsibility, and Business Managers tend to see it as a necessary part of the systems development process. It is hoped that, at the very least, the results of the study will convince them otherwise.

To facilitate a successful implementation, developers should make it their business to gain a clear understanding of who is likely to win and who is likely to lose from a potential information systems development (Hirschheim & Newman, 1991; Levine & Rossmoore, 1994). If developers ignore the politics endemic in large, intra-organizational developments, they risk the project becoming embroiled in a number of destructive, time-consuming disputes, and the ultimate failure of the development. Enid Mumford, a pioneer of the socio-technical paradigm, says that, in order to derive the benefits of the humanistic use of IT, an information systems design group should include representation from all interested users, and these users must be free to discuss their needs openly and to negotiate acceptable outcomes (Mumford, 2000). Mumford further suggests that this interaction should be guided by the knowledge of IT professionals. The research discussed in this chapter would suggest that this facilitation process should extend throughout the development of an information systems development.

The challenge for IT managers, then, is to maintain top management support for their development, *as well as* ensuring harmonious and homogenous support from the user base. This should involve more attention to potential conflict during user requirements analysis, and, during development, constant and candid communication with all user groups with developers acting as mediators among groups in conflict. Managing organizational politics and facilitating conflict resolution among user groups requires IT personnel to learn new skills and to implement new procedures. The challenge for researchers is to thoroughly investigate the problem associated with conflict and thereby provide a pathway to possible solutions.

Managing and resolving conflict in an information systems environment is clearly a difficult, challenging and time-consuming exercise, but the findings of this research study suggest that the rewards, in terms of higher success rates, should be worth the commitment.

In conclusion, it is worth pointing out that, although the research study was grounded in the information systems development environment, the technological revolution has merely exacerbated and highlighted existing problems of conflict as a response to change. While there is still much to be learned about conflict and we have not yet determined what the most effective solutions to the problems may be, the problem itself is not new:

"Let it be noted that there is no more delicate matter to take in hand, nor more dangerous to conduct, nor more doubtful in its success, than to set up as a leader in the introduction of changes. For he who innovates will have for his enemies all those who are well off under the existing order, and only lukewarm supporters in those who might be better off under the new" (Machiavelli, 1513).

REFERENCES

Ahituv, N., Neumann, S. and Riley, H. N. (1994). *Principles of Information Systems for Management* (fourth edition). Dubuque, IA: Wm. C. Brown, B&E Tech.

Checkland, P. and Scholes, J. (1990). *Soft Systems Methodology in Action.* Chichester: John Wiley & Sons.

Connors, E. (1994). IT is no longer a black art (editorial). *Managing Information Systems*, Winter, Special Issue, 8.

Davenport, T. H. (1994). Saving IT's soul: Human-centered information management. *Harvard Business Review, 72*(2), 119-131.

Davenport, T. H., Eccles, R. G. and Prusak, L. (1992). Information politics. *Sloan Management Review, 34*(1), 53-65.

Davis, G. B., Lee, A. S., Nickles, K. R., Chatterjee, S., Hartung, R. and Wu, Y. (1992). Diagnosis of an information system failure: A framework and interpretive process. *Information & Management, 23*, 293-318.

Dunford, R. W. (1992). *Organisational Behaviour: An Organisational Analysis Perspective.* Sydney: Addison-Wesley.

Ewusi-Mensah, K. and Przasnyski, Z. H. (1991). On information systems project abandonment: An exploratory study of organizational practices. *MIS Quarterly*, *15*(1), 67-86.

Gladden, G. (1982). Stop the life-cycle, I want to get off. *Software Engineering Notes*, *7*(2), 35-39.

Hirschheim, R. and Newman, M. (1991). Symbolism and information systems development: Myth, metaphor and magic. *Information Systems Research*, *2*(1), 29-62

Keil, M. (1995). Pulling the plug: Software project management and the problem of project escalation. *MIS Quarterly*, *19*(4), 421-447.

Laudon, K. C. and Laudon, J. P. (1997). *Management Information Systems: New Approaches to Organization and Technology* (fifth edition). New York: Prentice Hall College Division.

Levine, H. G. and Rossmoore, D. (1994). Politics and the function of power in a case study of IT implementation. *Journal of Management Information Systems*, *11*(3), 115-133.

Lyytinen K. and Hirschheim, R. A. (1987). Information system failures: A survey and classification of the empirical literature. *Oxford Surveys in Information Technology*, *4*, 257-309.

Lyytinen, K. (1988a). Stakeholders, information system failures and soft systems methodology: An assessment. *Journal of Applied Systems Analysis*, *15*, 61-81.

Lyytinen, K. (1988b). Expectation failure concept and systems analyst's view of information system failures: Results of an exploratory study. *Information & Management*, *14*, 45-56.

Machiavelli, N. (1513). *The Prince (1513), translated with an introduction by George Bull*, Penguin Classics, Harmondsworth, U.K., 1975.

Marakas G.M. and Hornik, S. (1996). Passive resistance misuse: Overt support and covert recalcitrance in IS implementation. *European Journal of Information Systems*, *5*(3), 208-219.

Markus, M. L. (1983). Power, politics and MIS implementation. *Communications of the ACM*, *26*(6), 430-444.

Martin, E. W., DeHayes, D. W., Hoffer, J. A. and Perkins, W. C. (1991). *Managing Information Technology: What Managers Need to Know*. New York: Macmillan.

Mintzberg, H. (1983). *Power In and Around Organizations*. Englewood Cliffs, NJ: Prentice-Hall.

Mumford, E. (2000). Technology and freedom: A socio-technical approach. In Coakes, E., Lloyd-Jones, R. and Willis, D. (Eds.), *The New Sociotech: Graffiti on the Long Wall*. London: Springer-Verlag for the British Computer Society.

Myers. R. H. (1986). *Classical and Modern Regression with Applications.* Boston, MA: Duxbury.

Newman, M. and Sabherwal, R. (1996). Determinants of commitment to information systems development: A longitudinal investigation. *MIS Quarterly, 20*(1), 23-54.

Newman, M. and Robey, D. (1992). A social process model of user-analyst relationships. *MIS Quarterly, 16*(2), 249-266.

Pfeffer, J. (1981). *Power in Organisations.* Marshfield, MA: Pitman.

Philipson, G. (1994). Information: A tool for all trades. *Managing Information Systems,* Winter, Special Issue, 13-16.

Pichault, F. (1995). The management of politics in technically related organizational change. *Organization Studies, 16*(3), 449-476.

Robey, D., Farrow, D. L. and Franz, C. R. L. (1989). Group process and conflict in system development. *Management Science, 35*(10), 1172-1191.

Robey, D., Smith, L. A. and Vijayasarathy, L. R. (1993). Perceptions of conflict and success in information systems development projects. *Journal of Management Information Systems, 10*(1), 123-139.

SAS Institute Inc. (1989). *SAS/STAT User's Guide, Version 6* (fourth edition). Cary, NC: SAS Institute Inc.

Sauer, C. (1993). *Why Information Systems Fail: A Case Study Approach.* Oxfordshire: Alfred Waller, Henley-On-Thames.

Smith, H., McKeen, J. D. and Staples, S. S. (2001). Risk management in information systems: Problems and potential. *Communications of the Association for Information Systems, 78*(13). [http://cais.aisnet.org].

Warne. L. (1995). Organisational power and information systems development: Findings from a case study of a large public sector project. *ACIS 95 Sixth Australasian Conference on Information Systems,* School of Information Systems, Curtin University, Perth.

Warne. L. (1997). Conflict as a factor in information systems failure. *ACIS 97 Proceedings of the 8th Australasian Conference on Information Systems,* School of Information Systems, University of South Australia, Adelaide.

Warne. L. (1998). Organizational politics and information systems development– A model of conflict. *Proceedings of the 31st Annual Hawaii International Conference on Systems Sciences IV,* IEEE Computer Society Press, Los Alamitos, CA.

Chapter VII

Concern Solving for IS Development

Mike Metcalfe
University of South Australia, South Australia

ABSTRACT

"Some make the deep seated error of considering the physical conditions of a country as the most important for its inhabitants; whereas it cannot, I think, be disputed that the nature of the other inhabitants with which each has to compare is generally a far more important element of success."
(Charles Darwin, *On the Origin of Species*, 1859)

Mitroff and Linstone's (1993) summit work, "The Unbounded Mind," reiterates the multiple perspectives epistemology that was introduced to IS by Churchman (1971). They explain the advantages of dealing with IS development problems as involving three domains of knowledge–technical, meaning objective; personal, meaning lifestyle and ethics; and organisational, meaning social constructions and politics. They argue these align with Freud's professional, personal and political layers of anxiety. This chapter focuses on the 'organisational' or 'political' domain, where the key is being able to deal with conflicting demands from stakeholders. The author recently returned from two years as adviser to the Deputy Premier of South Australia. This epitomises the typical working life of senior executives, who operate almost exclusively at this 'organisational' or political domain of analysis. His conclusion from that experience was that 'problem solving' in this domain should be relabelled 'concern solving,' as it was so much about dealing with stakeholders' concerns rather than objective problems.

THE ARGUMENT

The case for **not** thinking of **all** problems, especially IS development problems, as if dealing with an 'object' has now been extensively made in the IS literature. Butler (2000) provides one of the brief explanations, Mitroff and Linstone (1993) a more complete one that includes implications and comparisons. They explain the advantages of dealing with IS development problems as involving three domains of knowledge–technical, meaning objective, personal, meaning lifestyle and ethics; and organisational, meaning social constructions, politics. These, they argue, align with Freud's professional, personal; and political layers of anxiety. This chapter focuses on the second of these domains, the organisational domain. Knowledge, and therefore problem solving, in this domain is best treated as being socially constructed. In this context the chapter attacks the use of the words 'problem solving,' preferring instead 'concern solving.' This is not semantic but rather pragmatic; it changes the way problems are perceived and dealt with. It has been observed to cause a genuine realignment of thinking towards those that say they have a problem and away from the declared object of their concerns. In this problem domain it focuses thinking on the disease, not the symptoms. This includes concentrating more on listening and less on informing.

This chapter will first discuss the concept of 'concerns.' This is followed by a demonstration of the dominance of concerns-issues in the day-to-day activity of a senior manager by interpreting activities from that workplace. Last a simple application of the perspective will be presented. It is a concern-solving approach to IS project definition.

Wilson (1983) defines concern as "a readiness to exert influence: a readiness to act." A failure to be able to act often heightens concern. Use of the word "concerns" does come up in the IS literature. Baskerville and Wood-Harper (1998) use it frequently in their explanation of research, in particular action research, as "Area of Concern." This, they argue, needs to be determined up-front in any investigative process. This fits well with what is being argued here, in the sense that a problem is defined by first noting people's (area of) concerns. Keen (2000) also talks about exploring communities' concerns rather than "topics" when looking for research agenda. These he classifies as "classical (root metaphors), situational and immediate." He seems to be suggesting that a researcher should choose one of these. However, it may be more useful to think that a concern has to be studied through each of these lenses. Keen's work rather concentrates on "community concerns." In this chapter a more individualistic approach of individuals' concerns is taken to be a better level of analysis. Dewey (as cited in Argyris & Schon, 1996) uses the term "doubts" as the driver for human inquiry. This must be a similar concept to concerns.

Landry (1995) and Metcalfe and Powell (1995) argue that it is people's concerns (real interests) that they use to interpret the millions of messages they constantly receive from the environment. Which one signifies a problem that needs attention? We believe that these 'concerns' are the primary lens for new knowledge creation. The idea being that if you are concerned about something, then this 'determines' your priorities to the many messages your senses are receiving from the environment. For primal survival concerns, language is not paramount. For example, small children instinctively know to stay away from rows of sharp teeth. Concerns over being burnt either result from an action, like touching a fire, or from observing the panic-like actions of parents. More complex concerns, such as promotion at work, are socially constructed through dialogue (dialectic).

Concerns can therefore be classified as from nature (instinctive) or nurture (communicated). Barnes and Bloor (1982) argue that humans not only have, like all species, instinctive concerns, but also uniquely appear to have a concern anticipation and concern-solving disposition. At first thought it seems hard to understand why human beings would evolve such a disposition. Yet humans do seem to have an environmental competitive advantage in our desire, supported by our language skills, to create and solve problems of our own perception. For example, NASA scientists are mining for water (oxygen and hydrogen) on planets to allow the building of life support systems and for rocket fuel. Is there a problem here that "needs" to be solved? Extreme sports are another example, which involves solving the problem of how to get a safe thrill. However, if in place of thinking about the very objective concept of "problems" rather a more humanistic term like "threats," "worries" or "concerns" is used, than a "threat-solving" disposition does sound reasonable. Humans who anticipate threats may well have an evolutionary advantage. The word 'concerns' rather than the word 'threat' has been used simply because it is less 'threatening' in managerial-level discussions. Technological advancement itself can be seen as overcoming basic human concerns about controlling nature and food resources.

Wilson (1983) uses the term 'cognitive authority' to describe those people that influence our concerns. Influencing people's concerns may act to alter their information wants. Persuasion is really about altering people's concerns, a practice well versed in advertising. Managing an IS project, from design to implementation, can be perceived as becoming one of managing people's concerns. This will include appreciating those concerns, trying to clarify them, trying to satisfy them and trying to alter them. Put another way, project managers and specialists can act to alter the perceptions of those involved in the project, which in turn affects their concerns, all of which makes 'peoples' problem solving' a communicative action.

Concern Resolution Loop

An explanation of how the concern's approach is believed to alter the perception of the concern solving (i.e., decision-making) process has been attempted using the diagram below. The diagram incorporates:

1. A 'nurture' box which refers to the concerns introduced by other people.
2. A 'nature' box which refers to survival concerns.
3. Concerns generated from 'errors' or learned-from-doing feedback.
4. The argumentative (dialectic) research methodology by assuming that humans spontaneously make a claim (decisions) and then act (if only to recall) to confirm or disconfirm. If the claim cannot be tested satisfactorily by thinking to oneself, then communicative (dialectic) action is required. Note this contrasts with the idea that knowledge is created by first suspending decisions until after information has been collected.
5. Argyris and Schon's (1996) emphasis on 'errors' as the difference between espoused theory and 'theory in action,' that is, between what a person believed to be the way to deal with something and their thoughts when the consequential action does not work.
6. 'Action claims' are tested and learning occurs.
7. Argyris and Schon's (1996) concept of reflective loops.
8. All knowledge (information, data).

Starting from the top of the diagram, it is being suggested that we are born with survival concerns. We learn others from our families, friends and tutors. Upon receiving an external message (stimuli) through the senses, such as the presence of someone or food, these concerns motivate our brains to make assertions (claims, decisions) from which we decide to try some action. In babies this action might cause a missed grab. In an IS manager it may be a successful click on a menu or to build an ERP. This action may be just to move, to say something or to build

Figure 1: Concern resolution loop

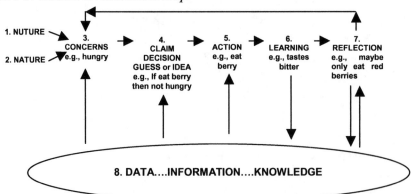

something. If the action is long enough, as in building something, then information will be sought to sustain the action. The action, regardless of whether it is successful, creates new knowledge (or perception) and will be followed by a period of reflection. The Argryis and Schon (1996) argument is that for complex tasks, this reflection should be explicit, sustained and collegiate to get maximum learning.

All stages in dealing with concerns need information and are of interest to the IS manager. These include the management of concerns (cognitive authority) to the storage of any newly created knowledge through the provision of rapid and relevant information when a claim needs to be tested. The complex part of the concern resolution process, sketched out in the diagram, is appreciating the layers and iterations going on at the same time at macro and micro levels. It is so pervasive that it is hard to envision, but a person is going around this loop hundreds of times a day, sometimes dealing with trivia and sometimes working on an innovative complex task. Consider a simplified example: while designing a new piece of software, an IS manager may be talking through options at a meeting and scratching her nose. In that sentence there are at least three iterations.

First, the nose scratching started with a sensory input of an itch. Concerned over the presence of a bug on her skin, the manager uses her memory to quickly come up with a possible action: she rubs her nose. Information from her fingertips suggests there is no bug. The rubbing worked, there was learning through action. No external information was required and a moment's reflection saves the experience in her memory.

Second, assume at the meeting someone boldly says, "lets take that section out of the program altogether." The manager's concerns make the thought (claim) jump into her mind that if this is done, her section may be adversely affected. She thinks about it for a while (information from her memory), asks a point of clarification (confirming information from outside) and then agrees, if it is put in writing (creating explicit knowledge). The whole meeting agrees and the manager reflects, maybe even making a note, on who said what, and why. She thinks that more information should really have been called upon before the idea was verbalised, but it was a good solution, one she might use herself sometime in some form in the future.

Third, the meeting above was part of the three monthly reviews of progress on a project the manager was working on. It involved designing a new piece of software. The project was the result of complaints about the old way of doing things. She had felt the need for something different. She started thinking about how best to do the changes, calling on some colleagues and reading the manual for a few suggestions. While not finished yet, she had learned a lot and was reflecting on what she had learned should be useful in the future.

In all three cases the manager is going through the 'concern resolution loop.' The main difference was the need for external information, beyond her memory, for the more complex tasks. The more complex the task, the more iterations were taken as the task was broken into smaller concerns and 'claims' (see Figure 1). Further, the more complex the task, the more formal the reflective process needed to become to reinforce the storage of memories.

The implication of the 'concerns resolution loop' is that it alters the IS design process. Design, under this perspective, starts with finding out people's concerns, or in a hierarchical organisation, determining what they should be concerned about in return for their remuneration. Satisfactory solutions occur when the stakeholders say their concerns have (for now) been alleviated.

It is being suggested that communicative action, in response to people's concerns, creates knowledge and determines information needs. Some empirical evidence is presented below that shows how many organisational 'problems' are really 'people's concerns' problems. An attempt is then made to show how this determines information needs. This should also provide an opportunity to reflect on how effective traditional MIS are in servicing these needs.

THE STUDY

Background

The opportunity arose to undertake a full-time, two-and-a-half year study of "problem solving in an executive strategic management setting," when the author was offered a job as adviser to the Deputy Premier of South Australia. The Minister was also the Treasurer, Minister for Mines and Energy, and the Minister for IT. It seemed an excellent chance to study 'modes of informing' and the opportunities for 'executive information systems.' This was analogous to Preston's study (1991) of factory managers, except that this was at an executive or 'Board' level. In terms of the study, there was an important difference as the researcher/consultant was a full-time member of the Minister's personal staff, fully responsible for the provision of useful, timely, information to a Minister who was working in an aggressive, information-dependent role. It was not an observation role, but one that tested the credibility and contribution of the researcher whose family income depended on making some contribution to the Office.

Therefore, the epistemological position was not one of observer independence, but rather more aligned to the principles of observer participation, with the researcher being an adviser to a small group of six making up the Minister's Office personal staff. While space limitations do not allow another methodological debate here, this type of study has the opportunity for reflective loops built into the day-to-day operations. As will be outlined below, the work day consisted of assisting with numerous projects. These ran in parallel over many months, each taking a day or two out of the week. This left a lot of time for reflection, both with those involved with the Minister, and alone. Indeed, formal and informal 'post mortems' on projects were common. From the author's consulting and employee experience, this was not untypical of many managers' working lives.

The job entailed helping the Minister deal with routine matters, such as questions from the public, but also there were a number of 'actions' or projects the Minister wanted his own staff to be directly involved with.

The Minister's Office is made up of the Minister, his appointments secretary, a liaison officer to ensure the smooth and timely flow of paperwork, a 'Chief of Staff'–in this case a ex-political journalist who was very much a political adviser–a media (or PR) adviser who was also an ex journalist, and the author who helped with 'commercial advice.' For example, the author's role included reading commercial contracts prior to the Minister signing them, informing the Minister of any delays or problems in the progress of projects, and interpreting the Minister's policy when public servants sought clarification to the progress of projects. In some cases this reached the point of joining the public servants as a negotiator on behalf of the Minister.

This work situation was unusual for organisational studies because it involved the policy function for large public service departments. The entire resources of the public service are at the Minister's control to turn his policy into practice. The Minister made use of all forms of knowledge: explicit, tacit, calculative, opinion, hearsay, experience and scientific detail, to make large impact, complex decisions in a politically charged, hostile atmosphere. The author's job included identifying problems, from the Minister's perspective, and to solve them to the Minister's satisfaction, that is, to address his concerns.

Being a politician is very much about being in tune with peoples' concerns. As a manager of a totally social process, success was defined by those involved. This contrasts with purely engineering tasks where some outcomes can be demonstrated objectively enough. With 'political solutions' the Minister had to define success depending on whether those with influence over him felt it was a satisfactory outcome. Saying that politicians are concerned with other peoples' concerns is not being a bit utopian. What is being suggested is that their advancement depends on the feelings of a select group of people, typically party members, or in case of a Minister, the Premier (Chief or Prime Minister). These 'colleagues' decide whether the MP has been successful. However, this may well be true for most, if not all, careers.

It is possible to underline the subjective view of problem solving by being a bit ironic about Vicker's appreciative systems. Vickers (1984) was referring to a manager's own appreciation of the world being altered, which is very much aligned with the concept of addressing 'concerns.' However, the Ministers dealt with in this study had a very acute sense that their role was to do things that *other people* appreciated. For example, the sale of public assets was not decided upon by following some pseudo-mathematical analysis. Rather, it was undertaken because the right people would be appreciative of the sale.

A Day in the Life of the Minister

The first general observation about working in the Office was the 'queen bee' nature of the job. The day was filled with meetings, and the evenings with signing off correspondence from the public service agencies. The Minister did not have a computer; those with computers used them to write speeches, letters or policy documents. There were no databases, no spreadsheets and no internet. Email, faxes, the telephone and yet more meetings filled the day. The job was about communication, in and out, not about calculations. Information came from experts' written or verbal reports. All discussions were aimed at minimising controversy and in addressing someone's concerns. If the Premier was concerned about something, that took priority. The Minister had concerns, as did the public, public servants and industry representatives.

Company representatives would arrange to meet with the Minister so they could outline their concerns or lack of them. Concerns had to be communicated and balanced. Stories carrying concerns were told by people claiming to represent large numbers of people. The more credible the story, which was rarely formally confirmed, and the greater number of people it claimed to involve, determined the priority given to the story. People's apparent accuracy, sincerity, past reputation and general level-headedness was also important in making the stories have influence.

There were almost no policy meetings in the traditional sense. Yet the author was impressed by the consistency of decision making as the Minister appeared to be working from a few general principles. The author interpreted these to be concern over the reduction of the State's financial liability, increasing sustainable economic activity and public servants forgetting to service their clients.

A typical day involved progressing numerous 'projects' or issues that the Minister had taken an interest in. These are listed below. In the language of the job, the author was simply charged with 'fix them' which meant negotiating them into no longer publicly controversial issues. Any media work or 'political' discussion with fellow MPs was done by the Minister. The author was left with the private commercial negotiations.

The Minister's Office was genuinely busy from 8am until 7pm, then catching up with the day's correspondence until 10pm at home. It was staffed by people with little experience in managing people under stress conditions. This made the mood of the office aggressive. There were public threats of dismissal, threats of incompetence, and public servants involved with the Office took stress leave; the job put stress on private lives. That said, the author has worked in various organisations for over 30 years and was impressed by the commitment of the staff, the quality of the work done and the very low number of errors made.

The Projects: The Problem of Norwood's Trees

The State-owned electricity utility was pushing the Minister to pass legislation to empower them to cut roadside trees in danger of touching overhead electricity wires. The utility wanted to cut back the trees to an extent that meant they would not have to revisit the tree for three or four years. As this considerably reduced the tree size, local residents in the established 'leafy suburbs' wanted a modest annual trim, but preferably the wires undergrounded. They were making it an election issue in a marginal seat.

It would be hard to present this 'problem' as an objective reality. It is about the concerns of all stakeholders. The utility was concerned with repair costs, and the residents with aesthetics. As 'owner' of the utility, the Minister tended to be more concerned about financial liability than aesthetics, but wanted an agreed outcome so as to not overly affect votes. A lot of knowledge was sought about tree growth rates, about treatments to slow down tree growth, about horizontal boring to underground wires and about the effect of tree branches growing between wires. Each side had their own numbers to support their arguments, none of which seemed to impress the other side. A lot was learned about how all the agencies involved operated, about tree growth and the law on owner's liabilities. At the end of the day, all sides compromised because of the threat of an election changing the balance of power in the Upper House. An independent arbitration process was established. It took many hours of meetings and a focus on stakeholder's needs, not on tree branches in wires.

The concerns resolution loop approach fits well with this problem. The role for IS includes the management of concerns, in the provision for information to test claims and in the preservation of explicit new knowledge. Concerns were altered for residents in ways now familiar, given the communications technology, such as newspapers, posters, letters, email and talkback radio. Domination of these allowed concerns to be manipulated and aggravated, both by the residents and the utility. During discussions, rapid access to authentic information on costs, such as undergrounding, may have speeded up the negotiations.

However, more information may have had the opposite effect if contrary views were found. Participants seemed to keep themselves informed by telephoning experts for estimates; for example, several horizontal boring companies, local and overseas, were contacted for approximate estimates. While the new procedures for tree cutting were captured in regulations, technology may have helped in capturing more of the tacit knowledge gained from the exercise.

The Uranium Mining Problem

The following project is one of many 'environment versus jobs' problems which arose, each with much the same concerns and issues. From the Minister's point of view, these tasks came down to staying on top of the media discussions to either counter the claims of environmentalists, or to alleviate the more conservative public's fears. On one occasion the Minister was pleased to note that even the radio announcers were asking the environmentalists how jobs were to be created if the ground could not be used. This marked, according to the office, the end of the dominance of environmental issues in favour of job-creation issues.

Uranium prices have fluctuated widely over the last 20 years. The demand is from the many strategic nuclear power plants around the world offering a power supply not dependent on fossil fuel. The latest mining technology is to find uranium in underground aquifers, pump down an acid mixture that makes the uranium separate from the surrounding rock, which mixes with the water so it can be pumped up to the surface and separated. There is a lot of environmental opposition to uranium mining normally, but here there was the opportunity to draw on people's concerns for water supplies. The State felt there was sufficient economic advantage to encourage this 'in-situ' leaching. The task for the Minister, after making the policy decision to encourage mining, was to manage, in a pro-development manner, responses to incidents publicised by the environmental movement.

These three 'problems' can hardly be called objective. Nature does not care if it is ruined, but fortunately many people do. The problem here was to balance development concerns with environmental ones. While there exists some dubious explicit knowledge about species under threat, there is little quantitative information that can inform this debate. It tends to come down to whether you see nature as an endless resource or rather as a complex inter-related web with humans presently being an overly dominant species. From the Minister's Office point of view, these projects provided a learning iteration of who is likely to do what to which media, and their likely response. It was therefore very much a communicative action issue.

The Competition Policy Problem

The State Government had signed up for a substantial compensation package from the Federal Government, designed to encourage enactment of their competition policy. The relevant part of this was for the State to review all its legislation for anti-competitive elements. This meant allowing competition against State monopolies, such as electricity supply, casino licences and various agricultural legislation, which limited trans-border competition, or else arguing the social benefits of having a monopoly. The main issue was corporatising the energy utilities for competition. This meant unravelling all the social programs which had been woven into the monopoly role, such as pricing structures, which did not distinguish geographic location. There was one price across the State regardless of transmission distance. Further, industry paid a higher rate than the 'mums and dads.' The Gas and Electricity Act had to be re-written, and the Upper House opposition parties had to be convinced that no voter backlash would follow.

From the Minister's Office this meant addressing the concerns of the Opposition, which included not raising the ideological concern over selling off public assets. A policy of not selling the utilities was announced. The agreement with the Federal Government had been signed off by the main opposition party, so they were concerned that would backfire on them if they now objected to the resulting new legislation. The minority party, which had the deciding vote, was concerned about the Green voters, so used the opportunity to float a sustainable energy policy. Any genuine concern for prices being shifted from industry to the 'mums and dads' was avoided, as was the issue of rural voters being disadvantaged. The whole process was a classic commercial passive-aggressive negotiation, with the stakeholders' concerns being addressed but missed ones not highlighted. After a modest amount of background negotiation, the legislation was passed in the House.

The Emergency Services Communications Problem

The police, ambulance and fire brigade were looking to upgrade and integrate their communication systems to digital, for more reliable coverage and to carry a lot more traffic, such as graphics files. The State had a mishmash of different systems, managed by a range of public service departments, including fisheries and the utilities. It was an innovative IT project which had the risk of blowing its budget. Moreover, attempts in London and Melbourne had been a disaster with their new systems simply not being clever enough to replace human operators. The State had a recent history of IT project blow-outs and of emergency services communications failures leading to death.

The concerns involved were about value for money, whether integration would rob the smaller departments of their autonomy, about a failure during an emergency and about the Minister losing control because of the technical nature of the project. In previous cases, one suspects public servants had received Cabinet permission for projects, knowing the budget estimates were too low, but relying on the Government becoming committed to the project. As so many Government agencies and commercial consulting companies were involved, the communicative action included getting people to meetings to get their agreement on any Cabinet Submissions required. The communicative action was thus to first create concerns about the complexity of this project and then to work through solving them. The project was still ongoing after the study finished, but cost blowouts were being reported.

The Leadership Challenge

The Minister's political party was divided over its preferred leader. A change of leadership meant a change of portfolios and, as it turned out, resignation. Halfway through the term of the Government, the majority vote of the party's MPs changed and a new leader was elected. The Minister was duly downgraded to a point where he chose not to re-stand for election. This story is being told because it is typical of office politics which presents a survival threat which puts a shadow over all other concerns in the workplace. The other projects had to be solved with this 'larger' concern in the background. The Minister went from being aggressive in pushing progress of these projects, to saying "don't bother me now."

IMPLICATIONS

Describing what was going on in this organisational setting as 'problem solving' would be misleading. Rather the term 'concern solving' would be more appropriate. The 'so what' is that this not only supports the social construction of knowledge through communicative action, but thereby suggests more concentration on developing IT solutions like group systems and collaboration software rather than just historic databases: de-objectifying knowledge is useful. The problem-solving and decision-making literature that concentrates on the argumentative process (Meyers and Seinbold, 1989) also supports this approach, although still assuming only objective knowledge.

In the examples above, calculative or analysis techniques, like spreadsheets, databases, budgeting, DCF, critical path analysis or market chain analysis, played no central role. The managerial tasks were about communicative action to manage the concerns of various groups of people. In some cases this was to make stakeholders concerned, and in others to alleviate those concerns. The *communications* revolution is assisting in the form of faxes, email, transport and telephone services. The people involved in these projects wanted to talk to each other, that is, dialectically share tacit knowledge. The demand for IT in this workplace was for easier and better communications, including travel, rather than for calculating machines. Silicon technology was required to communicate, not calculate. Any calculations were either contested or used as pawns in wider negotiations. The skill of managers was to use knowledge in negotiation, that is, in a dialectic argumentative process.

CONCERN DEFINITION

From the above experience and line of reasoning, the author has evolved a concern-solving approach to what otherwise might have been called 'problem' definition. This is presented here, in Diagram 2, to show how the concerns approach alters the language and focus of this task as compared to the technical or engineering problem approach.

This method has been developed, in parts, extensively over the last 10 years. It is intended to be a simple, fairly generic method that can be used in a wide range of projects for the purpose of concern definition. What is new about this method is the way the three parts–(1) the project definition diagram, (2) the argument, (3) the rich pictures–have been put together as a package focused on concern definition.

The Concern Definition Diagram (Figure 2) has been developed from Checkland's (1999) work, part of his soft systems toolbag, as "an organised use of rational thought." This has been reworked a little here to allow for the authors' own work on "concern solving" and Davidson's (1994) concerns about the validity of conceptual frameworks. The three parts of the diagram are the Object under consideration, the client's Concerns, and the evidence collection Method. The back arrows indicate that as the project is undertaken, the Object and Concerns may change.

The purpose of the diagram is to clarify the purpose of the project and hence enable the process of concern definition. Typically, and using a website as an example, the diagram can be used to say, "What exactly is the 'Object' under consideration?" Let's say the client's answer is "the corporate website's content." Next, the question is "What is it that "Concerns" you about this (website's content)?" Let's say the client's answer is "consistency across the organisation's departments." The "Method" is then introduced and its aim is to ascertain how evidence will be collected to address the client's concerns. This essentially represents an "inquiry" method, and it reflects the definition nature of most IS projects. In this example a typical method question for this is, "What evidence

Figure 2: The Concern Definition Diagram (PDD)

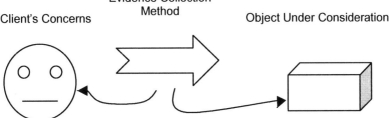

should be collected to convince?" The answer to this question may be a combination of experienced managers' opinions, comparative examples from other organisations and feedback from external customers.

The use of this simple approach to aid question formulation and hence concern definition has proven to be effective both in consultancies and research. The language of the question aligns with the interpretive approach as it acknowledges the presence of an objective physical world, and that the client has subjective concerns or a perspective that they want explored. The evidence collection method of the project analysis can be anything from the analysis of statistics, interviews, through to a comparative website analysis. However, under the multiple perspective approach, the intent is to utilise a method that seeks out diverse views. So if one experienced manager is interviewed and he/she responds by saying consistency is essential, then the respondent should be asked to name someone else who would have a totally different opinion. This search for diverse views is intended to inform the concern definition. Yet, paradoxically it can be difficult to know what evidence should be collected until it is known what conclusion (argument) is sought.

The Argument

Having considered the elements of the concern definition diagram, the next stage is to use these to state the project's argument. Importantly, by argument we mean reasoned debate not quarrelling. The aim is to try and set an "a priori" conclusion (argument) at the outset of a project. This aids with the concern definition by helping to identify the outcome sought. This approach also acknowledges that ultimately any concern definition will need to be presented in a way that persuades others that it is the correct way forward. Essentially, this is what the conclusion and recommendations of a project report do. As mentioned previously (and like the iterations involved in formulating a project report's conclusion and recommendations), the back arrows in Figure 2 indicate that while a project may start with an intended conclusion, the act of collecting evidence is expected to alter the choice of the final conclusion.

After drawing the concerns-solving diagram, the argument-setting process normally begins by simply asking those who claim to have a problem, "What is your argument?" Put in more familiar consulting terms, "What conclusion do you anticipate?" Using the example above, the concerned person may have already formed the opinion that a report will conclude, for example, that "the corporate website's pages should be more consistent." The advantage of having an explicit up-front argument is to focus the study in a way that one becomes clearer about what evidence is required and what actions would be irrelevant. So in this case, the interviewers will focus on consistency, not, say, customers' needs. If the concerned person is not clear about the "direction" of the conclusion, then the a priori argument can be written in a neutral form. In this case this would be "that the corporate website's pages should (or should not) be made more consistent."

To repeat, the most important point about the argument is that it is simply an opening (a priori) position, and the inquiry process is expected to alter the (posterior) argument (conclusion) and anything from minor editing, to a major redirection can be expected. However, it has still been found useful to act as if there is a clear conclusion at the start, provided it is understood not to be set in concrete. Furthermore, the argument method also includes an appreciation that the evidence collection is a process of informing a debate involving the concerned stakeholders as well as the analyst. Through discussion, socially constructed learning should take place. Ultimately, the concern definition is expected to benefit from an explicit acceptance that there is more than one interpretation, and a good constructive argumentative process can both reveal and incorporate this diverse knowledge (Mitroff and Linstone, 1993).

Rich Pictures (Concerns)

Checkland (1999), as part of his soft systems methodology, has suggested another evidence-collection tool that fits under the multiple perspectives and people-centred approach. While not quite as Checkland intended, the Rich Picture tool described here has been found to be useful in identifying stakeholders, their relationships and concerns, and thus directing the evidence collection exercise. The tool is used by bringing together a small group of one type of stakeholder (maybe the project owners) around a white-board to collectively draw a cartoon-type picture that shows all the people and entities that the group feel are involved in the argumentative process. With the website's pages this may include the owners, the customers, the web design staff, IT support staff and department heads. Next the relationship between them is shown as arrows. Last, the concerns of the people represented, either as individuals or as a group, are drawn on as "thought bubbles." The idea is to get what the present group thinks are their main concerns about the argument and what they guess are the main concerns of other stakeholders. The drafting of the group picture is intended to give participants a richer picture of the problem. When completed with one group, it has been found to be useful to go to other stakeholder groups and go through the same exercise, asking them to identify the concerns of others. At the end several pictures may have been drawn and it is worth showing the complete set to all stakeholders. In this way the people concerns become explicit.

The Rich Pictures can therefore also serve as a stakeholder-influence analysis. Many readers will be familiar with the idea of collecting demographics about stakeholders at the start of projects. However, it can be useful to extend this to focus on power and influence issues, the idea being to identify what influence over the project's progress the different stakeholders have, independently or in conjunction with each other. For example, while the demographics of customers may be included, so should the different stakeholders' choices and/or probable reactions. This analysis helps remind project owners of the political dimension of projects. This should not be treated as "silliness," but rather as a very real acceptance that different people have the right to have different perspectives.

CONCLUSION

This chapter has argued that 'concern solving' is a more useful description of managerial action than problem solving for problems like IS design that operate mostly in Mitroff and Linstone's (1993) organisational knowledge domain. This is more than semantics; it correctly refocuses IS development towards dialectic social construction rather than the knowledge collection, analysis and presentation, the latter being 'engineering' tools that are more appropriate for the 'technical' domain.

Concerns determine perceptions, interpretations and worldviews. Some are being 'hard wired' (from nature) and some 'soft wired' (from nurture), which includes those imposed by a childhood environment. These concerns drive a desire for action and/or information through reflection (Crosswhite, 1996; Wilson, 1983; Metcalfe, 1999). These actions inform (Argyris and Schon, 1996) through reflection. Therefore, concerns create problems, but it is a mistake to deal with people's concerns in a similar manner to physical problems.

REFERENCES

Argyris, C. and Schon, D. A. (1996). *Organisational Learning II*. Reading, MA: Addison Wesley.

Barnes, B. and Bloor, D. (1982). Relativism, rationalism and the sociology of knowledge. In Hollis, M. and Lukes, S. (Eds.), *Rationality and Rationalism*, 21-47. Oxford: Basil Blackwell Limited.

Baskerville, R. and Wood-Harper, A. T. (1998). Diversity in information systems action research methods. *European Journal of Information Systems, 7*, 90-107.

Butler. (2000). The con of knowledge. *Proceedings of ECIS 2000 Conference*.

Checkland, P. and Scholes, D. (1999). *Systems Thinking in Action*. Chichester: John Wiley & Sons.

Churchman, C. W. (1971). *Design of Inquiry Systems*. New York: John Wiley & Sons.

Crosswhite, J. (1996). *The Rhetoric of Reason*. Madison, WI: University of Winsconsin Press.

Davidson, D. (1984). *Inquiries into Truth and Interpretation*. Oxford: Oxford University Press.

Keen, P. (2000). Staff seminar held at Georges State University.

Landry, M. (1995). A note on the concept of problem. *Organizational Studies*, *16*(2), 315-327.

Metcalfe, M. (1999). Revisiting argumentative methodology. *Working Paper*, University of South Australia, Adelaide: COBAR.

Metcalfe, M. and Powell, P. (1995). Information: A perceiver-concerns perspective. *European Journal of Information Systems*, *4*, 121-129.

Meyers, R. A. and Seibold, D. R. (1989). Perspectives on group argument. *Communications Yearbook*, *14*, 268-302.

Mitroff, T. I. and Linstone, H. (1993). *The Unbounded Mind*. Oxford: Oxford University Press.

Preston, A. M. (1991). The problem in and of MIS. *Accounting Management and Information Technology*, *1*(1), 43-69.

Vickers, G. (1984). *The Vickers Papers*. London: Harper Row.

Wilson, P. (1983). *Second Hand Knowledge*. Westport, CT: Greenwood Press.

Section III

Linking the Human and Technical: Information Systems in Practice

Configuring the User, Configuring the System

Andrew Wenn
Victoria University of Technology, Australia

An Introduction—By Way of a Confession

I have a confession to make. I am a user. I use coffee shops to do much of my work. I would have been right at home in Restoration England where they provided a social hub for Londoners–hotbeds of political debate, society gossip and financial rumour. Not that I do much conversing; coffee shops are my special place to write (Wolcott, 1990). Sitting with a coffee on the table beside me, the slightly bitter taste of the last sip lingering in the mouth, the air permeated with the tantalising smell of roasting coffee, the hubbub of conversation and music playing softly in the background–this is where I do a great deal of my writing.

What does this talk of coffee shops have to do with an introductory section about human/technology interactions, you ask? Well, strangely enough, it allows me to firstly foreshadow (Creswell, 1998) talk about configurations–configurations of humans and technology. For you see, I can work using a number of configurations: I might just bring in a book and sit down with a coffee and read–the book has been produced using technologies that are situated elsewhere; I can bring the notebook and along with a pencil (a very simple technology (Bolter, 1991)) make notes or draw diagrams; or if I feel the need to have access to more resources, I could lug in a much fancier writing aid–a laptop–and write as I am doing now. Different configurations enable me to work in different ways, but with each one comes varying concerns of, for instance, portability, access and ease of use. It is one of the themes of this section that the different configurations between the human and non-human actors (farmers, computers, organisations, public servants, people wishing to pay bills, information systems designers, software, documentation) bring a variety of issues to system adoption and use.

Secondly it was while sitting in my local coffee shop pondering how I could introduce the material in this section that I overheard the following conversation.

F: " I have really never been able to make sense of the fact that to turn a PC off you have to go to 'Start'. It's just not logical ..."

M: "Well that's Microsoft for you. I keep trying to tell you that a Mac is much more logical."

F (scoffing loudly): "What! On your new iBook thingo I can't even find how to shut it down."

M: "You go to the Special Menu. It's perfectly logical–shutting down the computer is a special function so it makes sense to put it there."

F: "Doesn't make much sense to me, but I suppose once you have learnt how to use it and where everything is ..."

M: "Yes, but my point is that the Mac is easier to learn rather than some graphical interface that was cobbled together over the top of something that was a good idea in the early 1980s."

F: "umm. ..."

M (optimistically): "Besides in the new version of the operating system, Mac OS X, all of those functions are gathered together under the always-visible Apple menu."

The conversation turned to other things and I lost interest–I had found my little gem, the seed that would provide material for an introduction to this section of the book that is devoted to the user/technology relationship. A relationship that is, despite what technological determinists would have us believe, one whose nature changes, depending on local conditions, individual users and a variety of other social factors.

The conversation is interesting for a number of reasons, the continuing rivalry between PC and Macintosh users being the least of them.

Configurations

While there are a number of illustrative points about the socio-technical nature of information systems, it is just two that I wish to dwell on here. Firstly, notice how both participants refer to the fact we have to learn how to interact with the technology. Of course we are all probably familiar with this. How many of you reading this chapter have been on training courses where you may learn how to use a piece of software? How did you begin to master the mobile phone that is probably sitting on the desk beside you as you read this–quite possibly you read the manual. That is, you taught yourself.

The second thing is that there is expected to be an inbuilt logic to our interactions with technology. We need to be able to make sense of it. If we borrow Weick's idea of sense-making, then the pieces of the interface and the actions to be performed only provide a limited context which are "frequently inadequate to understanding what is happening in the system" (Weick, 1997). The **Start** button in the Windows interface provides a limited context; the user doesn't know, cannot access the reasoning behind the decision to place the **Shutdown** function in the **Start** menu. They have learned that to shut the system down, they have to click the **Start** button, which then brings up a menu from which they can select shutdown, but it fails to make sense.

The user has been configured by the technology. "The user's character, capacity and possible future actions are defined in relation to the machine" (Grint & Woolgar, 1997). I am sure that we have all come across the problems caused by not shutting a Windows-based machine down properly. The user is configured, has learned, to perform certain "sanctionably appropriate" (Grint & Woolgar, 1997) actions in response to the technology. Of course, there are those users (hackers in the old sense of the word) who try to bend the rules–go beyond what is sanctioned by the designers–and reconfigure the technology (hardware, software, firmware or whatever) so that it performs in new ways. A classic example of this is the French *Minitel* system (Feenberg, 1995; Rheingold, 1995). At other times, it may just be that the users appropriate the technology for purposes that are not regarded as appropriate in the circumstances. Here I am thinking of the way Public Access Internet in libraries has been appropriated by "backpackers" for email use rather than for the purposes of information retrieval and access that is regarded by many librarians as appropriate use (Wenn, 1999b).

Within the box that sits on your desk, the menus and arrangement of windows, in fact the whole interface design, are embedded certain assumptions that the designers have made about the users. They represent in many cases the first part of a complex relationship between technology and user, user and producer, and technology and producer. It is the variety, complexity and richness of these relationships that the three chapters in this section wish to explore.

Exploring the User/Technology Relationship

In a novel study that draws on theory from three areas–innovation diffusion, the technology acceptance model, and work that has been done on users and systems development outcomes–Teresa Lynch and Shirley Gregor argue that if we make users and their needs the principle focus and driver of systems development, then the chances of success are much greater. Their research looked at the adoption of intelligent support systems by the Australian farming community, an area where adoption rates of technology are very limited despite there being a number of products to choose from. What they discovered was that systems where the users were involved in the development process were, in general, more successful. In fact they state that when "users have a strong influence over systems features," the systems will be easier to use and "will be more truly useful to the users" (Lynch & Gregor, this volume).

Sandra Cormack and Aileen Cater-Steel state that cultural differences are one of the major sources of tension between IT professionals and businesses utilising IT. They identify six essential ingredients whose presence or absence helps determine the effectiveness of an IT-business relationship. Focusing on just the cultural aspects, the determining components are: mutual benefits, commitment to the relationship, predisposition, shared knowledge, dependence on distinctive competencies and resources, and organisational linkages. If, after an examination of the actors partaking in the relationship, some of the ingredients are lacking, the authors recommend introducing strategies to overcome this. However, they warn that there will be other factors that may exert an influence on the IT-business relationship such as politics and economics. So while they have researched one aspect of the socio-technical configuration, there is an unstated caveat that a more holistic approach could also be of value in reducing tensions between the parties.

One could also posit that organisational culture played a role in the failure to accept some of the intelligent support systems that Lynch and Gregor found. In this case we can discern possible lack of recognition, on the part of the system developers, of the shared benefits and a predisposition to develop the software for their own purposes rather than sharing and listening to what the users needed or would use.

Julie Fisher argues that usability can be thought of as how quickly and easily users may complete a task, but she finds that despite an increasing literature on usability, the human needs are not often considered when systems are built. She argues that people with a true understanding of human factors should be included from the very inception of a system alongside the technical. In the Bill Payment System she used as her case study, the human needs were considered from the start and efforts were made to understand the requirements of a wide variety of users including the disabled. Workflows and documentation were developed as the system was constructed, and interface design issues were explored throughout the development by team members who were employed because they were specialists in those particular aspects of human factors. By integrating these aspects into the design at inception, the Bill Payment System is considered a success both by the agencies who use it to collect monies and by the individual users who utilise it to pay their bills.

Conclusion

These three chapters illustrate just some aspects of the user/technology mélange. The coffee shop conversation illustrates some more. What emerges is that while many of the prevailing models of design and development of information systems assume that it is largely a matter for the supplier, this should not be the case. As McLoughlin says, one cannot and should not "downplay the human and organisational elements of system adoption" (McLoughin, 1999). Systems designers and consultants need to adopt a more humble approach–one that doesn't see them as experts with the solutions at their fingertips. User involvement is important. Likewise, those who teach systems design and implementation must also understand and work out how to engender in students an understanding of the complexity of the technology/user relationship. Once they have managed that, then they must encourage the development of effective collaborative relationships between producers, users and the technology. It is my belief that the issues raised by the following chapters are only those inscribed on the tip of the iceberg. Many others are below the waterline, but once we understand that a holistic socio-technical approach to comprehending information systems is more revealing, then we may yet be able to discover and manage them.

References

Bolter, D. J. (1991). *Writing Space: The Computer, Hypertext, and the History of Writing*. New Jersey: Lawrence Erlbaum and Assoc.

Creswell, J. W. (1998). *Qualitative Inquiry and Research Design: Choosing Among Five Traditions*. Thousand Oaks, CA: Sage Publications.

Feenberg, A. (1995). *Alternative Modernity: The Technical Turn in Philosophy and Social Theory*. Berkeley, CA: University of California Press.

Grint, K. and Woolgar, S. (1997). *The Machine at Work: Technology Work and Organisation*. Cambridge, UK: Polity Press.

McLoughin, I. (1999). *Creative Technological Change: The Shaping of Technology and Organisations*. London: Routledge.

Rheingold, H. (1995). *The Virtual Community: Finding Connection in a Computerised World*. Melbourne: Minerva.

Weick, K. E. (1997). Cosmos vs. chaos: Sense and nonsense in electronic contexts. In Prusak, L. (Ed.), *Knowledge in Organisations*, 213-226. Newton, MA: Butterworth-Heinemann.

Wenn, A. (1999b). *The Information Technology Complexity Game: How Librarians, the Internet and Patrons are Shaping the Libraries of Tomorrow*. School of Information Systems, Victoria University of Technology. Retrieved January 8, 2002, from the World Wide Web: http://www.business.vu.edu.au/infosyspapers/docs/1999/AWWP2.pdf.

Wolcott, H. F. (1990). *Writing up Qualitative Research* (Vol. 20). Newbury Park, CA: Sage Publications.

Chapter VIII

Technology-Push or User-Pull? The Slow Death of the Transfer-of-Technology Approach to Intelligent Support Systems Development

Teresa Lynch
Central Queensland University, Australia

Shirley Gregor
Australian National University, Australia

ABSTRACT

This chapter describes a study of the adoption of intelligent support systems in agriculture. The aim was to investigate the apparent low uptake of these systems and the approaches used in development–whether 'user-pull' or 'technology-push.' Data was collected for 66 systems, mainly through telephone interviews. An interpretative approach to research was adopted. The nature of user influence in the development process and the nature of the outcomes for the systems were found to be complex and multidimensional constructs. A pattern emerged showing the technology-push approach was associated with low levels of user influence in the development process and comparatively low levels of system impact. This relationship was more evident in systems developed by government organizations.

INTRODUCTION

There has been considerable effort and money spent on the development of intelligent support systems for Australian farmers, but few systems appear to be adopted for regular use. In this chapter it is suggested that this low uptake of intelligent support systems is due to the use of a particular approach in intelligent support systems development–a 'transfer-of-technology' approach. This paradigm involves a linear model for the dissemination of scientific knowledge. The aim is to 'transfer' knowledge generated by scientists to the farmer recipients. It appears this approach may still be widely used, despite many calls for more 'socio-technical' approaches to system development and knowledge transfer. In a socio-technical approach, users and their needs are the main focus and driver of systems development. That is, there is a 'user-pull' rather than a 'technology-push.'

Proponents of user-focused approaches argue for the involvement of users in the development process (Checkland & Scholes, 1990; Mumford, 1996). It is believed that participation of users in the system development process leads to systems that are truly useful to users because they better meet the needs of potential users. These approaches are participatory, have an adopter focus (Surry & Farquhar, 1997) rather than a developer, 'transfer-of-technology' focus and incorporate ideas from 'softer' systems methodologies (Checkland, 1981; Checkland & Scholes, 1990). That is, the developers focus on the needs and expectations of the users–the adopters of the technology–rather than on research and technical issues.

This chapter reports on a study that focused on the adoption of a certain type of software system, intelligent support systems, in Australian agriculture. For this study, intelligent support systems include expert systems and decision support systems–computer systems that can be used to assist in problem solving and decision making. The developers of these systems obviously perceive potential benefits to farmers from the use of these systems. There is, however, a body of literature indicating very limited adoption of intelligent support systems by farmers (Brown et al., 1990; Cox, 1996; Foale et al., 1997; Glyde & Vanclay, 1996; Greer et al., 1994; Hamilton et al., 1990; Hilhorst & Manders, 1995; Wilde, 1994).

Barrett *et al.* (1991) examined concerns that farmers were not using the intelligent support software developed for them. They believed that there had been limited acceptance of such systems because of lack of understanding by software developers of the decision-making process of farmers, inadequate user involvement in their development and improper problem definitions. Barrett et al. argued that there was a need to determine not only the critical success factors but also to define the logic used by expert producers when they make decisions. The beneficiaries of intelligent support systems were, they suggested, primarily the scientists or the programmers.

A study by Hilhorst and Manders (1995) into the reasons behind the slow penetration of knowledge-based systems at the farm level in The Netherlands suggested that there were pull and push factors at work. Knowledge-based system development was more research driven and knowledge driven; many times it lacked a user-pull. They cautioned that premature introduction of research-type systems may lead to very negative attitudes to knowledge-based systems and information technology in general. This concern is also expressed by Rogers (1995) who cautioned that "a negative experience of one innovation can damn the adoption of future innovations."

The questions addressed in the current study were:

(1)   What is the uptake of intelligent support systems in Australian agriculture?
(2)   What approaches are being used for intelligent support systems development–a technology-focused approach or a user-focused approach?
(3)   What are the outcomes of the different approaches used?

Answers to these questions will shed light on the varying approaches taken in systems development and the outcome for those systems.

BACKGROUND TO THE RESEARCH

This section gives more detail of the transfer-of-technology approach and presents an alternative paradigm that demonstrates why a user-focused approach should lead to more positive outcomes.

In the past, the task of achieving change in many agricultural communities has typically been approached using a transfer-of-technology approach (Ison & Ampt, 1992). In this approach a linear model of technology development is used–the extension officer transfers the information generated by scientists to farmers. The approach requires extension officers to visit farming groups and inform farmers of recent research findings and indicate how these findings could be implemented. The approach does not normally first determine whether, in fact, the information might be of importance to the farmer. The extension officer reports to the farmers the results of research with the belief that once the farmers learn about the research, they will change their farming practices.

The transfer-of-technology approach assumes that the areas of interest for researchers are also the areas of concern for farmers. It also assumes that farmers are interested in what the researchers have to say. While this approach is relatively simple, the low adoption rate of much of the information provided has led to a critical appraisal of the methodology as a mechanism for imparting information to farmers, particularly on complex farming issues (Bawden et al., 1985; Blacket, 1996; Clark, 1996; Doll & Francis, 1992; Gerber, 1992; Guerin & Guerin, 1994; Hamilton, 1996; Ison & Ampt, 1992; Lanyon, 1994; Okali et al., 1994; Scoones &

Thompson, 1994). The transfer-of-technology approach is efficient but ineffective when coping with complex issues such as sustainable agriculture and, it would seem, the use of intelligent support systems.

The current study investigated the development of intelligent support systems in order to gain some understanding of not only why these systems were developed but also how they were developed. That is, the study was interested in the reasons for the development of a given system and the approach taken in development in terms of focusing on the needs of users. The varying degrees and types of user involvement in system development and its impact on system outcome were explored.

The development and adoption of intelligent support systems in agriculture was examined in terms of the theory of diffusion of innovations (Rogers, 1962, 1983, 1995; Rogers & Shoemaker, 1971), the technology acceptance model (TAM) (Davis, 1993; Davis et al., 1989) and principles relating to user involvement in the development of information systems (DeLone & McLean, 1992; Ives & Olson, 1984). Drawing from these theories, the process of development, adoption and success or failure of intelligent support systems in agriculture is explained in terms of a dynamic conceptual framework (Figure 1).

The framework presented in Figure 1 proposes that characteristics of an operational software system depend in part on the development methods used to

Figure 1: Context-involvement-outcome model

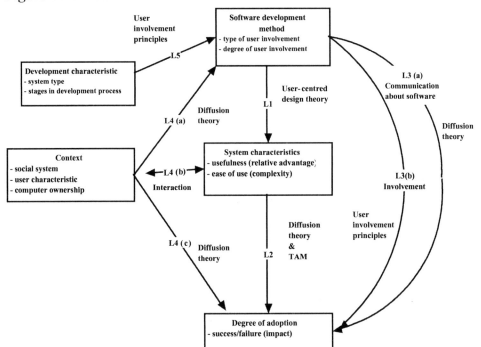

produce the system (L1 link). The degree of adoption of the system then, in turn, depends on a number of characteristics of the operational system (L2 link). In addition, aspects of the software development methods, such as user involvement and the communication processes, can affect the degree of adoption directly (L3 links). The broader social and organisational context in which systems are developed can influence the nature of involvement, the characteristics of the systems that are developed and the level or degree of adoption (L4 links). Finally, different types of systems and different stages of system development may require different degrees and types of involvement (L5 link). Each of these proposed relationships is based on underlying theory.

The first relationship (L1) arises from studies in the information systems field that discuss the importance of capturing the needs of users through user involvement in system development. In particular, approaches stressing user involvement are expected to lead to systems that better meet the needs of users in terms of ease of use and usefulness. However, if users are consulted only about the look and feel of the system and not about the nature or focus of the system then the system may be easy to use but not truly useful. Ives and Olson (1984, p.601) suggested that researchers, when looking at user involvement and information system success, should look at the "characteristics of the involvement process itself such as the degree and type of interaction." That is, there can be different degrees and types of involvement in software development, and the degree and type of involvement may influence the usefulness and ease of use of the software that is developed (L1 link). Different types of systems may require different degrees and types of involvement (L5 link).

The second relationship (L2) is based on the theory of diffusion of innovations and the related technology acceptance model, which provide for links between characteristics of an innovation (a software product) and its degree of adoption. The technology acceptance model proposes that systems that users perceive as useful and easy to use are more likely to be adopted than systems that are not perceived as useful and easy to use. These two characteristics are closely related to the characteristics of relative advantage and complexity–two characteristics that form part of diffusion theory.

In addition, diffusion theory provides insights into how communication channels among information providers and potential adopters can influence adoption levels (L3a link). Furthermore, diffusion theory contributes to our understanding of how the wider social systems into which innovations are introduced play a role in adoption outcomes (L4 links). For this current study, where the focus is on individual farmers adopting an innovation, as opposed to adoption within a medium to large organisation, diffusion theory provides a useful framework to begin understanding issues affecting software adoption. In fact, it gives rise to an understanding of why farmers may have failed to embrace intelligent support systems (Lynch et al., 2000). Diffusion of innovations indicates that communication is an important aspect of innovation adoption. Involvement of users in the development process would improve communication between farmers and developers and so potentially could lead to systems that are more useful to farmers and that are also easier to use. This would also lead to improved communication among farmers in relation to the software features and benefits. These improved communications channels could further lead to improved adoption outcomes.

From this conceptual framework, it is suggested that systems that are initiated from a research or developer's perspective, with limited farmer involvement, are unlikely to be adopted by farmers. A system developed using a technology-transfer approach would be less likely to be adopted than a system that was developed because of perceived need articulated by farmers. Systems developed from a technology-transfer perspective are more likely to reflect the decision-making style of the researcher or developer and not meet the needs and decision-making requirements of the farmer. Researchers and developers often structure their world in a way that helps them understand underlying mechanisms. The researchers' or developers' worldview is not necessarily compatible with developing the type of tools that could help farmers in their decision making. It is argued, therefore, that the reason behind why a system is developed influences the approach used in development and this in turn impacts on the outcome for that system.

Not all links developed in the framework will be discussed. The links that are the main focus of this chapter are L1, L2 and L3. That is, the focus is on the outcomes of involving or not involving users in software development in terms of system characteristics and system uptake. The reasons for the development of a system in the first instance and the system's outcomes are explored.

RESEARCH METHODOLOGY

Prior to this study, little was known about the development and the outcomes for many of the existing intelligent support systems in Australian agriculture. The initial intention was to study six systems in depth using a case study approach. The problem of how to determine which systems were representative of intelligent support systems outcomes in Australian agriculture was difficult to resolve. Given the caution by Benbasat et al. (1987) that case study site selection should be carefully thought out rather than be opportunistic, it was determined that a pilot study, in the form of a survey, would be helpful in determining how to proceed with case site selection.

A pilot study was undertaken with five systems in order to gain some understanding of (1) how to select representative systems and (2) the best approach for collecting data that would provide insights into relevant issues. The pilot study involved in-depth telephone interviews with developers or managers of the five systems. The richness of the data collected led to the conclusion that the best way to proceed with this study was through in-depth telephone interviews with a relatively large number of systems.

Given this, data were collected on 66 intelligent support systems through telephone interviews. This sample represents all identified intelligent support systems within Australia where up-to-date contact details were available. The interviews were open-ended in nature and were conducted, in the main, with a developer or a manager of each of the systems. This in-depth survey approach combined elements of both case study methodology and survey methodology. Following data collection from individuals involved in the development of the system, the data were examined for themes and coded accordingly.

In a second stage in the research, two of the intelligent support systems studied in the first stage of this study were examined in greater depth by interviewing users of the two systems. Again the data gathered were examined and then coded according to the main research themes.

In order to investigate the impact of the differing scenarios on system outcomes, it was necessary to code the data so that some organised meaning could be extracted from the many pages of interview transcripts. Each transcript was coded in terms of attributes considered important for this analysis. These key attributes were drawn from the conceptual framework as well as from the transcripts as they were coded. The attributes were derived from data that were both quantitative and qualitative in nature. For example, system attributes included number of systems sold, cost and current status. Assigning values to these attributes was straightforward. However, determining how to rate, for example, the impact that a system had, or the degree of user involvement was a more subjective process due to the nature of the data collected. These attributes relate more to how the system was developed and the outcome for the system. A systematic and ordered approach was required not only in assigning values for the more complex and subjective attributes but also in determining which attributes were important and the real nature of the more complex attributes (Lynch & Gregor, 2001).

It became clear during the coding of the interview data that the notion of user involvement needed very careful consideration. This construct appears to be complex and multi-dimensional. That is, when looking at user involvement, both the type and degree of user involvement are important.

NATURE OF USER INVOLVEMENT

A distinction was made between user involvement and user influence. User influence is a complex construct that involves determining the degree of user influence in relation to at least two aspects of system development. These two aspects are: (i) type of user involvement and (ii) degree of involvement. These two factors determine the degree of influence that users have in system development.

(i)   **Type of user involvement**. This attribute records the type of the user involvement–ranging from none to consensus. The differing types of user involvement are drawn from Mumford's (1979) work but modified in relation to this study. The three types of involvement, from least to most direct are: (a) consultative–consulted with users from time to time or consulted with users after the system was developed, (b) representative–involvement of users through a reference group or a testing group of selected users and (c) consensus–involvement of users through working groups that involved many users on an on-going basis. Involvement was principally observed during development and maintenance. Involvement of users prior to the development phase, that is, during requirement gathering, was not mentioned by the interviewees when asked to describe how the system was developed.

(ii) **Degree of user involvement**. The construct of user involvement was indicated by involvement in development, involvement in testing and whether user feedback, as a result of using the system, was incorporated into the system. From these three ratings, a value was assigned to the attribute "degree of user involvement." For example, if users had been involved in a minor way in testing then the degree of user involvement was minimal. If users had been involved in testing but the system had been changed to incorporate user feedback as well, then user involvement would be scored as reasonable–depending on the nature of the changes made. Generally, the extent of user involvement was clear from reading the transcripts. The above process made the assigning of values more systematic.

(iii) **Degree of influence**. Degree of influence is gauged by reference to type of involvement and the degree or depth of involvement. Both these factors impact on influence. Involvement, for example, may be consensual in that all users are involved but the developers may not talk with users that often–maybe just a couple of times and maybe only about superficial issues. Therefore, the degree of influence that users had over the system may not be that extensive. For this example, the type of involvement would be consensual but the degree of involvement would be low, resulting in, most probably, low user influence.

Type of user involvement + Degree of user involvement → Degree of influence

If there was no user involvement of any type, then clearly users had little or no influence on system features. If a few users were involved in testing at the end of the system development or input was sought but not really incorporated, then this was seen as token involvement and coded as weak influence. If the views of many users were incorporated from the conceptual stage and the software was continually refined as a result of user feedback, this was seen as extensive influence.

Data were analysed using a mainly qualitative approach. An interpretive approach to coding the interview transcripts was used that required many passes through the transcripts allowing the principal issues and constructs to emerge from the data. Simple statistics are presented in order to summarise the findings and help understand the issues involved. As with any qualitative analysis, there is a certain amount of subjectivity in assigning values to some attributes, and in categorizing responses. Clear definitions of constructs were developed and categories were clearly defined to enhance the internal validity of coding. In addition, the coding of the data was checked by an independent researcher to increase consistency.

RESULTS

Before discussing the results of this study in terms of reasons behind development, degree of user involvement and system outcomes, a brief overview of all 66 systems is given. The systems covered a wide range of agricultural applications including weed identification, irrigation scheduling, and determining pest and disease levels in a variety of crops.

Fifty-three (80%) of the 66 systems were classed as decision support systems, the remainder were expert systems. Of the 66 systems, 37 (56%) were still in use. Thirty-eight systems (58%) had minimal to no user involvement. Eight systems (12%) had user involvement regarded as extensive. Only 19 systems (29%) had used project management when developing the system. Project management was rarely what would be regarded as 'conventional' information systems project management.

Government Versus Non-Government Development— The Technology-Transfer Culture

Of the 66 systems included in the study, 56 (85%) were developed in government organisations. This supports the findings of Hilhorst and Manders (1995) who concluded that most systems in Dutch agriculture were developed in government organisations, that is, in a non-competitive environment. As indicated, only 10 of the 66 systems were developed by private organisations or individuals. These 10 systems had to compete with systems that were developed outside of the commercial environment. Fifty-two systems (79%) were either free or priced at $500 or less. All the systems distributed for free or for $250 or less were developed by government organisations.

Table 1 examines the outcome for these 66 systems, in terms of system impact and whether the system was developed by a government or non-government organisation. For this study, impact was determined by examining the adoption levels (high, medium, low), market share (%) and other information that gave some indication of the impact that the system had among users. A formal coding strategy was used to code the outcome of each system (Lynch & Gregor, 2001). The process of determining the factors that constitute the formation of a complex construct, such as impact of a system, was the result of many passes through the data. The approach taken was to read through the transcripts to identify occurrences of particular constructs, and to re-define and re-read when new nuances in understanding of the construct were found.

From Table 1 it is clear that systems developed by non-government organisations had a better outcome in terms of the impact of the system than those systems developed by government organisations. For non-government organisations, 70% of the systems were coded as high impact systems compared to 19.6% for government organisations. The qualitative data indicated that, in general, developers of systems in government organizations were less likely to involve users in the development process. Thus, users had little or no input into system features resulting in systems that were less useful and easy to use (L1 link). Because of the lack of involvement, potential users were also less likely to know about the features of the finished system (L3(a) link).

Table 2 examines the reasons behind the development of the systems in relation to the type of organisation, either government or non-government, for all 66 systems included in the study.

Clearly, individuals in government organisations were more likely to develop a system from a technology-transfer perspective than individuals in non-government organisations. For government organisations, 48.2% of the systems were developed as a tool for technology-transfer, while for non-government organisations, only 10% were developed as a tool for technology-transfer. Clearly, almost by definition, systems developed from a developer's perspective, that is, a technology-transfer perspective, are less likely to involve users. From Figure 1 it would be

Table 1: Relationship between developer type and impact (66 systems)

Developer	Impact of system					
	High	Reasonable	Low	Not clear	Too early	Total
government	11 (19.6%)	21 (37.5%)	13 (23.2%)	7 (12.5%)	4 (7.1%)	56 (100%)
non-government	7 (70%)		3 (30%)			10 (100%)
Total	18	21	16	7	4	66

Table 2: Relationship between developer type and development focus (66 systems)

Developer	Why developed						
	Saw need[1]	Saw need & TT[2]	Technology transfer	Market strategy	Modelling tool	Unclear	Total
government	19 (33.9%)	6 (10.7%)	27 (48.2%)		3 (5.4%)	1 (1.8%)	56 (100%)
non-government	6 (60%)	2 (20%)	1 (10%)	1 (10%)			10 (100%)
Total	25 (37.9%)	8 (12.1%)	28 (42.4%)	1 (1.5%)	3 (4.5%)	1 (1.5%)	66 (100%)

Note. [1] Saw need ≡ Perceived need; [2] TT = Technology-transfer

anticipated, therefore, that systems developed from the developer's perspective would be less likely to be useful and easy to use than systems developed with user involvement (L1 link) and therefore, less likely to be adopted (L2 link).

Intelligent support systems developed in government organisations may be developed for a variety of reasons. For example, they may be seen as tools for transferring knowledge to highly technical staff members or they may be research tools. In these cases, a technical tool may be seen as not only acceptable but desirable.

In this context, the data were re-analysed and the 38 systems targeted specifically at farmers, rather than research staff or extension staff, were examined.

Table 3 displays the data for the 38 systems in terms of the reason for developing a system and the organisational type, government or non-government, where the system was developed. For the 38 systems targeted at or used by farmers, those systems developed by government organisations, as opposed to non-government organisations, were more likely to be developed as a technology-transfer tool (35.5% versus 14.3%).

Table 3: Relationship between developer type and development focus (38 systems)

Developer	Why developed				
	Saw need[1]	Saw need & TT[2]	Tech transfer	Unclear	Total
government	15 (48.4%)	4 (12.9%)	11 (35.5%)	1 (3.2%)	31 (100%)
non-government	4 (57.1%)	2 (28.6%)	1 (14.3%)		7 (100%)
Total	19 (50%)	6 (15.8%)	12 (31.6%)	1 (2.6%)	38 (100%)

Note. [1] Saw need ≡ Perceived need; [2] TT = Technology-transfer

In addition, Table 4 shows that for the 38 systems targeted or used by farmers, 36.8% of those systems developed because of a perceived need were coded as high impact systems while only 8.3% of those systems developed as a tool for technology-transfer were coded as high impact systems. Systems developed as a technology-transfer tool were more likely to be coded as low impact systems (33.3%) than systems developed because of a perceived need (21.1%). *AVOMAN* was the only system that was developed as a technology-transfer tool and had a high impact level. The system had extensive user involvement, however, and is discussed in further detail later.

In summary, these results support the arguments made earlier and represented diagrammatically in Figure 1. In particular, Table 4 shows that a user-focused development approach is more likely to lead to a system with greater impact (L1, L2 and L3(b) links). In addition, the user-focused approach is more likely to be found in non-government organisations, while the government developers are more likely to have a transfer-of-technology approach (Tables 2 and 3). Thus, it is perhaps not surprising that the systems developed in government organisations also tended to have less impact (Table 1).

In the next section, the nature of the user-focused approach and the involvement of users are discussed in more detail.

DEGREE OF INFLUENCE OF USERS

There can be a difference between user involvement and user influence. It is argued that involvement alone is not adequate to ensure that users have any major influence over the focus of the system or on system features. Rather 'degree of influence,' as previously discussed, is seen as the important factor. Table 5 explores the relationship between user influence and the reasons why a system was

Table 4: Relationship between development focus and impact (38 systems)

Why developed:	Impact of system					
	High	Reasonable	Low	Not clear	Too early	Total
Saw need[1]	7 (36.8%)	6 (31.6%)	4 (21.1%)	2 (10.5%)		19 (100%)
Saw need & TT[2]	1 (16.7%)	2 (33.3%)	2 (33.3%)		1 (16.7%)	6 (100%)
Technology transfer	1 (8.3%)	6 (50.0%)	4 (33.3%)		1 (8.3%)	12 (100%)
Not clear			1 (100%)			
Total	9 (23.7%)	14 (36.8%)	11 (28.9%)	2 (5.3%)	2 (5.3%)	38 (100%)

Note. [1] Saw need ≡ Perceived need; [2] TT = Technology-transfer

developed without regard to whether the system was developed by a government or non-government organisation.

Eight (66.7%) of the 12 systems developed as a technology-transfer tool had user influence ranging from none to weak. As indicated earlier, one system initially developed as a tool for technology-transfer had a high degree of user involvement resulting in users having a strong influence over system design. Seven (36.9%) of the 19 systems developed from a perceived need had user involvement ranging from none to weak. That is, if the system is developed from a technology-transfer perspective, the users are less likely to have any influence over system features. Users had absolutely no influence on design features for six (50%) of the 12 systems developed from a technology-transfer perspective.

Table 6 shows the relationship between the degree of influence users had over design features and the impact of the system.

Looking at the systems that fell into the two extremes of impact level–high and low–a pattern emerges. The majority of systems coded as high impact had user involvement that was in the range of moderate to strong. Only one high impact system, *Feedlotto*, had weak user influence. The developer of this system intentionally developed a very simple system because he perceived that there were many programs on the market that were too hard to use, especially given the skill base of targeted users. The ease of use of the software was the reason identified for the success of the system. The outcomes for this system suggest that the degree of user involvement is not as important for simple systems.

For the high impact systems, users had consultative, representative or consensual involvement–although for many systems the type of user involvement changed over time. For the high impact systems, users had, in general, a higher degree of

Table 5: Relationship between development focus and degree of influence of users (38 systems)

Why developed	Degree of influence								
	Strong	Mod to strong	Mod-erate	Weak to mod	Weak	No influence	Not applic-	Not clear	Total
Saw need[1]		3 (15.8%)	4 (21.1%)		4 (21.1%)	3 (15.8%)	3 (15.8%)	2 (10.5%)	19 (100%)
Saw need & technology transfer		2 (33.3%)	1 (16.7%)		1 (16.7%)	1 (16.7%)	1 (16.7%)		6 (100%)
Technology transfer	1 (8.3%)	1 (8.3%)	1 (8.3%)	1 (8.3%)	2 (16.7%)	6 (50.0%)			12 (100%)
Not clear								1 (100%)	1 (100%)
Total	1 (2.6%)	6 (15.8%)	6 (15.8%)	1 (2.6%)	7 (18.4%)	10 (26.3%)	4 (10.5%)	3 (7.9%)	38 (100%)

Note. [1] Saw need ≡ Perceived need

Table 6: Relationship between degree of influence and impact (38 systems)

Level of Impact	Degree of influence users had over system design							Total
	Strong influ-ence	Mod-erate to strong	Mod-erate influence	Weak to mod-erate	Weak influ-ence	No influ-ence	NA* or Not known	
High	1	2	3		1		2	9
Reasonable		3	2	1	1	3	4	14
Low					5	5	1	11
Not clear						2		2
Too early		1	1					2
	1	6	6	1	7	10	7	38

* NA – Not applicable

influence over system design than in the low impact systems. Of the nine systems coded as high impact, all but one were developed because of a perceived need. The one system developed not from a perceived need perspective was *AVOMAN*. The original intention for this system was to build a decision support system as a mechanism for technology-transfer. However, extensive user involvement significantly changed the approach taken in development.

From the analysis, all the systems coded as low impact were systems where users had either weak or no influence over system design. For these systems identified as low impact systems, developers appear to have built systems: (1) without consideration of the needs of their target audience, (2) without consideration of how to reach their target market and (3) without consideration of maintenance issues. For four (36%) of the 11 systems coded as low impact systems, the reason given for development was exclusively as a tool for technology-transfer. Two other systems were developed as tools for technology-transfer and also because of a perceived need. Only four (36%) of the 11 low impact systems were developed entirely from a 'perceived need' perspective.

Reference to the transcripts gave insights into situations where there was no user involvement in system design and yet the system was successful. These systems were simple systems and had been designed specifically with ease of use in mind and had been developed because of a perceived need rather than from a technology-transfer perspective. Many factors impact on system outcomes–user involvement and the degree of influence that users have during system development are just two factors. The results of this study, however, support the theme that user involvement is a contributor to the degree of success of an information system project. The degree of user involvement can be related back to the underlying reasons for developing the software in the first instance. That is, if researchers or developers are thinking in terms of the software from their own perspective, then they are less likely to involve users with resulting poor outcomes. The findings support the propositions that involvement of users leads to more successful systems in terms of impact and adoption levels.

Some developers have learned from their mistakes. Some interviewees felt they had learned that developing these types of systems was just not worth the effort. Other developers commented on their misunderstanding of the users' needs and their naïve approach to system development and the corresponding expectations about the systems.

We were of the opinion that if you put a package out there, then people would use it. We see this as naïve now.

To summarize, when development approaches are examined in detail, we find that the transfer-of-technology approach was associated with a low level of a complex construct we have designated as 'degree of user influence' (Table 5). Low degree of user influence in turn was associated with low level of impact of systems (Table 6). These findings give a deeper insight into why the transfer-of-technology approach has less than desirable outcomes.

To gain even deeper understanding of the issues surrounding development approaches, degree of influence of users on system design features and system outcomes, further details were collected on two systems.

ILLUSTRATIVE VIGNETTES

The study investigated the users' view of two intelligent support systems, *AVOMAN* and *GrainCrop* (alias). The outcomes for these two systems are tied back to the reasons for the system's development and the approach taken in system development. Initially both systems were developed as a tool for technology-transfer.

AVOMAN

The developers of *AVOMAN* initially conceived of a decision support system to act as a vehicle for technology-transfer.

There were many years of research on avocados, but grower uptake and application of results was poor–they were not using the information. We were looking for a technology-transfer approach that was novel.

However, while initially intending to use the system as a tool for technology-transfer, a technology-transfer approach was not taken in the development of the system.

Prototype approach. Not sure where we were headed when we first started. Lots of testing with the three prototypes. Beta ver 1, 1995, 128 testers; beta ver 2, 1996, 191 testers; beta ver 3, 1997, 247 testers. There were 14 regional productivity groups. These groups were used for testing. As well, farm walks were undertaken. The development group was strongly focused on better adoption and usability. Growers helped with the development of the software.

As a result of interaction with users, the system was changed to be more than a decision support system. *AVOMAN* is a decision support tool that advises farmers on the optimum level of fertiliser application required for a given orchard. It provides growers with management tools and information for improving avocado orchard productivity and fruit quality. It is both a record-keeping tool and a decision aid tool. In fact, user involvement and influence completely changed many system features. Users rated its record-keeping facilities and reporting facilities as very useful for them in managing their farms. The system is in line with the recommendation of Lewis (1998) in terms of providing users with systems falling along a continuum of their prior experiences. Many avocado farmers wanted a comprehensive record-keeping facility that would allow them to issue reports for quality assurance. *AVOMAN* allowed them to do this. Adding a decision support facility to this record-keeping tool was a practical solution to encouraging farmers to use the records they had already kept to assist them in their decision-making in relation to chemical applications. The farmers were able to use the one software package for both record keeping and decision making. This approach overcomes previously reported problems where farmers are required to enter the same data into different software packages. This approach is congruent with the findings of Gill (1995) who reported that "expert systems embedded within conventional systems (i.e., enhanced conventional systems) showed significantly higher rates of maximum usage and current development than those of standalone systems" (p. 67).

The system was coded as a high impact system where user involvement was high and of a consensual nature resulting in users having a high degree of user influence on system features.

Thus, while *AVOMAN* was originally intended as a vehicle for technology-transfer, interaction with users changed the focus of the system. This outcome is unusual, as most of the systems investigated in this study that were developed as a tool for technology-transfer had minimal to no user involvement. The involvement of the users changed not just the look and feel of the system, but the focus of the system.

Feel it is our (producers) product–because of involvement. It was a team effort. Producers put a lot of effort into it as well. There is joint ownership.

GrainCrop

The other system where users were interviewed was *GrainCrop*. *GrainCrop* is a grain growth simulator. It is a decision support tool with some record-keeping facilities. The reasons why *GrainCrop* was developed were given as:

A paper-based version of the concepts was released–the software developed from there. It allowed the researchers to compile research information into one product. There were major changes in 1993/4–put on a programmer to rewrite in C. There were major changes to the interface at this stage.

In relation to how the system was developed, the following information was given: The extension team, with the aid of a programmer, developed it. Initially, a self-taught programmer developed the program. There was user testing done on changes.

From the interview transcript, the developer of the system described user involvement in such a way that it appeared to be representative in nature. It appeared that users were involved through reference groups or testing groups of selected users. After interviewing users, however, the degree of user influence on design features appeared to be weak to moderate. A technology-transfer approach was taken in the development of this system. The system was coded as a moderate impact system even though adoption levels were low, reaching only 4% of the target audience. Information on different varieties of grain and frost risk are provided in pamphlets that are put out by the Department of Primary Industry each season based on information generated by the *GrainCrop* system. The information is fairly broad and general, and for many farmers this is sufficient. Therefore, the impact of the system is higher than the adoption levels would indicate.

Users had varying opinions in relation to most aspects of the system. Some users found the system useful in decision making while others felt that they did not gain much from using it. Some users found it a useful tool for record keeping whilst others were disappointed with the record-keeping side of the software. In general, there was a sense that for many users the system did not match their way of thinking in terms of managing their data and making their farming decisions. While the system met some of the farmers' needs, there were aspects of it that were clearly not in line with how some of the farmers thought about their farming process.

The new version–they have tried to go too far. It is too complicated. You also need to have a planting date in order to do a simulation run. This is not the way I like to operate........ I was going to ring up and let them know. They have sorghum and all sorts of things. What the hell do we want to know all that for?

Outcomes for AVOMAN and GrainCrop

It is not appropriate to make a direct comparison between the adoption levels of *AVOMAN* and *GrainCrop*. Certainly *AVOMAN* had a better adoption level of targeted users (25%) than *GrainCrop* (4%). Many factors influence adoption levels, for example the availability of generic information generated by the *GrainCrop* system may have impacted on its adoption levels. Although, it could be equally argued that if farmers were aware of the value of the information generated by the *GrainCrop* package, it would raise their awareness of the software and encourage them to use it. Another reason for not making too direct a comparison between the adoption levels of the two software systems is that there may be different reporting requirements by the two industries–the avocado and grain industries. Nonetheless, it was very apparent from interviews with users that users of *AVOMAN* had a high level of trust in this system. This level of trust was not as apparent to the same extent for users of *GrainCrop*. Cox (1996) argues, in fact, that the criteria for success should not be in terms of units sold but rather to "the critical insights gained through improved communication of the different perspectives of researcher and farmer" (p.376). If this is the criteria used to gauge success of a system, then *AVOMAN* would be considered significantly more successful than *GrainCrop*.

There appears some evidence that the developers of *GrainCrop* convened the reference groups from, as proposed by Woods et al. (1997), a perspective that focused on their own purposes rather than to build an enduring relationship with the farmers based on joint purposes. For *AVOMAN* the relationship seems to have been more enduring.

The developers of AVOMAN took an adopter-focused approach to system development. The outcomes for this system, in terms of user acceptance, usefulness and ease of use, were better than the outcome for GrainCrop. The developers of GrainCrop took a technology-transfer approach to the development and delivery of the system despite some involvement of potential users. The differing outcomes for the two systems support the proposition that by involving users in system development, the systems are more likely to be useful and easy to use (L1 link) and, therefore, more widely adopted (L2 link).

CONCLUSIONS AND FUTURE TRENDS

The study supports the anecdotal impressions that, despite the many intelligent support systems that have been developed, few have been widely adopted. The study confirms previous work in that a significant number of systems were developed because of a research or developer-push rather than a user-pull. This was particularly true for systems developed by government organisations. This knowledge is important in that it can guide future development of intelligent support systems in Australian agriculture.

In addition, the study clearly demonstrated that intelligent support systems targeted at farmers are, in general, more successful when users are involved in the development process. A trend was found between the transfer-of-technology approach and lower degrees of user influence on the development process, which was in turn related to lower levels of system impact. In addition, the transfer-of-technology approach and associated poorer outcomes were more prevalent in government organisations.

This study has extended work on user involvement and system outcomes. It has drawn together work from three areas–Rogers' diffusion theory, the technology acceptance model, and principles surrounding the involvement of users and system outcomes. Most prior research in the information systems area has investigated only two of the above three features in any one study. There appears to be little work on examining the three aspects of (1) involvement, (2) system characteristics and (3) outcomes in the one study. Work in the area of user involvement and system outcomes has generally not investigated whether user involvement has impacted on the usefulness and ease of use of the software (Cavaye, 1995; Ives & Olson, 1984), and how this may impact on system outcomes. The study has also investigated the reasons behind system development and the resulting impact on outcomes. The results support the relationships presented in the context-involvement-outcome framework (Figure 1). In particular, the study has shown that the approach taken in software development influences system outcomes (L3 links). By involving users in system development, the system will be more useful to the user and will be easier to use (L1 link). Software that is useful and easier to use generally is more widely adopted and has a higher impact (L2 link).

From the investigation of the system, *AVOMAN*, it is apparent that when users have a strong influence over system features, then the system will be easy to use, but more importantly will truly be more useful to users. It is not a perception of usefulness–the system is truly useful.

The outcomes of this study are of interest not only to developers of intelligent support systems in agriculture but also for developers of other types of systems. In particular, the outcomes of this study will be of interest to developers of non-mandatory systems used outside of large organisations.

There is currently a move towards placing some intelligent support systems onto the World Wide Web (Georgiev & Hoogenboom, 1999; Jensen et al., 2000; Zhu & Dale, 2000). The intention is that users will interact with these systems and the underlying data via the Web. The outcomes from this study are relevant to the development of intelligent support systems for use over the World Wide Web. It will still be important to capture the needs of users–regardless of how the system will be delivered. In fact, it is important that developers do not continue to develop systems from their perspective. If this happens then users may be 'turned off' using these types of systems over the Web–and again, an opportunity will be lost.

REFERENCES

Australian Bureau of Statistics. (2000). Use of Information Technology on Farms, Australia (Report 8150.0): Australian Bureau of Statistics.

Barrett, J. R., Thompson, T. L. and Campbell, W. P. (1991). Information requirements and critical success factors for corn/soybean decision support systems. *Proceedings of the American Society of Agriculture Engineers*, 7491-7501. Chicago, Illinois, December 17-20.

Bawden, R. J., Ison, R. L., Macadam, R. D., Packham, R. G. and Valentine, I. (1985). A research paradigm for systems agriculture. *Proceedings of the Agricultural Systems Research for Developing Countries. ACIAR Proceedings No. 11*, 31-42. Richmond, N.S.W., May.

Benbasat, I., Goldstein, D. K. and Mead, M. (1987). The case research strategy in studies of information systems. *MIS Quarterly*, September, 369-386.

Blacket, D. (1996). From Teaching to Learning: Social Systems Research into Mixed Farming (Project Report Q096010), Emerald: Department of Primary Industry.

Brown, J. D., Walsh, J. and Pfeiffer, W. C. (1990). Experts systems in agriculture: An assessment of their success. *Proceedings of the 3rd International Conference on Computers in Agricultural Extension Programs*, 264-269. Florida, USA, January 31-February 1.

Cavaye, A. L. M. (1995). User participation in system development revisited. *Information and Management, 28*, 311-323.

Checkland, P. (1981). *Systems Thinking, Systems Practice.* Chichester: John Wiley & Sons.

Checkland, P. and Scholes, J. (1990). *Soft Systems Methodology in Action.* Chichester: John Wiley & Sons.

Clark, R. A. (1996). Sustainable Beef Production Systems Project: Beyond Awareness to Continuous Improvement Part 1 (Project Report Series Q096002), Rockhampton: Department of Primary Industries.

Cox, P. G. (1996). Some issues in the design of agricultural decision support systems, *Agricultural Systems, 52*(2/3), 355-381.

Davis, F. D. (1993). User acceptance of information technology: System characteristics, user perceptions and behavioral impacts. *International Journal Man-Machine Studies, 38*, 475-487.

Davis, F. D., Bagozzi, R. P. and Warshaw, P. R. (1989) User acceptance of computer technology: A comparison of two theoretical models. *Management Science, 35*(8), 982-1003.

DeLone, W. H. and McLean, E. R. (1992). Information systems success: The quest for the dependent variable. *Information Systems Research, 3*(1), 60-95.

Doll, J. D. and Francis, C. A. (1992). Participatory research and extension strategies for sustainable agricultural systems. *Weed Technology*, *6*, 473-482.

Foale, M., Carberry, P., Hochman, Z. and Dalgliesh, N. (1997). Management of dry-land farming systems in North Eastern Australia. How can scientists impact on farmers' decision-making? *Agricultural Science*, May-June, 34-37.

Georgiev, G. A. and Hoogenboom, G. (1999). Near real-time agricultural simulations on the Web. *Simulation*, *73*(1), 22-28.

Gerber, J. M. (1992). Farmer participation in research: A model for adaptive research and education. *American Journal of Alternative Agriculture*, *7*(3), 118-121.

Gill, T. G. (1995). Early expert systems: Where are they now? *MIS Quarterly*, March, 51-80.

Glyde, S. and Vanclay, F. (1996). Farming styles and technology transfer: Sociological input in the development of a decision support system for viticulture. In Lawrence, G., Lyons, K. and Momtaz, S. (Eds.), *Social Change in Rural Australia*, 38-54. Rural Social and Economic Research Centre, Central Queensland University, Rockhampton, Queensland, 4702, Rockhampton.

Greer, J. E., Falk, S., Greer, K. J. and Bentham, M. J. (1994). Explaining and justifying recommendations in an agriculture decision support system. *Agricultural Systems*, *44*, 217-235.

Guerin, L. J., and Guerin, T. F. (1994). Constraints to the adoption of innovations in agricultural research and environmental management (a review). *Australian Journal of Experimental Agriculture*, *34*, 549-571.

Hamilton, N. A. G. (1996). *Learning to Learn with Farmers: An Adult Learning Extension Project. Case Study: Queensland, Australia 1990-1995*, Landbouw University, Wageningen, The Netherlands.

Hamilton, W. D., Woodruff, D. R. and Jamieson, A. M. (1990). Role of computer-based decision aids in farm decision making and in agricultural extension. *Proceedings of the Climatic Risk in Crop Production: Models and Management for the Semiarid Tropics and Subtropics*, 411-423. Brisbane, July 2-6.

Hilhorst, R. and Manders, R. (1995). Critical success (sic) and fail factors for implementation of knowledge based systems at the farm level. *Proceedings of the 2nd Symposium on Artificial Intelligence in Agriculture*, 275-287. Wageningen, The Netherlands, May 29-31.

Ison, R. L. and Ampt, P. R. (1992). Rapid rural appraisal: A participatory problem formulation method relevant to Australian agriculture. *Agricultural Systems*, *38*, 363-386.

Ives, B. and Olson, M. H. (1984). User involvement and MIS success: A review of research. *Management Science, 30*(5), 586-603.

Jensen, A. L., Boll, P. S. and Pathak, B. K. (2000). Pl@nteInfo (R)–A Web-based system for personalised decision support in crop management. *Computers and Electronics in Agriculture, 25*(3), 271-293.

Lanyon, L. E. (1994). Participatory assistance: An alternative to transfer of technology for promoting change on farms. *American Journal of Alternative Agriculture, 9*(3), 136-142.

Lewis, T. (1998). Evolution of farm management information systems. *Computers and Electronics in Agriculture, 19*, 233-248.

Lynch, T., and Gregor, S. (2001). User involvement in DSS development: Patterns of influence and system impact. *Proceedings of the 6th International Society for Decision Support Systems (ISDSS'01)*, 207-217. Brunel University, West London, UK, July 2-4.

Lynch, T., Gregor, S. and Midmore, D. (2000). Intelligent support systems in agriculture: How can we do better? *Australian Journal of Experimental Agriculture, 40*, 609-620.

Mumford, E. (Ed.). (1979). *Consensus Systems Design: An Evaluation of this Approach.* Gromingen: Sijthoff and Noordhoff.

Mumford, E. (1996). *Systems Design–Ethical Tools for Ethical Change.* Houndmills: Macmillan Press.

Okali, C., Sumberg, J. and Farrington, J. (1994). Farmer Participatory Research: Rhetoric and Reality, Intermediate Technology Publications, on behalf of the Overseas Development Institute, London.

Rogers, E. M. (1962). *Diffusion of Innovations.* New York: The Free Press.

Rogers, E. M. (1983). *Diffusion of Innovations* (third edition). New York: The Free Press.

Rogers, E. M. (1995). *Diffusion of Innovations* (fourth edition). New York: The Free Press.

Rogers, E. M. and Shoemaker, F. F. (1971). *Communication of Innovations: A Cross-Cultural Approach* (second edition). New York: The Free Press.

Scoones, I., and Thompson, J. (Eds.). (1994). *Beyond Farmer First: Rural People's Knowledge, Agricultural Research and Extension Practice.* London: Intermediate Technology Publications.

Surry, D. W. and Farquhar, J. D. (1997). Diffusion theory and instructional technology. *Journal of Instructional Science and Technology, 2*(1).

Wilde, W. D. (1994). Australian expert systems for natural systems. *AI Applications, 8*(3), 3-12.

Woods, E. J., Cox, P. and Norrish, S. (1997). Doing things differently: The R, D,&E revolution. *Proceedings of the Intensive Sugarcane Production: Meeting the Challenges Beyond 2000*, 469-491.Wallingord, UK.

Zhu, X., and Dale, A. P. (2000). Identifying opportunities for decision support systems in support of regional resource use planning: An approach through soft systems methodology. *Environmental Management, 26*(4), 371-384.

Chapter IX

Prescription to Remedy the IT-Business Relationship

Sandra Cormack and Aileen Cater-Steel
University of Southern Queensland, Australia

ABSTRACT

Even though organisations are highly dependent on information technology (IT), many organisations have reported an unhealthy relationship between business and IT professionals. Establishing an effective relationship between these two disparate groups is essential for organisational success in today's competitive global economy. Despite many attempts to improve the IT-business relationship, tensions still exist. The cultural differences between business and IT have recently been blamed for these tensions.

Through the application of relevant organisational behaviour theories, the cultural characteristics of the IT group that effect the IT-business relationship can be identified. Research shows that the IT culture is such that mutual benefits are not derived from the relationship, IT and business groups have a poor attitude towards cooperation, there is a lack of shared knowledge between business and IT, and there is a lack of organisational linkages between business and IT. As a starting point for reconciliation between business and IT, this chapter provides insights into how tensions in the IT-business relationship can be minimised through understanding and managing the IT culture.

INTRODUCTION

Since the introduction of computers in the early 1960s, many organisations have reported a troubled relationship between business and information technology

(IT) professionals. Some 40 years on, and despite many attempts to resolve the troubled relationship, tensions still exist. These tensions have, in recent times, been attributed to the cultural differences between business people (those who use IT) and IT people (those who make IT work).

Establishing an effective relationship between these two disparate groups is essential for organisational success in today's competitive global economy. In an effective relationship, IT and business professionals work together to understand business opportunities, determine needed functionality, choose among technology options and decide when urgent business needs demand sacrificing technical excellence for immediate, incomplete solutions (Rockart, Earl & Ross, 1996).

This chapter examines the troubled IT-business relationship from a cultural perspective. Firstly, six ingredients necessary for an effective IT-business relationship are explored. Secondly, some of the more typical characteristics of IT groups are identified. Then, the effects of each of these cultural characteristics on each of the six essential ingredients of an effective relationship are discussed. As a starting point for reconciliation between business and IT professionals, insights are provided as to how tensions in the IT-business relationship can be minimised through managing the IT culture.

SIX ESSENTIAL INGREDIENTS OF AN EFFECTIVE IT-BUSINESS RELATIONSHIP

There have been many models developed by researchers and practitioners to explain the behaviour between groups in organisations. One of these models, developed by Henderson (1990), specifically describes the partnership between business and IT professionals in organisations. This model, illustrated in Figure 1, has two dimensions:
1. Partnership in context–key factors necessary for a long-term relationship;
2. Partnership in action–key factors that create an effective day-to-day working relationship.

Figure 1: Six determinants of a partnership (Henderson, 1990, p.10)

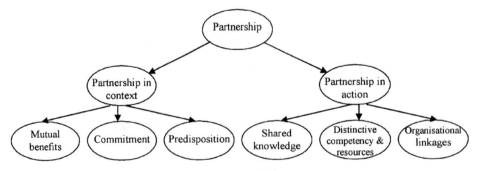

To sustain an effective relationship over time, three key ingredients were found to be necessary: mutual benefits, commitment to the relationship and predisposition. To establish an effective day-to-day relationship, three key ingredients were also deemed to be necessary: shared knowledge, dependence on distinctive competencies and resources, and organisational linkages. These six ingredients are now discussed.

Mutual Benefits

For a relationship to be sustained over time, it is necessary for the two parties of the relationship to specify and agree on three types of mutual benefits: financial contribution, operations efficiency and quality of work life.

The relationship can be helped by articulating the financial contribution of IT to achieve business objectives, such as increased revenue and efficiency, or decreased costs. Improvements in product and service delivery, such as improved systems delivery times, contribute to an effective relationship, as does a positive working environment which improves the quality of work life.

Commitment

In addition to mutual benefits, a commitment to achieving organisational goals and objectives from both sides helps sustain a partnership over time. There are three indicators of commitment: shared goals, incentive systems and contracts. Shared goals provide ongoing motivation and a common ground for negotiation where goal conflicts arise. An appropriate incentive system reinforcing shared goals also fosters commitment. In addition, contracts, although ineffective as an enforcement mechanism, indicate some willingness of the partners in a relationship to commit.

Predisposition

Predisposition relates to the attitude towards cooperation between business and IT groups (Subramani, Henderson & Cooprider, 1998). Two conditions that indicate predisposition are trust, and existing attitudes and assumptions.

Groups work better together in an atmosphere of mutual trust. Trust is built on track record and personal relationships, and is a shared expectation that IT and business groups will meet their commitments to each other (Nelson & Cooprider, 1996). There are four dimensions of trust: similarity, prolonged interaction, appropriate behaviour and consistent behaviour (Bashein & Markus, 1997). People tend to trust others who are similar, have common interests and a common language. Trustworthiness takes time to develop, hence the need for prolonged interaction. Repeated intergroup relations build trust, as does developing personal

184 Cormack & Cater-Steel

relationships at all levels of the organisation. Appropriate behaviour in the light of the other's expectations builds trust. Behaviour against the norm may result in negative impressions. Consistent behaviour makes people appear predictable, which can promote trust. Consistency includes a reputation for fulfilling past commitments and for matching promises with deliveries.

The second condition of predisposition, existing attitudes and assumptions, is based on the assumption that if members of the partnership believe they can help each other, then they will develop cooperative attitudes.

Shared Knowledge

Having an understanding and appreciation of the work environment of the other member in the partnership can lead to a better relationship (Henderson, 1990). However, this shared knowledge must be more than mere communication of facts and knowledge of each other's activities and skill bases. It must extend to a deeper level of understanding of the other's needs, constraints and contribution to organisational goals (Nelson & Cooprider, 1996). Knowledge gaps can lead to differences of interpretation, which may lead to conflict (Hirschheim, Klein & Newman, 1991).

The primary responsibility of many IT groups is to deliver IT solutions based on the requirements of the business. This creates the need for a common knowledge base between business and IT groups. Shared knowledge can be acquired through effective education and work experience from both a technical and business perspective (Earl, 1989; Nelson & Cooprider, 1996). Also, shared knowledge can be gained through repeated periods of positive communication, social interaction, attaining trust and goal achievement. However, too much shared knowledge can also become a problem. For example, as the business group becomes more knowledgeable about IT, this reduces their dependence on the IT group. As a result, the business group may distance themselves from the IT group, resulting in a lack of cooperation and incidences of intergroup conflict.

Dependence on Distinctive Competencies and Resources

Organisational groups are often dependent on each other for achieving goals. Group dependence on each other for information, assistance or coordinated action can foster both cooperation and conflict between groups (Boulding, 1957; Irwin & More, 1994; Choi & Kelemen, 1995; Robbins, 1998; Ivancevich & Matteson, 1999). Opposing forces are stimulated when one group is dependent on another, which may result in tension when it comes to decisions (Smith & McKeen, 1992). For an effective day-to-day relationship, groups must learn to accept dependence on each other's skills and resources.

Organisational Linkages

Organisational linkages result when organisational processes intertwine, information is freely exchanged between groups and social relationships are established. For an effective relationship to develop, both business and IT people must be part of the decision-making process. Opportunities for social interaction between groups in organisations can help develop group relations, as social activities provide an environment for workers to interact and talk about their work, which can lead to a greater understanding and appreciation of the work environment of each group (Nelson & Cooprider, 1996).

With an understanding of the six essential ingredients of an effective relationship, we now move on to look at the cultural characteristics of IT groups in organisations, and the effects of these cultural characteristics on the IT-business relationship.

CHARACTERISTICS OF IT GROUPS IN ORGANISATIONS

Organisational culture models provide an excellent starting point to better understand the characteristics of the IT group in organisations. One such model represents culture as a web, as illustrated in Figure 2. The centre circle, the paradigm, represents a core set of values, beliefs and assumptions common to the organisation. These values, beliefs and assumptions are reflected through the outer

Figure 2: The cultural web of an organisation (Johnson & Scholes, 1993, p.61)

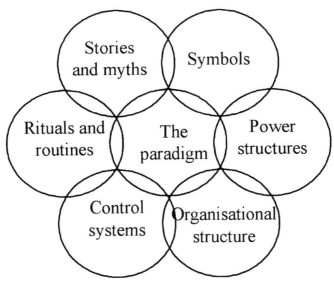

circles, which represent the cultural elements of stories and myths, symbols, power structures, organisational structures, control systems, and rituals and routines (Johnson & Scholes, 1993).

Stories are tales told by members of an organisation. Symbols refer to the type of language used, logos, and office layouts. Power structures reflect the powerful managerial groupings in an organisation. Organisational structures refer to the way in which an organisation works. Control systems emphasise what is important in the organisation, and rituals and routines define the way work is done.

This cultural model was applied to understand the culture of IT groups in organisations (Cormack, 2001). In-depth interviews, structured around these six cultural elements, were conducted with a total of 32 senior business and IT professionals in five Australian organisations. The next part discusses the cultural characteristics of the IT group that emerged from these interviews, and the effects of these characteristics on the six essential ingredients of an effective relationship.

Organisational Structure

Organisational structure reflects the "formal structures within an organisation which impact on organisational behaviour" (Ward & Peppard, 1996, p.55). Organisational structure is one factor likely to increase intergroup conflict, as it may create or reinforce intergroup differences in goals, values and perceptions (Boulding, 1957). Two aspects of organisational structure emerged from the interviews in relation to the IT group in organisations: the role of IT, and the positioning of IT.

Role of IT

Over the years, the role of IT in an organisation has evolved from a process-oriented backroom function, to a strategic, information-oriented function (Ward & Griffiths, 1996). Traditionally, the IT function played a support role. Now, IT has matured to a stage where it is an important aspect of everyday business and an integral part of everyday life (Keen, 1991).

However, in some organisations, IT is still viewed as a support function and as such is not considered to be critical to organisational success (Avison, Cuthbertson & Powell, 2000). This has a negative effect on three ingredients of the IT-business relationship. When IT is not seen to be contributing to organisational goals or the bottom line, *mutual benefits* are diminished. Also, in a support role, the IT group may develop separate goals to the organisation, demonstrating the IT group has little *commitment* to the relationship. Further, if IT is not viewed as being critical to organisational success, the business may not involve IT people in business activities, thus restricting *organisational linkages*.

In organisations where IT is considered to be of strategic importance, IT receives much more devotion (Lucas, 1984; Raghunathan & Raghunathan, 1989).

A strategic role demonstrates the importance of IT to the organisation with respect to *mutual benefits*: it demonstrates recognition by the organisation of IT's contribution to the bottom line and also to the goals of the organisation. Also, if IT is viewed as being critical to organisational success, then business management will ensure that IT people are involved in organisational activities, strengthening *organisational linkages*.

One factor, problematic of the changing role of IT from a support to a strategic role, and having a negative effect on the IT-business relationship, is that the role change may not have been communicated to the business. Many business managers understand the role of human resources, finance and administration in an organisation, but not the role of IT. This suggests a lack of *shared understanding* by the business of the role of IT.

If an effective IT-business relationship is desired, the IT group should be viewed within the organisation as a strategic business partner. This strategic role can be promoted through words and action.

Positioning of IT

The positioning of IT is measured by the rank of the chief information officer (CIO) or IT director in relation to the senior managers within the organisation. The positioning of the CIO in an organisation has been suggested to influence the effectiveness of the IT group (Raghunathan & Raghunathan, 1989).

The CIO reporting to top management has several advantages. Reporting to and interacting with top management can help to overcome the problems of the IT group not knowing what the objectives of the organisation are, clarifying *mutual benefits* and improving IT *knowledge* of business activities. It can increase the likelihood of IT management participating in organisational strategy formulation, improving *organisational linkages*. It can promote communication between business and IT at the top level, increasing business appreciation, understanding, motivation and perceptions of IT, thus improving business *knowledge* of the activities of the IT group. These qualities can be fostered by a CIO if the CIO has direct access to these senior executives. This is more easily accomplished if the CIO is at the same reporting level as other executives (Raghunathan & Raghunathan, 1989).

However, the CIO is often not part of the executive management team. IT groups are frequently positioned and structured to manage IT rather than to support the business (Ward & Peppard, 1996). This has a negative effect on the IT-business relationship. The IT department is often remote from the key decision makers in some organisations (Watson, 1989; Keen, 1993), restricting *shared knowledge* between business and IT. Attempting to align the IT department more closely with the working requirements of the business has long been the source of irritation in companies (Howarth, 1999). Without this alignment, the CIO has difficulty gaining access to top management (Doll & Ahmed, 1983), restricting *organisational linkages*.

To improve the IT-business relationship, the CIO should be positioned where he/she has direct access to the senior executives of the organisation and the senior executives have direct access to the CIO. Management should encourage the regular and frequent exchange of information between the senior executives of the organisation and IT management, enabling business executives and IT managers to become more aware of each other's activities and work environments. In addition, organisations should encourage the joint involvement of business executives and IT management in social and organisational processes.

Stories and Myths

The second cultural characteristic, stories and myths, refers to what is communicated by organisational members to others about the way things work. These stories may be the truth or variations of the truth (Ward & Peppard, 1996). The history of an organisation is often communicated through stories, and these stories create images and values that are then shared by members of the culture (Davies, 1991).

Horror Stories

At the executive level, few CEOs defend IT and many relay horror stories of lost revenue, failed initiatives and missed opportunities. Senior management tell stories of IT not delivering on promises and that IT does not understand the business (Wang, 1994; Ward & Peppard, 1996). Internal clients have lost patience with long systems development times, inflexible interfaces and cost overruns. The proliferation of these stories is not surprising, as IT projects are notoriously late, over budget and deliver about half to one-quarter of what was initially expected (Selig, 1991; Harrison, 2000).

Horror stories have a damaging effect on the IT-business relationship. They can dampen the enthusiastic support of users and managers (Cannon, 1994), and as a consequence, the business becomes less *dependent* on IT. Unrealistic promises and frequent problems with IT systems and support create a feeling of disappointment (Selig, 1991). Stories of poor IT performance affect the credibility of the IT group (Rockart et al., 1996), reducing the trust of the business group in the IT group, hence affecting *predisposition*. Horror stories also result in IT staff being excluded from major decision making in organisations (Bashein & Markus, 1997), reducing *organisational linkages*.

In contradiction, horror stories may also have a positive effect on the IT-business relationship. For example, horror stories may improve *organisational linkages* when the business group turns bad experiences into cooperative situations by becoming more involved in IT activities to prevent further disasters.

Success Stories

Few IT success stories are told in organisations. Those that are told relate mostly to legendary IT leaders and IT mavericks, and the IT people in organisations that 'save the day' when problems arise. Having legendary leaders and successful systems implementation can enhance the track record of IT (Ward & Peppard, 1996; Rockart et al., 1996). Success stories have a positive effect on the IT-business relationship in relation to *predisposition*, as the attitude towards cooperation improves when people hear positive reports.

To foster an attitude towards cooperation between business and IT professionals, organisations should focus on promoting IT success stories among members through newsletters, intranet and staff awards.

Symbols

The third cultural characteristic, symbols, includes words, gestures, pictures or objects that carry a particular meaning. Symbols play an important part of organisational life, helping to reduce uncertainty, facilitate interaction and communication, clarify relationships and make people more comfortable with their surroundings (Hofstede, Neuijen, Ohayv & Sanders, 1990; Hirschheim & Newman, 1991). Four key symbols were found to characterise the IT group: communication, staff turnover, characteristics and skills, and physical location.

Communication

Communication involves looking at both what is said and how it is said (More, 1990). A large proportion of conflict that arises in an organisation is a consequence of poor communication (Vecchio, Hearn & Southey, 1996). Both what is communicated, and the chosen means for communication, can influence opposition. Problems with communication may retard collaboration and stimulate misunderstanding, resulting in conflict (Robbins, 1998).

Like other professions, IT people have their own specialised jargon which is often meaningless to others (Rubin, 1991; Kennedy, 1994; Ward & Peppard, 1996). The use of jargon results in poor communication and frustration between business and IT (Keen, 1993; Nelson & Cooprider, 1996), restricting *shared knowledge* and *organisational linkages*.

Distorted communication, resulting from restricted communication or the restricted flow of communication, also causes frustration. IT has a reputation for distorted communication (Hirschheim et al., 1991). The dialog between business and IT tends to be limited, restricting *shared knowledge* and *organisational linkages.* Receiving information is seen as a reflection of trust, and without the sharing of information, this trust (*predisposition*) is damaged (Australian Quality Council, 1994). IT people tend to be secretive, and promote a mystique about the use of technology (Kennedy, 1994). More and more business managers are demanding information from IT, specifically relating to the economics of IT, better control of costs and more evidence of business value. Without this information, business managers may oppose IT initiatives (Keen, 1991).

Many business people are also poor communicators, contributing to an ineffective relationship. IT people often have difficulty getting their messages understood due to the different priorities and concerns of business management (Keen, 1993). "It's very hard to explain a lot of things in computing terms to senior management. They don't know a lot about computing" (Wilson, 1996, p. 49).

Ineffective communication between business and IT results in tension in the IT-business relationship (De Brabander & Thiers, 1984). The relationship between business and IT is enhanced when jargon is avoided and through the free flow of information. Open communication builds trust, and also increases the knowledge of other groups.

Staff Turnover

The IT industry suffers from a high staff turnover rate (Paré, Tremblay & Lalonde, 2000; Information Age's archive, 2000/1). High staff turnover creates many problems in the IT-business relationship. When staff move on, they take knowledge with them which newcomers must take time to learn (Robbins, 1998). *Shared knowledge* is lost and *organisational linkages* are broken. One reason for high staff turnover is that technologists often pursue their own goals, not organisational goals (Vecchio et al., 1996), demonstrating a lack of *commitment* to the goals of the organisation.

To minimise staff turnover and enhance the IT-business relationship, organisations should take action to retain staff. Some strategies for consideration include rewards for staff, recognition for good work, increased involvement of IT staff in business activities, and increased training for IT staff in both business skills and IT skills. Further, to minimise the impact of staff turnover, organisations should consider strategies to capture knowledge of IT staff and pass this knowledge on to others. Business can lessen the impact of IT staff turnover by appointing business people to manage IT projects, and by providing adequate training to help users become more independent in relation to IT support.

Characteristics and Skills of IT Professionals

IT people are renowned for being highly technical. Many view themselves as technology specialists. This is not surprising, as IT people are trained to apply or advance technology and solve technology problems (Davies, 1991; Smith & McKeen, 1992; Broadbent, Butler, Hansell & Dampney, 1993; Bushell, 1996; Ward & Peppard, 1996; Fletcher & McCann, 1997; Jackson & Wilson, 1999). Many see their future in IT, and therefore have more loyalty to their profession than the organisation for which they work. Also, IT professionals work in a discipline that changes rapidly and skills become outdated quickly. They are therefore motivated to learn state-of-the-art IT to retain their marketability (Wang & Barron, 1995).

This technical tendency of IT professionals can create problems in the IT-business relationship. Due to their technical orientation, IT professionals are often criticised for their lack of *business knowledge* (Kaiser & King, 1982; McFarlan, 1990; Rockart et al., 1996). IT professionals tend to pay attention to the technical and methodological issues of business problems, and overlook the social, political and psychological issues (Bushell, 1996). This evidence suggests a misalignment of IT and organisational goals, or a lack of *commitment* by the IT group to the goals of the organisation.

The reverse is also true: the IT-business relationship is enhanced when an IT group is recognised for their technical skills. Possessing technical skills promotes a feeling of *trust*. If effective relationships are to be built between business and IT, then organisations should strive towards an IT team with both technical and business skills (Rockart et al., 1996). Technical skills and the ability to relate to users are equally important (Tomes, 1996). Organisations can encourage hybrid managers such as a business manager with a sound understanding of IT, or an IT staff member with strong business skills.

Physical Location of IT Professionals

The physical location of IT professionals can both enhance and damage the IT-business relationship. The relationship can be enhanced though a decentralised IT structure, where an organisation has IT staff located through- out the organisation, not in a separate department (Ward & Peppard, 1996; Broadbent et al., 1993; Jackson & Wilson, 1999). This structure increases opportunity for *shared knowledge* between the two groups and also increases *organisational linkages*. One means of getting business and IT groups to better understand each other is co-location (Smith & McKeen, 1992). When IT professionals work day to day with their business counterparts, personal and professional relationships form, as does a positive attitude (*predisposition*) towards each other (Field, 1997).

A poorly implemented decentralised IT structure can also damage the IT- business relationship. Reporting relationships become confused, and stan- dards become difficult to implement, priorities become difficult to manage, strategies tend to move in isolation, and it is very hard to manage and coordinate IT activities (Keen, 1993).

A centralised IT structure in an organisation may cause problems in the IT-business relationship, especially in cases where the IT group is located away from the core business area. When IT and business groups are physically separate, there are less opportunities for social interaction between IT and business people, and less involvement by each group in the activities of the other group. In a centralised structure, *organisational linkages* between business and IT are reduced, as is *shared knowledge*.

An effective IT-business relationship is enhanced through a clearly defined and managed decentralised structure, where roles and reporting relationships are clearly defined and communicated.

Rituals and Routines

Most groups in organisations exist to provide a number of products and services to clients. Over time, such groups develop rules, procedures and practices to deliver these products and services. These rituals and routines constitute the fourth cultural characteristic. Some of these procedures are written down, but many are unwritten rules of thumb. IT professionals spend most of their working life operating in a product or service delivery role, governed by a number of standards or methodologies (Fletcher & McCann, 1997). Three of the more commonly reported IT procedures introduced by IT groups in organisations are the Help Desk procedure, IT purchasing procedures and the systems development methodology. These procedures are aimed at providing better service to customers, protecting organisations from lawsuits, ensuring all computers are compatible, and that networks and computers can be interconnected (Smith & McKeen, 1992).

Although IT standards and procedures can assist software developers in delivering software solutions that meet the customers' needs on budget and within the required timeframe (Robey & Markus, 1984; Rubin, 1991), they can also cause conflict with business people. Educating business managers and staff to act consistently with IT standards and procedures for provision of quality IT services has been a big problem for IT groups (Broadbent et al., 1993).

IT standards and procedures may be viewed by business professionals as efforts by IT to recreate monopolies and regain the control that IT professionals initially enjoyed (Smith & McKeen, 1992; Keen, 1993). This influences the *predisposition* of the business people toward IT people, and may result in less trust. Also, because IT people work within standards and procedures, the output of their work is highly structured, and the timing of their solutions does not always meet the needs of business. Business plans typically have shorter implementation cycles than IT plans, and hence the business becomes frustrated with the lack of short-term results. The business may view IT as not contributing to organisational goals and also not enhancing the quality of their work life, hindering *mutual benefits*. Also, business people may be less inclined to approach the IT group, therefore reducing *organisational linkages*. In addition, many managers have the belief that the responsibility for IT development should rest with IT, thus showing little interest in IT. This lack of involvement has hindered software development, having a negative effect on the IT-business relationship by creating a barrier to *shared knowledge* and *organisational linkages*.

Where business people are not educated in the benefits of standards and procedures implemented by the IT group, an uneasy relationship can result between business and IT. High levels of involvement are required by business people in the development and execution of IT procedures for a healthy relationship to be sustained between these two groups. Business professionals can become more involved and knowledgeable in the systems development process through the creation of joint processes in the organisation and the joint involvement by both business and IT groups in these processes.

Further, the IT group must design systems in terms of client business goals rather than in terms of technology goals. IT professionals can make major gains by shaping their work to contribute directly to the achievement of business goals. The IT group must be adequately resourced to follow standards and procedures introduced. For example, in the case of the Help Desk, it must be adequately resourced to meet the demands of business people. Also, Help Desk staff need to be customer focused and technically competent.

Control Systems

The fifth cultural characteristic is control systems which reflect the degree of control the business or IT has over the information resources of the organisation. Control systems highlight what is valued by the organisation (Ward & Peppard, 1996). Three types of control systems relate to the IT group in organisations: strategic, project and financial control.

Strategic Control

For IT success, both IT and business groups must have responsibility for IT (Earl, 1989). A good business plan can only be developed and executed through a partnership between business and IT, and therefore it should be the business managers, not the technology leaders, managing IT at the strategic level (Selig, 1991).

However, in many organisations, responsibility for the IT strategy still lies with the IT group (Colquhoun, 2001). Many senior managers distance themselves from IT, reducing *organisational linkages*. They are puzzled by IT, uncomfortable about their lack of understanding, not of the technology, but of the key decisions on how to exploit it. This lack of familiarity sometimes creates anxiety for managers when dealing with IT. Also, continued emergence of new technologies contributes to further management discomfort in managing IT, leading to a difficult IT-business relationship (Keen, 1991). Surrendering IT decisions to technical experts can prove disastrous in relation to *mutual benefits* and *commitment* to the relationship. Under such circumstances, IT management and business management may have different objectives, and a misalignment between business and IT plans may result.

For an enhanced IT-business relationship, both IT and business professionals must be involved in the strategic direction of IT. A joint planning process helps to bridge the gap between the business and IT groups, builds better communication between these two groups, enhances the probability of IT success, and results in much better cooperation between IT and business management (Boynton & Zmud, 1984; Ein-Dor, Segev, Blumenthal & Millet, 1984; Saaksjarvi, 1988; Byers & Blume, 1994).

Project Control

Similar to the control of IT at the strategic level, the success of projects is linked to the active involvement of business, especially at the project management level. Unfortunately, it is typical for IT professionals to build systems without keeping management adequately informed, and for management not to ask questions (Rubin, 1991), damaging *organisational linkages*. In many instances, responsibility for a business-related project is assigned to an IT professional, instead of the business manager responsible for that business function (Hann, 1992). Without business ownership and involvement, the resulting systems may be user unfriendly, overly technical, over-engineered or isolated from the business objectives of the project (Brookes, Grouse, Jeffrey & Lawrence, 1982), impacting on *mutual benefits*. Projects which do not meet user expectations erode user confidence, and the IT group faces credibility problems when it repeatedly fails to meet user expectations for developing successful applications on time and within budget, affecting *predisposition*. Therefore, where a business project has an IT component, IT must become a business priority, not a technical support function (Doll & Ahmed, 1983; Keen, 1993).

In order to minimise tensions in the IT-business relationship, business professionals, as well as IT professionals, must develop high levels of project management skills. Additionally, an organisation should develop and implement joint project management procedures that involve both business and IT people in project management and control.

Financial Control

To minimise tensions in the IT-business relationship, business and IT groups should create and participate in joint planning processes in relation to IT expenditure. This can be achieved through joint planning workshops, joint project management, joint cost/benefit analyses, improved reporting and communication of IT expenditure, and joint meetings where IT expenditure is reviewed. Sharing responsibility for IT expenditure strengthens *organisational linkages* and *shared knowledge* between business and IT professionals.

Power Structures

The sixth and final cultural characteristic relates to power structures. Organisational power has many definitions. These include the ability to influence the behaviour of another (Lucas, 1984; Vecchio et al., 1996), the capacity to achieve outcomes (Walsham, 1993; Hensel & Schkade, 1995), and the "capacity to influence another person or group to accept one's own ideas or plans" (Greiner & Schein, 1988, p.13).

Power imbalances between business and IT can lead to problems. Discontent can arise between groups with different power structures, resulting in dysfunctional behaviour and a lack of cooperation that in turn reduces the effectiveness of groups. Departments can grow to resent powerful groups in organisations, and may attempt to reduce their power through blame and non-cooperation. Without cooperation from the business, it is difficult for IT to provide good service or design good systems (Lucas, 1984; Vecchio et al., 1996).

IT groups can have high levels of power in four circumstances. Firstly, they can have a high level of position power, where the CIO is a senior executive of the organisation. The higher in the organisation, the greater the power to affect and influence organisational behaviour (Raghunathan & Raghunathan, 1989). Without influence at the top, it is impossible to make a significant difference. If an IT manager is not as senior in an organisation as other managers, the IT manager may not have the power to influence others in the organisation, contributing to tensions by restricting *organisational linkages*. In addition, *mutual benefits* are not derived from the relationship. In many organisations, senior management does not regard IT as essential for making a significant contribution to the firm. Therefore IT is often omitted from key planning and decision making related to the missions of the organisation, and IT is viewed as having a lack of influence and power on the important decisions of the firm (Lucas, 1984; Keen, 1993).

Secondly, an IT group in an organisation can also exert power in situations where the organisation is dependent on the IT group. Groups can acquire interdependence power by supplying resources which other people become dependent upon. IT is a resource many people value, and hence the IT group should have high levels of resource dependence power (Vecchio et al., 1996; Lucas, 1984; Markus & Bjorn-Andersen, 1987). Interdependence power is also measured by the extent to which one group is connected to other groups; the more connections, the more power (Lucas, 1984). IT groups are in a position to touch every part of a company, giving them the potential to be a force for alignment and cohesion, and assume more power (Robey & Zmud, 1992; Jackson & Wilson, 1999). The IT group should have high levels of interdependence power, contributing to an effective IT-business relationship in terms of *organisational linkages* and *dependence* on distinctive competencies and resources.

Thirdly, IT groups may also have high levels of expert power. When individuals or groups have specialised skills or knowledge that others do not, and are able to direct or influence others, expert power results (Vecchio et al., 1996; Robbins, 1998). IT departments are perceived to have power based on their expertise, and this can be both good and bad (Hensel & Schkade, 1995; Earl, 1997). They can use their expertise to make recommendations and deliver solutions for the benefit of the organisation (Markus & Bjorn-Andersen, 1987), enhancing *mutual benefits*. They are ideally placed to facilitate others coping with technology (Robey & Zmud, 1992), enhancing *shared knowledge* and *organisational linkages*. On the other hand, expert power can give one group advantage over the other to pursue its own interests and satisfy its own needs, demonstrating a lack of *commitment* to the relationship, resulting in conflict (Hirschheim et al., 1991).

However, the expertise of business people in relation to IT is rapidly increasing, so the expertise gap between business and IT professionals is reducing, shrinking the expert power of IT professionals. The net result is reduced *organisational linkages* and reduced *dependence* on the IT group, and hence the IT-business relationship suffers.

Lastly, IT groups can also have information power. Information power results from having and using information to implement change (Vecchio et al., 1996). It is believed that the gatekeepers of information possess power (Hensel & Schkade, 1995). Given that the IT department is central to the distribution of information in an organisation, and that information is power, IT should have influence in organisations (Markus, 1984; More, 1990), promoting *mutual benefits* and *organisational linkages*.

As the ideal situation for an effective IT-business relationship is equal power bases, in organisations where the IT group has high levels of power, the IT group needs to exercise caution as to how it uses this power. Business managers should be educated in how to recognise high levels of power and learn how to manage technological innovation (Lucas, 1984). Further, although the IT group should have high levels of power, this power base is often overshadowed by delayed IT implementations and cost overruns. The benefits of high levels of power are therefore not realised by the IT group, and the IT-business relationship suffers as a consequence. To minimise tensions in the IT-business relationship, IT professionals need to become responsive so that they are meeting the needs of the business in a timely manner.

PROPOSED CULTURE FOR AN EFFECTIVE IT-BUSINESS RELATIONSHIP

Having identified the effects of specific cultural characteristics on the IT-business relationship, those characteristics that reflect positively on the IT-business relationship can be separated from those characteristics that reflect negatively on the IT-business relationship. With this knowledge, organisations can develop strategies to implement cultural change to foster a healthy IT-business relationship.

Summarising the discussion above, characteristics of the IT culture predicted to have a positive effect on the IT-business relationship are:

- a structure where IT plays a strategic role and the CIO is a senior executive of the organisation;
- success stories promoted about the IT group;
- a decentralised IT structure where IT professionals are physically located with business colleagues;
- open communication, low staff turnover, technically competent IT staff with a good business understanding;
- user-friendly standards and procedures developed jointly by business and IT;
- joint involvement by IT and business in setting the IT strategy and managing projects;
- equal power structures.

Conversely, the IT culture is likely to work against the IT-business relationship where the IT culture reflects:

- a structure where IT plays a support role and the CIO does not have access to the senior executives of the organisation;
- many horror stories about the IT group;
- extensive use of IT jargon and a failure to share information with the business;
- high staff turnover in the IT group and a lack of business knowledge;
- unfriendly standards and procedures imposed on the business;
- lack of involvement by the business in IT strategic planning and project management;
- unequal power bases.

CONCLUSION

This investigation into the troubled IT-business relationship provides insights into some of the cultural characteristics of the IT group that may contribute to this troubled relationship.

To enhance the IT-business relationship in their own organisations, practitioners and managers can review the presence or absence of the six essential ingredients of an effective IT-business relationship: mutual benefits, commitment to the relationship, predisposition, shared knowledge, dependence on distinctive competencies and resources, and organisational linkages. Where ingredients are lacking, they can introduce strategies to increase the degree of presence of these ingredients. Alternatively or additionally, managers can foster an IT culture with characteristics proven to have a positive effect on the IT-business relationship.

However, practitioners desiring to use the results of this research to improve the IT-business relationship, should be aware that factors other than cultural differences may result in intergroup conflict. Such factors include political behaviour and external influences. Also, an organisation that copies the culture of a successful organisation's culture may not realise the same success: the Japanese business culture, although successful in Japan, failed when introduced in America (Choi & Kelemen, 1995). Therefore, the findings of this research should not be applied without consideration of the environment in which the organisation operates.

Instead of paying lip service to culture, or applying new technology to business problems, or manipulating a few priorities and calling this cultural change, organisations must take the concept of culture more seriously (Schein, 1996). This research, by describing the effects of the themes of IT culture on the six ingredients necessary for an effective IT-business relationship, enables organisations to better understand how the IT-business relationship can be affected by the IT culture. As a starting point for cultural change, this research suggests an ideal IT culture that organisations may wish to consider to minimise tensions in the IT-business relationship.

REFERENCES

Australian Quality Council. (1994). Cultural Imprints. [*Brochure*]. Australia.

Avison, D. E., Cuthbertson, C. H. and Powell, P. (2000). The strategic value and low status information systems. *Proceedings of the Australian Conference on Information Systems*, Brisbane, Australia.

Bashein, B. and Markus, M. L. (1997). A credibility equation for IT specialists. *Sloan Management Review*, (Summer), 35-44.

Boulding, K. E. (1957). Organisation and conflict. *Journal of Conflict Resolution*, *1*, 122-134. In Hinton, B. L. and Reitz, H. J. (Eds.), *Groups and Organisations*. (1971). Graduate School of Business, Indiana University, Belmont, CA: Wadsworth Publishing Company, Inc.

Boynton, A. C. and Zmud, R. W. (1984). An assessment of critical success factors. *Sloan Management Review*, (Summer), 17-27.

Broadbent, M., Butler, C., Hansell, A. and Dampney, C. N. G. (1993). Business value, quality and partnerships: Australasian information systems management issues. *Australian Computer Journal*, *27*(1), 17-26.

Brookes, C., Grouse, P., Jeffrey, R. and Lawrence, M. (1982). *Information Systems Design*, 8-10. Sydney: Prentice Hall.

Bushell, S. (1996). Birth of a salesman. *IT Casebook*, (July), 28-31.

Byers, C. R. and Blume, D. (1994). Tying critical success factors to systems development. *Information & Management*, *26*(1), 51-61.

Cannon, J. A. (1994). Why IT applications succeed or fail. *Industrial and Commercial Training*, *26*(1), 10-15.

Choi, C. J. and Kelemen, M. (1995). *Cultural Competences: Managing Co-operatively Across Cultures*. England: Dartmouth Publishing Co. Ltd.

Colquhoun, L. (2001). Selling the IT story. *Managing Information Strategies*, (April), 32-34.

Cormack, S. (2001). Effects of the culture of the information technology group on the IT-business relationship. *MIT*, University of Southern Queensland, Australia.

Davies, L. (1991). Managing the human context of information systems: Culture and information systems. Paper presented at the *Australian Computer Society Half-Day Seminar Workshop Series*, May, Brisbane, Australia.

De Brabander, R. and Thiers, G. (1984). Successful information system development in relation to situation factors which affect effective communication between MIS users and EDP specialists. *Journal of the Institute of Management Science*, *30*(2), 137-155.

Doll, W. J. and Ahmed, M. U. (1983). Diagnosing and treating the credibility syndrome. *MIS Quarterly*, (September), 21-32.

Earl, M. J. (1989). *Management Strategies for Information Technology*. UK: Prentice Hall International Ltd.

Earl, M. J. (1997). A quantity of qualities. *CIO*, (November).

Ein-Dor, P., Segev, E., Blumenthal, D. and Millet, I. (1984). Perceived importance, investment and success of MIS, or the MIS zoo–An empirical investigation and a taxonomy. *Systems, Objectives, Solutions*, *4*(2), 61-67.

Field, T. (1997). IT/business alignment. *CIO*, (December), 18-19.

Fletcher, B. and McCann, M. (1997). The partnership process or relationship management for IT business managers. *Systems Thinking*. Australia.

Greiner, L. E. and Schein, V. E. (1988). *Power and Organisation Development*. Reading, MA: Addison-Wesley Publishing Co.

Hann, J. (1992). The role of executives in project management. *The Source, Qld: Australian Computer Society*, (August), 12-13.

Harrison, P. (2000). Diagnosis: IT myopia. *CPA News*, *5*(5), 4.

Henderson, J. C. (1990). Plugging into strategic partnerships: The critical IS connection. *Sloan Management Review*, *31*(3), 7-18.

Hensel Jr., M. C. and Schkade, L. L. (1995). Computers, power and organisations: A game theory perspective. *Journal of Information Technology Management*, *6*(2), 23-28.

Hirschheim, R., Klein, H. K. and Newman, M. (1991). Information systems development as social action: Theoretical perspective and practice. *International Journal of Management Science*, *19*(6), 587-608.

Hirschheim, R. and Newman, M. (1991). Symbolism and information systems development: Myth, metaphor and magic. *Information Systems Research*, *2*(1), 29-62.

Hofstede, G., Neuijen, B., Ohayv, D. D. and Sanders, G. (1990). Measuring organisational cultures: A qualitative and quantitative study across 20 cases. *Administrative Science Quarterly*, *35*(2), 286-310.

Howarth, B. (1999). So what's so special about IT? *Business Review Weekly*, (December 17), 56-59.

Information Age's Archive Hold Editorial Trove. (2000/2001). *Information Age*, (December/January), 38.

Irwin, H. and More, E. (1994). *Managing Corporate Communication*. Australia: Allen & Unwin Pty Ltd.

Ivancevich, J. M. and Matteson, M. T. (1999). *Organisational Behaviour and Management* (fifth edition). New York: Irwin/McGraw-Hill.

Jackson, S. F. and Wilson, R. K. (1999). Information technology and organisational alignment. *Aviation Informatics*, *8*(1), 24-25.

Johnson, G. and Scholes, K. (1993). *Exploring Corporate Strategy* (third edition). UK: Prentice Hall International Ltd.

Kaiser, K. M. and King, W. R. (1982). The manager-analyst interface in systems development. *MIS Quarterly*, (March), 49-59.

Keen, P. G. W. (1991). *Shaping the Future: Business Design Through IT*. Cambridge, MA: Harvard Business School Press.

Keen, P. G. W. (1993). Information technology and the management difference: A fusion map. *IBM Systems Journal*, *32*(1), 17-39.

Kennedy, S. (1994). Why users hate your attitude. *Informatics*, (February), 29-32.

Lucas, H. C. (1984). Organisational power and the information services department. *Communications of the ACM*, (January), *27*(1), 58-65.

Markus, M. L. (1984). *Systems in Organisations: Bugs + Features*. New York: Ballinger Publishing Company.

Markus, M. L. and Bjorn-Andersen, N. (1987). Power over users: Its exercise by system professionals. *Communications of the ACM*, *30*(6), 498-504.

McFarlan, F. W. (1990). The 1990s: The information decade. *Business Quarterly*, *55*(1), 73-79.

More, E. (1990). Information systems–people issues. Paper presented at *Macquarie Information Systems and Teaching: An Industry Briefing*, April, Australia.

Nelson, K. M. and Cooprider, J. G. (1996). The contribution of shared knowledge to IS group performance. *MIS Quarterly*, *20*(4), 409-429.

Paré, G., Tremblay, M. and Lalonde, P. (2000). The impact of human resources practices on IT personnel commitment, citizenship behaviours, and turnover intentions. *Proceedings of the International Conference on Information Systems*, Brisbane, Australia.

Raghunathan, B. and Raghunathan, T. S. (1989). Relationship of the rank of information systems executive to the organisational role and planning dimensions of information systems. *Journal of Management Information Systems*, *6*(1), 111-126.

Robbins, S. P. (1998). *Organisational Behaviour* (eight edition). Upper Saddle River, NJ: Prentice Hall.

Robey, D. and Markus, L. (1984). Rituals in information system design. *MIS Quarterly*, (March), 5-15.

Robey, D. and Zmud, R. (1992). Research in the organisation of end-user computing: Theoretical perspectives from organisational science. *Information Technology & People*, *6*(1), 11-27.

Rockart, J. F., Earl, M. J. and Ross, J. W. (1996). Eight imperatives for the new IT organisation. *Sloan Management Review*, (Fall), 43-55.

Rubin, R. S. (1991). Save your information from the experts. In Blodgett, T. B. (Ed.), *Information Infrastructure*, 99-101. Boston, MA: Harvard University.

Saaksjarvi, M. (1988). Information systems planning: What makes it successful? *Proceedings of the Australian Computer Conference*, 523-542. Sydney, Australia.

Schein, E. H. (1996). Three cultures of management: The key to organisational learning. *Sloan Management Review*, (Fall), 9-20.

Selig, F. F. (1991). Managing information technology in the nineties. *Information & Management*, *21*(5), 251-255.

Smith, H. A. and McKeen, J. D. (1992). Computerisation and management: A study of conflict and change. *Information & Management*, *22*, 53-64.

Subramani, M. R., Henderson, J. C. and Cooprider, J. (1998). Examining IS-user partnerships: A socio-cognitive perspective. *Unpublished*, April 29.

Tomes, C. (1996). The changing face of IT recruitment. *Network World*, (February), 28-30.

Vecchio, R. P., Hearn, G. and Southey, G. (1996). *Organisational Behaviour* (second edition). Australia: Harcourt Brace & Company.

Walsham, G. (1993). Reading the organisation: Metaphors and information management. *Journal of Information Systems*, 3, 33-46.

Wang, C. B. (1994). *Techno Vision*. New York: McGraw-Hill, Inc.

Wang, E. T. G. and Barron, T. (1995). The decision to outsource IS processing under internal information asymmetry and conflicting objectives. *Journal of Organisational Computing*, 5(3), 219-253.

Ward, J. and Griffiths, P. (1996). *Strategic Planning for Information Systems* (second edition). England: John Wiley & Sons Ltd.

Ward, J. and Peppard, J. (1996). Reconciling the IT/business relationship: A troubled marriage in need of guidance. *Journal of Strategic Information Systems*, 5(1), 37-65.

Watson, R. T. (1989). Key issues in information systems management: An Australian perspective–1988. *Australian Computer Journal*, 21(2), 118-129.

Wilson, E. (1996). Sparks fly in meeting of minds. *The Australian*, (November 19), 49.

Chapter X

Human Factors and the Systems Development Process

Julie Fisher
Monash University, Australia

ABSTRACT

Internet systems have the potential to reach a huge and unknown audience. How easy a system is to use will usually determine its success or failure and consequently the business and yet the human factors elements of systems are rarely considered. Usability describes the ease with which people can use a system to complete a task. It is often the case however that development teams focus more on the technology and less on the users when designing systems resulting in software that is not useable and therefore does not satisfy users' need. This chapter presents recent research, which examines one approach to developing a web-based information system and demonstrates how the composition of the development team through the inclusion of people with an understanding of user needs is important to the quality of the final product and ultimately the success of the system.

INTRODUCTION

In an age where Internet systems reach a huge and largely unknown audience and businesses are competing for customer attention, the accessibility and usability of an Internet-based system will be critical to its success. Usability in the context of information systems is usually thought of as how users can quickly and easily complete a task. The usability aspects–the human element of systems–however, are often not considered when systems are built.

Often development teams focus more on the technology and less on the users when designing systems resulting in systems that do not satisfy users' needs. People with technical skills frequently dominate systems development teams; people with skills that focus on the human factors aspects of systems are rarely included. This often results in the failure of the system. Grudin (1991) notes that as the cost of computers fell and user numbers increased, expectations of usability also grew. Technology costs continue to fall and, coupled with a rapid growth of Internet-based, e-commerce systems, we can see an increasing expectation on the part of users that these systems will be easy to use and businesses expect corresponding returns. In this chapter I will argue that there are two sides to producing an effective information/e-commerce system, the technical /functional side and the human side. For a system to be successful from a user's perspective the development team must include people with not just technical skills but also human factors skills. A case study will be used to illustrate how the development of a system that meets the users needs can be achieved through the inclusion of people with human factors skills.

WHY SYSTEMS SUCCEED OR FAIL

There has been much written about information systems (IS) success and failure. Oz and Soski (2000) define failure of an information systems development (ISD) project as either the project being abandoned or the system not fully utilised by the intended users.

Much of the work to date on why systems succeed or fail has focused on the technology and, according to Mitev (2000), takes a very positivist approach to investigating the issues. Mitev argues that there is a lack of understanding of the wider issues involved, and the context and people for whom the system has been built.

Mitev's argument is supported by research undertaken by Oz and Sosik (2000) who determined, from a survey of IS executives, that leadership, clear goals and clear communication were more important for IS project success than the technology.

In a detailed assessment, Delone and McLean (1992) identified six major categories for measuring **system success**; these are system quality, information quality, use, **user satisfaction**, individual impact and organisational impact.

This paper focuses on the users and the extent to which those elements of a system that contribute to usability and success from a user's perspective can be better managed through the development process. Specifically the areas determined by Delone and McLean (1992) are:

- use
- user satisfaction
- individual impact.

The Users' Perspective of System Success

A system that is technically and functionally correct gas the measures of a successful system; the other measures, though, are how easily users can use the system and how satisfied they are with it. Unless the users can use the system and use it effectively and fully, the system cannot be deemed to be a success because the users will not want to use it. What then are the elements of an information system that make it successful from a user's perspective? The literature suggests a number of factors that contribute strongly to users rating a system as successful; these are the human factors or the human side. Table 1 presents some of these elements.

SYSTEM DEVELOPMENT TEAM SKILLS

To ensure that the needs of the users are met and the human factors and usability elements of a system are designed appropriately, the systems development team needs to include people with a wide range of skills. The traditional composition

Table 1: Factors contributing to user satisfaction

Reason for Success or Failure	**Research**
Understanding of user requirements and the user perspective during the development process	Axtell et al., 1997; Shah, Dingley & Golder, 1994; Shand, 1994
The effectiveness of the communication (between users and developers)	McKeen et al., 1994; Oz & Soski, 2000; Schmidt et al., 2001
Users' involvement in the development process and the effectiveness of their involvement	Ballantine et al., 1996; McKeen et al., 1994; Schmidt et al., 2001; Whyte et al., 1997
The quality and accessibility of the user information	Shand, 1994; Torkzadeh & Doll, 1993
The ability of users to use the system–**ease of use**	Ballantine et al., 1996; Grudin, 1991; Mitev, 2000; Shah et al., 1994; Shneiderman, 2000
The quality and appropriateness of the design of the **user interface**	Davis et al., 1992; Ditsa & MacGregor, 1997; Mitev, 2000; Whyte et al., 1997

of a development team includes people with skills such as systems analysis, systems design, programming, communication and problem-solving skills. The focus is primarily on the technical skills. The basis of this information comes from a range of sources including Simon (1994), Misic (1996), and Turner and Lowry (1999). It should be noted that these skills are also the primary skills taught in Australian university information systems courses and recognised by the Australian Computer Society (Underwood & Maynard, 1996). It is also assumed that similar courses elsewhere in the world focus on similar skills.

If, however, the factors that relate to users rating the system a success are important, then there are other skills that are needed. Some of the key skills needed for developing the human elements of a system are detailed in Table 2.

In some cases the systems development team will have people with some of these skills. There are surgeons who have good patient psychology support skills, rock musicians with business skills and even board members of sports teams who have the ability to coach. More often than not, however, the skills professional people have are those skills they were specifically trained in. Therefore we should not expect that every systems development team will have people who possess all the skills needed to produce both a technically and functionally correct system and one that meets the needs of the majority of users.

Table 2: Skills needed to design human elements of systems

Profession	Skills
Technical communicators	Written and oral communication Understanding of users Understanding of text layout and design. (Avison & Fitzgerald, 1995; Grudin, 1991; Mathieson, 1993; Preece et al., 1994; Shah et al., 1994; Shand, 1994 A)
Interface designer	Understanding screen layouts Design of icons Understanding users' workflow Use of colours. (Grudin, 1991a; Preece et al., 1994; Shand, 1994)
Graphic designers	Understanding how to colour Design of graphics, charts, illustrations (Hager, 2000; Preece et al., 1994)
Ergonomics	Understanding how people should work (Preece et al., 1994)

AN ILLUSTRATIVE CASE STUDY

To illustrate the importance of the skill set of the development team members to the success of systems, a case study based on recent research has been selected. The case study examines the development of a large system, a multimedia web-based bill-paying system developed for an Australian state government.

The research that forms the basis of this chapter was part of a larger research project that involved an investigation of success factors in systems development. The research included interviews with the key personnel and users for each system and examined, among other things (the role of technical communicators, user participation in development) the usability aspects of systems.

For the Bill Payment System, interviews were conducted with the project manager, human factors people and users. The users interviewed included agencies joining the system (agency clients) and bill-paying customers (users). The interviews involved both semi-structured and structured questions, including Likert-scale-type statements (for more details see Fisher, 1998, 1999a). A total of eight interviews were conducted resulting in approximately five hours of tape recorded material. The data was analysed using a meta matrix as described by Miles and Huberman (1994). A matrix "is essentially the 'crossing' of two lists, set up as rows and columns" (Miles & Huberman 1994, p. 93). "Meta-matrices are master charts assembling descriptive data from each of several cases in a standard format" (Miles & Huberman 1994, p. 178). The use of a meta-matrix allows data to be analysed in a number of ways. Miles and Huberman (1994: 246-253) argue that conclusions that generate meaning (making and interpreting findings at different levels of inference) can be drawn using these techniques.

CASE STUDY: BILL PAYMENT SYSTEM

Overview

There is much evidence in the literature to suggest that the larger and more complex a system is, the greater the chance of failure (Schmidt et al., 2001). This system was a risk for the government: it was large, there were numerous stakeholders, it was a new and very innovative system, and it was developed over quite a long timeframe. The system was designed to provide *"agencies and services of the government online. Customers can pay for services over the Internet or through multi-media kiosks or through the integrated voice response telephones" (Project Manager).*

The system provides a means by which users can pay a range of bills to a number of agencies through the one interface. For the user the transactions appear to be conducted through a single interface; users are unaware that they are in fact communicating directly with the agency's systems. See Figure 1 for the system structure. The website was launched at the start of 1997.

The system initially allowed customers to pay for a range of services such as electricity bills, council dog licences, council rates and water charges. The system also provided other facilities such as registering a change of address, enrolling to vote and ordering a new garbage bin. The system has since been extended and now users can, for example, purchase tickets for events, pay parking fines and book a licence test. For the system to be successful, it must be widely used, universally accepted and have a high level of usability. Providing kiosks in places such as shopping centres enables people without the Internet to access the system.

Systems Development and Development Team Members

The system's website describes the project as 'pioneering electronic service delivery.' The project was a significant one, the team comprised of 35 to 40 people employed full time for approximately a year. A Rapid Application Development method based on the in-house methodology of the contracted development company was used.

Figure 1: System structure

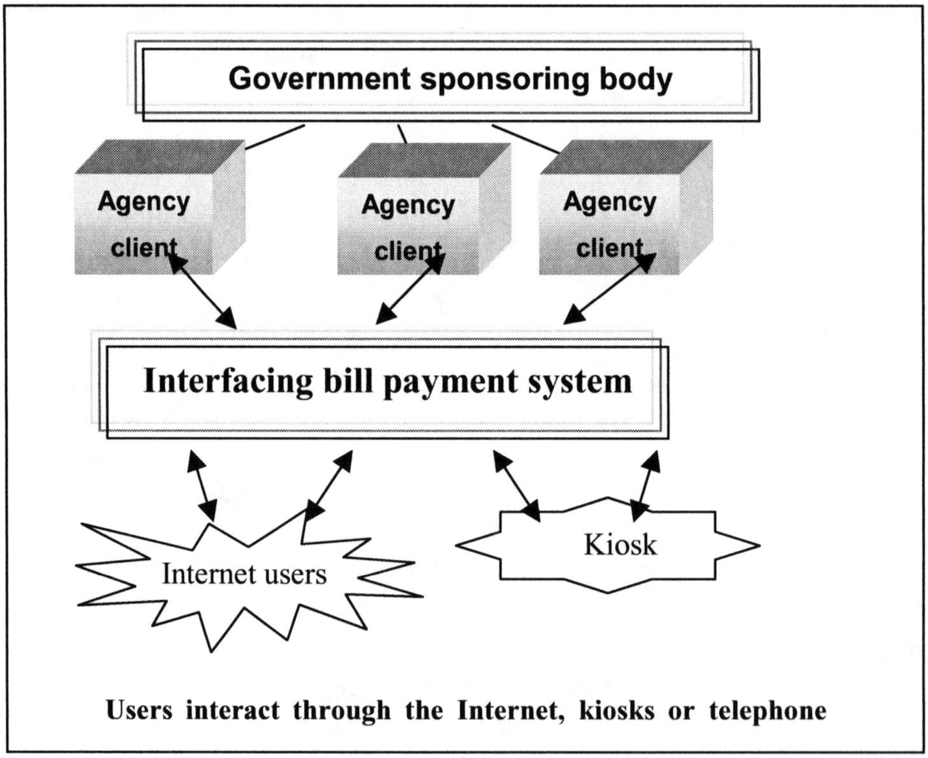

A complex issue for the project has been that it required a system to be designed that had to communicate with a range of systems from many government and non-government agencies and, at the same time present a consistent interface to the users.

It was recognised at the outset that if the system was to be successful, it had to be accessible to the widest possible group of people, customers, council residents, users, clients, taxpayers, pensioners, etc., consequently a broad range of people with specific human factors skills were included on the development team. The project manager in explaining the decision to include people with a human factors perspective said:

"That was the major driver in many respects. Trying to make things workable and consistent whether it be the screens or the help or whatever else they did. The whole thing was consistency, readability, usability, and because of that it is an essential part of the system. If we didn't have that then it would have taken longer to develop and be harder to maintain, so in that respect it was an important function that they played."

Table 3 lists the titles of the specialists focusing on the human factors aspect of the system, the number involved (in brackets), the roles they played and the skills they brought to the team.

Table 3: Human factors team members

Title and Number	Role	Skills
Technical communicators (3)	Wrote or edited the error message text, wrote system messages and some online help. Communicated with users.	Writing, layout, editing, communication and facilitation skills.
Graphics designers (2)	Designed the graphics used on the site. Contributed to the interface design.	Graphical design skills.
Disability expert (1)	Consulted on design issues to do with access for the disabled.	Understanding of users, particularly disabled users.
User interface designers (3)	Designed the user interface. Contributed to the help screens, graphics.	User interface design, understanding of users' perspective, graphics, workflow skills.
User facilitator (1)	Worked with users, arranged usability testing.	Communication skills.

Management of the Human Factors Elements

The list of elements contributing to systems success, presented in Table 1, will be used to highlight the contribution of the human factors people to the development process and the response of the users to the system. The first three elements cover the process side of the development and include understanding the user requirements, communication between development team and users, and the management of the users' involvement in the development process. The second part covers the usability elements of the system; these are: the user information, ease of use and the user interface design.

Understanding User Requirements and User Perspective

Understanding the user requirements of a system and understanding the perspective the users have of a system are important factors that strongly contribute to system success. There is ample evidence of this. Schmidt et al. (2001) report on their study involving an investigation into software project risk factors. Among the top three risks identified, of a list of 29, was not understanding the user requirements. Axtell et al. (1997) investigated user participation in a development project and found that because users were not involved enough in the process, their perspective was not well understood and this issue was a factor in the failure of the system.

Two different groups of users are identified as involved in the Bill Payment System. The first group includes the agencies that link into the system: the councils, water authorities, electricity suppliers, etc. The second group of users is the general community that uses the system to pay bills, purchase goods and services. Understanding the user requirements was focused on the first group, the agency clients, and this was the responsibility of both the technical communicators and the user facilitator. Each agency client had quite specific and different requirements, so from the development team's perspective, it was a challenge to ensure that the needs of such divergent users were met. It was expected that the system would ultimately have over 200 agencies involved, and with such a large number, the developers were very conscious of ensuring that there was consistency across the screens and across the system.

> "*Every one took the users' perspective, consistency across all agencies and across Maxi and it was important that they [the technical communicators] communicated when required when they were dealing with the agencies that this has to be consistent.*"

The technical communicators were responsible for creating a series of storyboards and mock-ups of the system that described for the agencies what the system would look like. Storyboards were the basis for agency clients' comments and feedback. In describing this, one technical communicator said:

"More than feedback we have sat down and agreed, and have got consensus on that text. Line by line. The agencies were the users. Often they would take the mock ups off the wall and they would take them back to their company and then have a meeting about them and bring them back with sticky paper all over them. Very iterative process."

Understanding the users and having a strong user perspective was, for the developer, critical to the success of the system.

User Response to Understanding Their Requirements and Perspective

Generally the users (agency clients) believed that the developers had understood their requirements. At the initial stages of the project, there were five different agencies including a water authority, electricity supplier and the road traffic authority.

The process as described was generally regarded as effective from the agencies' perspective; a staff member from one of the agencies who was involved in the project said:

"We did get initial storyboards about how the transaction would flow and we had a session here to show those who know about it here and then we took it back to them. Everything was taken on board. When we had concerns often the concerns had already been thought about and they had an answer for us."

This was supported in the post-project review by Likert-scale-type statements relating to user participation in the process. When asked their view on whether the developers had understood their perspective, they very strongly agreed. The users felt that they had been listened to and their comments taken seriously.

User-Developer Communication

Oz and Soski (2000) concluded from their study that clear communication was more important in predicting the success of IS projects than the hardware and software. Further, they argue that research often ignores the importance of user-developer communication.

In the case of the Bill Payment System, the developers were very aware of the need to ensure that communication between the different groups was effective. Again the users in this case were the agencies. The user-facilitator and the technical communicators played a critical role in ensuring that communication channels between the users and the development team were kept open. This was managed formally through the requirements documentation and a request change control system. As changes were requested the user-facilitator worked with the agencies and the development team on the changes that were identified as being needed. One of the technical communicators described how, from his perspective, the facilitation and communication role operated.

*"The users gave us an order requirements document. It is a crucial role.
Going back and forth on the actual requirements document as we were
designing the system there had to be a constant communication going
on, otherwise we would have ended up with a system that did not
satisfy what the people wanted because not everything they put in
the order was possible.   Not everything we wanted to do was
desirable to them so we had to talk a lot."*

User Views on Communication

Each of the agencies had a person responsible for coordinating the feedback
to the development team through the user-facilitator. The feedback was both from
the agency clients as well as the businesses. The agencies communicated with the
development team on many aspects of the system, the error messages, online help,
screens, business interfacing, workflow, etc. One agency client said:

*"The developers were really keen for input. We were given screens to
look at and comment on. We had meetings with the technical communicator. We commented on screens and online help. We talked to them
and clarified a few issues about the error messages."*

One of the other agency clients commented that the facilitator was not a
developer and this was an advantage because they were able to talk more easily
to the person. When asked to rate the effectiveness of the communication and
the extent to which their comments were taken seriously, the users rated both
very highly.

User Involvement

Effective user involvement in systems development is regarded as an important
factor in system success and has been the subject of much research (Doll & Deng,
2001; McKeen et al., 1994; McKeen & Guimaraes, 1997). Lack of adequate user
involvement was ranked fourth from a list of 29 system development risk factors by
Schmidt et al. (2001).

Participation from the agency clients was critical to the success of the project.
The approach taken by the development team was a very iterative one as previously
described. The interface design consultants, the facilitator and the technical
communicators all worked closely with the agency clients. No aspect of the system
was finalised until the client group was satisfied that it met their needs.

User Views of Involvement

McKeen et al. (1994) concluded from their research that where a system has
a high level of complexity, effective user participation is crucial to success. The Bill
Payment System is very complex because, as described earlier, it is required to

interface with a diverse range of other systems and yet present to users a consistent look and feel.

The agency clients were very involved and believed they had been able to participate effectively. A series of statements was put to the users relating to how they participated, how much they were listened to and how well the developers met their needs. Overwhelmingly the response was that they either agreed or agreed strongly with the statements. For them it had been a very positive process.

User Information

User information includes all text-based information a user might require to successfully interact with a system. Without adequate information it is usually impossible for a user to interact with a system effectively (Mathieson, 1993). In the case of the Bill Payment System (as with most web-based systems), hard copy documentation was not an option. All information for users had to be delivered through online help and system and error messages. The technical communicators, in consultation with the agencies, wrote the system and error messages. The developer described this as: *"The technical communicators did not necessarily write the system and error messages, but what they did is agree to them or edit them or make them so they are useable for users."*

The technical communicators were responsible for writing the online help, however the system was designed to be used with a minimal need for help. In the words of one of the technical communicators: *"There is not a lot of online help. There are some assistance topics with particularly complicated screens but in general the system relies on being intuitive."*

Online help was delivered primarily through icons on the screen users could click on; the interface design team created the 'look and feel' of the buttons but the technical communicators wrote the text. The agencies reviewed the online help information but had minimal input; the developers needing to ensure consistency across the system felt it appropriate to limit the agencies' input.

User Response to the User Information

Although the agency client users had input into the user systems message information, the users most needing effective information were the broader community of users. The agency clients were pleased with the quality of the information, and they recognised the need for the messages to be simple: *"It did explain where to go and how to use it. It will explain to the user what is going on. We don't want people walking away from the system not knowing what went wrong."*

The difficulty for the development team was to ensure that all users could understand the information, and it was not surprising therefore that the response of the broader community of users was mixed. Some thought the user information was very helpful and others thought it was too simple. In the words of one user: *"I thought the online help was quite good although in places it was a bit basic."* Another user reflected that the system *"accommodates one kind of user who is a naive user who has never used a system before."* The users however did understand the online help, and as the system was designed to be intuitive and to require minimal help the online help was really there for those who have little experience or are reluctant users of technology.

System and error messages are a constant source of frustration for users (Grudin, 1991; Heneghan, 1996), most frequently written by programmers in a language or code that users cannot understand and with little understanding of the user's needs (Fisher, 1999b).

The error messages for the Bill Payment System however were well regarded by all the users, both agency clients and the broader community of users as these comments illustrate:

- "Yes I thought the messages were good, I always knew, basically where I was and what I had to do next."
- "It does explain things well; it didn't come up with a shocking error code or something you couldn't interpret."
- "It has got a lot of prompts, like it will tell you if there is a receipt jammed in the printer or something."

From the users' perspective the user information, while often viewed as very simple, was effective and useful, and all agreed or agreed strongly with the statements relating to the quality of the error messages, online help and system messages.

Ease of Use

System usability is how easy a system is to use. "Usability means that the people who use the product can do so quickly and easily to accomplish their own tasks" (Dumas & Redish, 1994, p. 4) "Usability is an attribute of the entire package that makes up a product–the hardware, software, menus, icons, messages, manual, quick reference, online help and training" (Dumas & Redish, 1994, p. 6). These elements are all important for the users to be able to successfully complete a transaction. Shneiderman (2000) observed that there is a high level of frustration and anger among users with regard to technology. He argues that there is therefore a need to pursue a goal of 'universal useability,' to ensure the highest use of technology.

The technology aspects of the Bill Payment System were in the hands of the developers; however, responsibility for the usability elements fell to a number of groups: the technical communicators, the graphic and interface designers, and the disability expert.

The technical communicators conducted usability testing, and a wide range of users participated in the usability tests. The project manager described the process: *"The technical communicators got the users in from outside and they sat with these users. People from off the street, people from old people's homes and wherever else. They put them through the system to see what sort of problems they were coming up with and this was then conveyed back to the developers."*

From the usability testing results, the technical communicators would raise 'observation requests,' that is as a result of the observations through the testing, changes were requested of the development team. Unless it was technically not possible to make the changes, the development team would adopt what was recommended.

The story boards were also part of the usability testing process for the agencies–taking the storyboards to the agencies and getting their input. An agency client commented: *"We had a big say in the flow of work, a useability session on it. The result was some major changes were made."*

The development team had a very strong focus on how easy the system is to use to the extent that the system was designed, as far as was possible, to cater for disabled groups including sight-impaired people. A specialist from the United Kingdom was brought in specifically to provide input into this aspect of the system.

"The person from the UK consulting company was blind and so had very good empathy with disabled groups and she has had to deal with them through other projects. She could take a position and say 'if you don't do it this way, you are going to have some trouble with this group of people.' Sometimes she thought these groups had expectations that were too high for the system and what it could offer. She knows the limitations of the system and some of these groups had no idea of what the limitations of this system were and demanded a lot more than the system could offer. This made it very difficult. She prepared us well for those eventualities." (Project Manager)

User Response to Ease of Use

It is not surprising, given the strong usability focus taken by the development team, that the ease of use of the system was ranked highly by the broader community of users. One of the difficulties of the system and for the design team is that the Bill Payment System allows users to move to other web sites such as the Registry of Births, Deaths and Marriages. The users do not always realise that they have 'left' the Bill Payment System. One user said:

"I really like the general concept of the web site. At times, for example in the births and deaths section, it takes you unexpectedly to their web site to find out the cost of a certificate and this was a little confusing.

*But generally the screens were clear and not cluttered. The buttons
were well labelled in a language I could understand. Sometimes there
were a few too many steps, but I guess if you were not familiar with the
technology, this would be helpful."*

The agency clients found the system both easy to use and reliable. In the words
of one agency person: *"The system does everything. It is very simple to use so
I would say we are satisfied. The bill payment side is successful. We were
getting inquiries about whether or not people could pay using the Internet so,
in terms of customer service it is successful."*

When asked to respond to statements relating to ease of use of the system, all
users either agreed or agreed strongly with the statements.

DESIGN OF THE USER INTERFACE

Preece et al. (1994, p. 7) make the point that:

*"Producing computer systems that are straightforward to use means
that system designers have to think beyond merely what capabilities the
system should have. They also need to consider the interaction that goes
on between users and a computer system."*

It was recognised by the Bill Payment System development team that the user
interface would be the critical component in terms of the usability of the system. The
project manager reflecting on who should do such work commented that:

*"It is a particular skill designing web pages and kiosk type of pages
because it is a public interface. The programmers don't have that skill
and nor should they; we don't expect them to be in that sort of league
at this stage. These people [the interface design group] are professionals
at it–they are doing web pages so they have all the skills, they know what
works and they know what doesn't work and how to do attractive screens
to get people to come along in the first place and how to explain things."*

The people responsible for the interface were those also responsible for
the other usability aspects of the system, the technical communicators and the
graphic and interface designers. The team was responsible for everything from
the graphics, the icons and buttons, the colour combinations, work flow,
consistency of screens, etc.

The process for designing the interface through mock ups of the screens helped
illustrate the workflow. Once the design team was satisfied that they were on the
right track, they used a drawing package to produce an electronic version, again
taking these back to the users for their approval. Only when the team was sure the
users were happy with the design was the development team provided with the
screen design and told to 'do it.' The developers built the screens from these designs

and only if the technology could not support the design did the system vary from what the users approved.

User Response to the Interface

Not surprising, given that the users found the system easy to use, the users regarded the interface as well designed. When presented with Likert-scale-type statements exploring issues such as consistency, icon design and user friendliness, the users overwhelmingly agreed or agreed strongly that the interface was well designed.

DISCUSSION

There are many measures of system success, but in particular this chapter has focused on; use, user satisfaction and individual impact. The Bill Payment System is regarded as successful because:

- *Use*: At the time of writing this, the system had been in operation for four years and although slow to start, by the end of 2000 celebrated its one-millionth transaction. Transactions per month are in excess of 70,000. The City of Melbourne's published statistics on use further demonstrate the success of the system from the perspective of use. In 1999, 61,000 transactions for the City were conducted through the Bill Payment System representing $3.8 million. In 2000 this had grown to nearly 200,000 transactions, representing in excess of $16 million worth of business processed through the system. Payment of parking fines grew from 932 in 1999 paid online to over 100,000 twelve months later. The system appears to be a particularly effective way to make low value, ad hoc payments such as parking fines. It should be remembered that users have alternative payment methods; they are not forced to use the system.
- *User satisfaction*: The agency clients who were interviewed were satisfied with the system, and it is assumed that because they continue to be involved and because other agencies have since joined, that this is still the case. It can be concluded that the users are satisfied with the system demonstrated by the level of use and from the ratings users gave the system when interviewed.
- *Individual impact*: This is not as easily measured; however, as the use of the system continues to grow, it can be assumed that users find the system useful. it has therefore had an impact on them in terms of the ease with which they can pay their bills.

Why Was the Bill Payment System Successful?

To achieve success in a project of this size is difficult given the risks involved with a totally new use of technology that the Bill Payment System represents. There will be many factors that contributed to the success of the system, not the least of which is that it works from a technical perspective. However, the development team's strong focus on the human elements of the system must also be regarded as a contributing factor. The three issues identified through this case study are:

- *Involvement of human factors people*: The developers identified from the start a need to involve people with skills other than technical. Of the total number of people on the development team, 10 or 25% were people with human factors skills. They had a strong focus on the people issues, the 'human element.' Avison and Fitzgerald note:

  "*Although not simple, the technological aspects are less complex than the human aspects in an information system, because the former are predictable in nature. However, many information systems methodologies only stress the technological aspects. This may lead to a solution which is not ideal because the methodologies underestimate the importance and complexity of the human element.*" (Avison & Fitzgerald, 1995, p. 41)

- *Reverse approach to design:* The most common approach to developing the human aspects of systems has been to hand the design of the user information, the user interface–that is the human elements–over to the developers. User documentation is usually written after the system is finished. The user interface is likely to be presented to users after it has been designed. The reverse was the case with Bill Payment System. The development team made sure the interface design, user information and workflow worked from the users' perspective before it was coded. Only after the users had accepted the mock-ups were the screens given to the technical people for building. The technical people played little or no part in the design of the user interface, user information or workflow of the system.

- *Strong focus on usability and the people issues*: Shneiderman (2000) notes that: "Designing for experienced frequent users is difficult enough, but designing for a broad audience of unskilled users is a far greater challenge" (Shneiderman, 2000, p. 85) This was essentially what the Bill Payment System development team were trying to achieve. Involving experts such as interface designers, graphical designers and disability experts maximised the chance of the system being 'universally used.'

The Bill Payment System case study illustrates that for a system to be successful both technical and human factors skills are required. Figure 2 describes this.

Figure 2: Including the human factors side in systems development

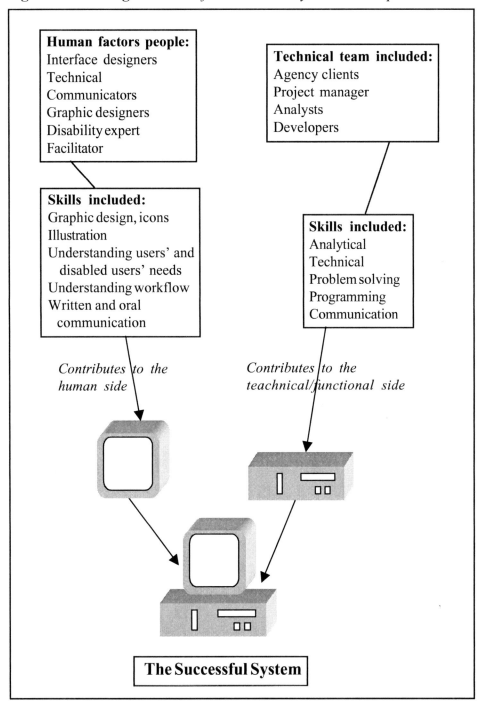

Human factors people:
Interface designers
Technical
Communicators
Graphic designers
Disability expert
Facilitator

Technical team included:
Agency clients
Project manager
Analysts
Developers

Skills included:
Graphic design, icons
Illustration
Understanding users' and
  disabled users' needs
Understanding workflow
Written and oral
  communication

Skills included:
Analytical
Technical
Problem solving
Programming
Communication

*Contributes to the
human side*

*Contributes to the
teachnical/functional side*

The Successful System

CONCLUSION

The traditional view of IT development teams is that the technical people on the team adequately cover the human factors skills. However, technically competent systems will fail if the usability is not acceptable particularly where users have alternatives through a competing web site. There is now ample evidence, illustrated through the case study presented in this chapter, that systems development must adequately resource and design for usability, in the broadest sense. Budget and resource constraint is no excuse, since to skimp in this key area is to place the entire system investment at risk for the ultimate reason that the users simply are not satisfied with it.

REFERENCES

Avison, D. E. and Fitzgerald, G. (1995). *Information Systems Development: Methodologies, Techniques and Tools* (second edition), *1*. London: The McGraw-Hill Companies.

Axtell, C., Waterson, P. and Clegg, C. (1997). Problems integrating user participation into software development. *International Journal of Human-Computer Studies, 47*(2), 323-345.

Ballantine, J., Bonner, B., Levy, M., Martin, A., Munro, I. and Powell, P. L. (1996). The 3-D model of information systems success: The search for the dependent variable continues. *Information Resources Management Journal*, Fall, 5-14.

Davis, G., Lee, A., Nickles, K., Chatterjee, S., Hartung, R. and Wu, Y. (1992). Diagnosis of an information system failure. *Information and Management, 23*, 293-318.

DeLone, W. and McLean, E. (1992). Information systems success: The quest for the dependent variable. *Information Systems Research, 3*(1), 60-95.

Ditsa, G. and MacGregor, R. (1997). Our mousetrap's fine: So why aren't people beating a path to our door. *Information Resources Management, 10*(3), 28-39.

Doll, W. and Deng, X. (2001). The collaborative use of information technology: End-user participation and system success. *Information Resources Management Journal, 14*(2), 6-16.

Dumas, J. and Redish, J. (1994). *A Practical Guide to Usability Testing*. Norwood: Ablex Publishing Corporation.

Fisher, J. (1998). Defining the role of a technical communicator in the development of information systems. *IEEE Transactions on Professional Communication, 41*(3), 186-199.

Fisher, J. (1999a). The value of the technical communicator's role in the development of information systems. *IEEE Transactions on Professional Communication, 42*(3), 145-155.

Fisher, J. (1999b). The importance of user message text and why professional writers should be involved. *Australian Computer Journal, 31*(4), 118-123.

Grudin, J. (1991). Interactive systems: Bridging the gaps between developers and users. *IEEE Transactions on Computers*, (April), 59-69.

Hager, P. (2000). Global graphics: Effectively managing visual rhetoric for international audiences. In Scheiber, P. H. (Ed.), *Managing Global Communication in Science and Technology*, 21-43. New York: John Wiley & Sons.

Heneghan, B. C. (1996). Error messages are your friends. *Intercom, 43*(3), 3.

Mathieson, K. (1993). Effective user documentation: Focusing on tasks instead of systems. *Journal of Systems Management*, (May), 25-27.

McKeen, J., Guimaraes, T. and Wetherbe, J. (1994). The relationship between user participation and user satisfaction: An investigation of four contingency factors. *MIS Quarterly, 18*(4), 427-451.

McKeen, J. D. and Guimaraes, T. (1997). Successful strategies for user participation in systems development. *Journal of Management Information Systems, 14*(2), 133-150.

Miles, M. B. and Huberman, M. A. (1994). *Qualitative Data Analysis* (second edition). London: Sage.

Misic, M. (1996). The skills needed by today's systems analysts. *Journal of Systems Management, 47*(3), 34-37.

Mitev, N. (2000). Toward social constructivist understandings of IS success and failure: Introducing a new computerized reservation system. Paper presented at the *Twenty-First International Conference on Information Systems*, Brisbane.

Nichols, M. C. (1994). Using style guidelines to create consistent online information. *Journal of the Society for Technical Communication, 41*(3), 432-438.

Oz, E. and Soski, J. (2000). Why information systems projects are abandoned: A leadership and communication theory and exploratory study. *Journal of Computer Information Systems, 41*(1), 66-80.

Preece, J., Rogers, Y., Sharp, H., Benyon, D., Holland, S. and Carey, T. (1994). *Human Computer Interaction*. Reading, MA: Addison-Wesley.

Schmidt, R., Lyytinen, K., Keil, M. and Cule, P. (2001). Identifying software project risks: An international Delphi study. *Journal of Management Information Systems, 17*(4), 5-36.

Shah, H., Dingley, S. and Golder, P. (1994). Bridging the culture gap between users and developers. *Journal of Systems Management*, (July), 18-21.

Shand, R. M. (1994). User manuals as project management tools: Part I–
   Theoretical background. *IEEE Transactions on Professional Communication, 37*(2), 75-80.

Shneiderman, B. (2000). Universal usability. *Communications of the ACM,
   43*(5), 85-91.

Simon, H. (1994). The executive as decision-maker. In Arnott, D. and O'Donnell,
   P. (Eds.), *Readings in Decision Support Systems*, 59-64. Melbourne:
   Department of Information Systems, Monash University.

Torkzadeh, G. and Doll, W. (1993). The place and value of documentation in end-
   user computing. *Information and Management, 24*, 147-158.

Turner, R. and Lowry, G. (1999). Educating information systems professionals:
   Towards a rapprochement between new graduates and employers. Paper
   presented at the *Australasian Conference on Information Systems*, 1049-
   1058. Wellington, New Zealand.

Underwood, A. and Maynard, G. (1996). ACS guidelines for the accreditation of
   courses in universities at the professional level. Paper presented at the
   Australasian Conference on Information Systems, Hobart, Tasmania.

Whyte, G., Bytheway, A. and Edwards, C. (1997). Understanding user
   perceptions of information systems success. *Strategic Information
   Systems, 6*, 35-68.

Section IV

Human Issues:
The Lessons from
and Applications of
Social Theory

The Human Side of Information Management

Steve Clarke
University of Luton, UK

I start this section introduction with a confession: I do not see human issues in information management as a "particular perspective," or a "counter to the prevailing technological view," or as any other of the many arguments for or against this approach to the domain. For me, information systems (IS) *are* human activity systems.

I invite the readers of this section to bear with me for a while, and consider what it might mean to see IS in this way. Consider, for example, what might happen if the computers containing the so-called information had no human beings to use them; consider whether there was such a thing as an information system before technology existed...

Ultimately, it seems self-evident to me that information is something which passes between human beings in social interaction: computers, filing cabinets, administrative systems and so on may help *facilitate* or *enable* this interaction, but fundamentally it remains a human concept. In three different but interrelated ways, the authors of the chapters within this section explore this concept.

Michael Arnold begins by presenting a case study of an information system currently under construction, which he critiques from the perspectives offered by three social theorists: Habermas, Foucault and Latour. For my part, it seems fundamental that, if we are to see IS as systems of people in social interaction, a grounding in social theory is an essential constituent. Mike does a sterling job of not only opening up the ideas of the three key contemporary theorists to those new to the subject, but of situating those ideas firmly within IS through the use of an interesting case study analysis.

Paul Drake and I, in the next chapter, aim to demonstrate how, in a very practical sense, a Kantian approach, together with the interpretations of it by critical thinkers, can be applied in questioning the basis for a theory and practice of information security. It is argued that the dominant approach to the subject applies instrumental reason in producing *objective knowledge,* and that this leads to an impoverished view when compared with the insights generated through practical reason. Practical reason, with its critically informed search for that which *ought* to govern our social world, has the potential to free us from the rule-based traps we have fallen into.

This leads to the proposition that a *critically normative* approach to information security be developed, based on relevant social theoretical constructs, and focusing primarily on critical theory. The aim must be to build a system of information security based on a critically informed dialectic, where the normative content of the system, its boundaries and the material conditions within which it is presently perceived, are all open to challenge and debate. All those involved in and affected by the system of concern should participate, with an emphasis on information sharing rather than restricted access to information, and with the overall objective of determining what the system *ought to be*, not what it *is*.

Finally, Arthur Tatnall looks at a socio-technical approach to IS through actor-network theory.

Following an ideology close to my own, Arthur argues that information systems is a socio-technical discipline involving both human and non-human entities, and that information systems implementations are complex activities almost inevitably involving some form of technological innovation. This casts the more techno-logical approaches to building information systems as "simplistic," and serving to conceal rather than acknowledge important interactions between human and non-human actors.

Arthur applies actor-network theory in a selection of case studies, the findings of which do much to support the value of this approach.

In conclusion, it is argued that an actor-network approach avoids the need to consider the social and the technical, and thus human and non-human actors, in different ways, but rather focuses on the way that human and non-human actors interact with each other. In showing how these interactions may lead to the formations of stable networks, actor-network theory offers a useful way to handle the complexity of such studies.

I hope you enjoy reading these different accounts as much as I have enjoyed my involvement in editing them for inclusion in this book.

Chapter XI

Systems Design Meets Habermas, Foucault and Latour

Michael Arnold
University of Melbourne, Australia

ABSTRACT

This chapter begins with a review of the theoretical foundations that are common in the systems design literature, before moving to draw upon the work of three prominent social theorists to analyse and critique a particular case of information systems design. It is argued that in different, but complimentary ways, each theorist offers systems designers compelling insights to guide their work. In particular, it is argued that Habermas' understanding of "Ideal speech"; Foucault's understanding of "power/knowledge" and "discipline"; and Latour's understanding of systems as "networks"; confirms that social theory is able to offer systems designers concrete recommendations to guide their work.

INTRODUCTION

This chapter presents a case study of an information system currently under construction, and critiques the design decisions that have been made from the perspectives offered by three prominent social theorists–Habermas, Foucault and Latour. It is argued that in different but complimentary ways, each theorist offers conceptual tools and insights that enable specific inferences to be drawn about the system's functions and features. These insights confirm that social theory is able to offer systems designers concrete recommendations to guide their work, and is able to offer critics of sociotechnical systems a theoretical contextualisation for their analysis.

A BRIEF REVIEW OF THEORY

Information systems design and research is a diverse practice with its own internal tensions and fracture-lines. It does not speak with one voice, and it is not homogenous. Different theoretical and philosophical assumptions position the IS designer and researcher in an orientation to her work; different questions are asked in different places, different forms of information and argument are regarded as constituting evidence, evidence is dealt with in different ways, thus drawing out different characteristics of the case. A theoretical orientation points to what might be attended to, what one might expect to find, how one might recognise it and what its implications may be. It offers an orientation to analysis, in that it provides a number of powerful and well-developed concepts, and a language by which those concepts might be explicated and applied in particular circumstances. Although most designers and researchers do not explain or justify their theoretical assumptions (Iivari, Hirschheim, & Klein, 1998, p.176), theory remains vital to IS design, and to an understanding of the implications of IS design, and IS designers and researchers are encouraged to be explicit in bringing forward the use of theory (Iivari et al., 1998; Mingers, 1984; Orlikowski & Baroudi, 1991; Preston, 1991; G. Walsham, 1995).

Of all the theoretical approaches, IS design and research has most clearly been shaped by positivism (Iivari et al., 1998), and today positivism remains hegemonic (Vickers, 1999). Positivists see their work as a continuation of a 300-year tradition, flowing from the European Enlightenment through to Modernity, in which reason displaces custom and superstition, and increases our possession of Truth, and therefore our power over our world and our fate (Wilson, 1997). This positivist approach is manifest most notably in the Natural Sciences; and IS design and research, though not a classical science, is traditionally built around the realist metaphysics of classical science. At the heart of the differences between positivism and other theoretical approaches are the answers that are given to the ontological question (what exists?) and the epistemological question (how do we know it?). The positivist answer to "What exists?" is "an objective, law-abiding universe," and the answer to "how might we know it?" is "through the application of the scientific method, composed of formal propositions, disprovable-hypothesis testing, use of quantitative data in both experimental and field work, use of controlled and uncontrolled variables, logic and calculation, and reproducible techniques" (Introna & Whitley, 1997; Klein & Myers, 1999; Wilson, 1999).

The contribution of positivist theory to IS design method and practice is most apparent in the so-called "hard methods" or "structured methods" of systems design (Wilson, 1999), which self-identify as objective and scientific rather than humanist, and characterise successful design in instrumental terms of measurable effectiveness and efficiency. Information is structured data, humans are rational and goal seeking individuals, and an organisation is a sequence of business processes and data flows. The success of structured information system design methodologies over the last 30 years is said by its practitioners to rest upon the development and maintenance of these positivistic principles (Wilson, 1999, p.161).

But for its critics, positivist theory and structured methods are associated with a singular lack of success, not just in humanist terms, but also in the terms it has set for itself. Business systems are argued to have failed to deliver increased efficiencies, productivity, return to shareholders and other measures one might reasonably apply (Landauer, 1997), and the structured methods associated with their development are said to be characterised by failure rather than success, despite huge investments in technology and impressive advances in hardware capacity (Lyytinen, 1991). The absence of clear data supporting the effectiveness and efficiency of these systems opened up the "productivity payoff" debate in the 1970s, and it continues today (Dewan & Kraemer, 2000; Gimlin, Rule, & Sievers, 2000; Lucas & Adenso-Diaz, 2000; Mahmood & Mann, 2000; Sheridan, 2000).

But positivism is not the only game in town, and many attempts have been made to draw-out and analyse the significance of non-positivist methodologies in IS research and design methodology. A brief survey of these attempts follows.

Geoff Walsham reports that the importance of social issues related to IS design has been increasingly recognised over the last decade, and that non-positivist methodologies are finding a place in research and design practice, and in the literature (Walsham, 1995). In line with common practice in the information systems literature, he uses the term "interpretivist" to refer to non-positivist practices (though many non-positivists will argue that positivism is no less interpretivist than "interpretivism"). Walsham points to Mingers' examination of the variety of philosophical positions that underpin the "interpretivist" approach (Mingers, 1984), and provides examples of phenomenological work (Zuboff, 1988), ethnomethodology (Suchman, 1987) and hermeneutics (Boland & Day, 1989; Lee, 1994). In other work, Walsham (1995) returns to the examples of phenomenology and hermeneutics, and adds to the list Soft Systems Methodologies (Checkland, 1981; Checkland & Scholes, 1990), Heideggers Phenomenology (Winograd & Flores, 1986), Ecological Studies (Schneiderman & Carroll, 1988), Foucault's social theory (Orlikowski, 1991) and Gidden's Structuration Theory (Orlikowski & Robey, 1991).

Lyytinen (1991) approaches IS design methodologies through a hierarchical model of three tiers. The most fundamental level, described by the author as the "technology context," is where the ontological stance is realism, the epistemological stance is positivism and the objects that inhabit the level are abstractions. This is the level that is "closest to the machine" (Ullman, 1995) and closest to the Enlightenment/Modernist ideals of certainty, truth and power. But the next tier provides for a "language context" which acknowledges that information systems are not comprehensible solely through structured system representations such as dataflows and decision tables, but also require attention to the symbolic function embedded in the behaviour of the system. Communications theory, language theory and linguistics, psychology, theories of perception and representation, semiotics, grammatology, Piaget's schema, Skinner's stimulus and response model, and symbolic interactionism have all made contributions at this level. The "organisational context" is the third tier, seen to be dependent on both the technical and the symbolic, and focuses on the forms of sense-making, and systematic relationships and interactions between people. Psychology, economics, political science, sociology, anthropology, management theory and organisational theory are disciplines contributing theory at this level.

Orlikowski (1992) uses two axes to locate theoretical approaches to information systems. "Scope" is taken to refer to the ontology of technology and "role" is used to refer to technology's relation to its context. Using "scope" as a lever the author differentiates between technology *qua* hardware, and social technology, and using "role" identifies a "technological imperative model," a "strategic choice model," a "social constructionist model," a "Marxist model" and a "trigger model." Numerous references are cited as examples of each model. The author's original contribution to the field is to suggest and illustrate the advantage of a "structuration model," based on Giddens social theory of structuration (Giddens, 1984), in which technical and social elements, structure and agency interact recursively rather than linearly.

Iivari, Hirschheim and Klein also attempt to provide a structure for a review of design methodologies by using a coarse unit of analysis to identify contrasting philosophical assumptions (Iivari et al., 1998). Rather than focusing on methodologies as distinct entities–as say, Berg does (Berg, 1998)–the authors group methodologies into "approaches" to systems design, each approach being a paradigmatic class of related methodologies, differentiated on the basis of respective ontologies, epistemologies, research methodologies and ethics. Five contrasting approaches to the realist orthodoxy are identified and discussed–the interactionist approach, the speech-act approach, the soft-systems approach, the trade unionist approach and the professional work-practice approach.

Ang claims that the work of Hirschheim, Klein and Lyytinen in framing and classifying research in the IS field (Hirschheim et al., 1996) has called into question the hegemony of the positivist approach (Ang, 1996, p. 65). Hirschheim, Klein and Lyytinen draw upon social action theory, in particular Habermas and Etzioni, to explore the intellectual structures of IS research in general and IS design in particular. The authors suggest that the field has grown from one informed by classical management discourse (e.g., Ackoff, 1971), which in turn was founded on systems theory, to one which may be characterised as a "fragmented adhocracy," in which there is a diversity of "intellectual communities," spread across domains, orientations, object systems and development strategies (Hirschheim et al., 1996).

Meanwhile, the positivists also acknowledge alternative positions, albeit through attempts to demolish them. Wilson, a fierce defender of positivism and structured methods, sets up a binary consisting of realist research methodologies and their associated "hard" design methodologies on the one side, and on the other, relativist methodologies and "Emancipatory Information Systems Design" methods (Wilson, 1997, 1999). Examples of these "spurious socio-technical design techniques" (Wilson, 1997, p. 202) are given–"soft system methodology," "institutional democracy design," "rational augmentation design," "participatory design" and "consensual communication development."

Another fierce defender of the positivist orthodoxy is Tsoukas, who provides a three-part model distinguishing between a "positivist systems perspective," an "interpretive systems perspective" and a "critical systems perspective" (Tsoukas, 1992). The latter is further divided into a "contingency view" and a "fundamentalist view," and although most fire is directed at the "fundamentalist" version of the critical systems perspective, one strongly suspects that he has little time for the contingency view either, or for that matter, the Interpretive Systems Perspective.

In summary then, what does the literature tell us about the state of play in respect of IS design and research, and theory? At the simplest level of distinction, IS design and research methodologies have been categorised as positivist at the centre, and interpretivist at the margins. The IS research literature continues to be characterised by work from the positivist school, and orthodox IS design and development methods continue to be resolutely realist and instrumental. Around the margins though are now arrayed a varied collection of design and research methods, including computer-supported cooperative work, soft systems design, participatory design, user-centred design, end-user computing, democratic design and the Scandanavian or Trade Union fields. These design methods are informed by non-positivist theory derived from speech-act and phenomenological approaches, ethnomethodological and anthropological approaches, social constructionism, social determinism, structuration perspectives and actor network theories.

The purpose of this brief review is not to negotiate between the alternatives and bring about a peaceful resolution (as Lee, 1999, for example, intends), nor to argue for the victory of one particular ontology and epistemology (as does Tsoukas, 1992, for example), but to set the scene for what follows by reminding the reader that theoretical positions in the IS field are now both disputed and various, that debate on their relative merits continues, and to suggest that this diversity might be inclusive of social theory, the subject of this chapter.

My motivation for calling upon aspects of social theory for this exercise (rather than say, Information Theory, Cybernetics, Chaos Theory, Game Theory–or any number of alternative orientations) is the now familiar conceptual premise that interprets information systems as socio-technical systems (Law, 1991). In this view, technology such as *KeyBuilding* is deeply implicated in shaping the social conditions social theory seeks to illuminate. Social theory may bring IS design to account for this by lifting it from a technical and instrumental context, and repositioning it among social concepts. But at one and the same time, the social context is deeply implicated in IS design, and needs to be brought to account for that. We therefore have a mutually contingent symmetry. We can see the social in the technical, and the technical in the social.

The theories that have been chosen for this case study are drawn from the work of Habermas, Foucault and Latour. For those with a background in the humanities or Social Theory, and for those in IS design with an interest in non-positivist positions, these writers' ideas will need no introduction. This may not be the case for all readers however, and accordingly, I have tried to provide clear and straightforward accounts of the aspects of their work that are relevant to a critique of software (drawing in the main upon Skinner, 1985; Danaher et al., 2000; Habermas 1998; Law, 1991; Law & Hasard, 1999; Foucault, 1973). Before introducing the social theorists though, the software itself needs to be introduced.

KEYBUILDING: A CASE STUDY

KeyBuilding is part of an integrated suite of software products to be marketed to homeowners and the home building industry by an Australian company called Keyvision. The designer's intention is that *KeyBuilding* gather and archive the informational resources that are generated and required by all participants and stakeholders in a domestic building project. *KeyBuilding* thus integrates, co-ordinates and archives the process of building. The system begins its work when a client sits down with a builder or developer to discuss the client's requirements. Concept and isometric drawings, display examples, floor plans, power and hydraulics plans, shade diagrams, finishes and appliances are represented in a variety of forms. Estimates and running totals of costs are calculated and maintained throughout the process of design and specification, and all warranties, materials specifications and guarantees are stored and cross-referenced as selected. To this point the system might be described as a *"Design, Specification and Customer Management System."* As contracts are signed and construction commences, the system relocates (metaphorically and physically) to the building site, and provides a single comprehensive information resource and reference point to builders, contractors, tradespeople and other stakeholders. In addition, key landmarks, deliverables and documents are prompted in sequence, and agreed variations are stored and cross-referenced. In this phase the system might be described as a *"Process Coordination and Project Management System."* When construction is complete and the owners take possession and move in, the system relocates again, and becomes a fixed asset of the home, for the total life of the building. The homeowner uses the system to access wiring diagrams, paint codes, material definitions and guarantees, appliance warranties and operating instructions, contact details of contractors and suppliers, and so on, and the system is updated to account for renovations and alterations. At this stage the system might be described as a *"Home Manual and Building Archive."*

THE THEORISTS

Jurgen Habermas (1929 -), Michel Foucault (1926 - 1984) and Bruno Latour (1948 -) are certainly among the most influential social theorists of the latter half of this century, to a point where all those who work in social theory have to work with their ideas, or around them, or against them. I have chosen to try to work with all three in this chapter, despite the fact that Habermas and Foucault in particular were in bitter opposition to one another, and that Latour takes a different approach again on many important issues. I make no attempt to reconcile these theories, or to argue that one is privileged over another. Indeed, the differences in their perspectives are useful in that each draws out different aspects of the software, while also emphasising different aspects of our social condition.

Habermas and KeyBuilding

Habermas' project has been to explicate the circumstances in which *rationality* might prevail in both public and private spheres. Important to this project is his conceptualisation of the "ideal speech situation," in which communication is undistorted, and rational consensus is the outcome. Habermas' theory has excited interest in IS research and IS design, particularly in respect to communicative action at the requirements stage (see for example Auramaki, Hirschheim, & Lyytinen, 1992; Janson, Woo, & Smith, 1993; Johannesson, 1995; Klein & Truex, 1995).

Before going on to outline the conditions for ideal speech, it should be made clear that Habermas did not set out to dream-up a set of utopian conditions out of the clear blue sky and wishful thinking. Nor are the conditions for ideal speech a set of moral guidelines or strictures. Rather, Habermas contends that the conditions for ideal speech are implicit in all speech, and are assumed in all communicative action. That is to say, underpinning the very capacity to communicate is an implicit capacity to engage in undistorted communication, and an assumption that the requirements for this can and may be met in any given circumstance. In this sense the notion of ideal speech is pragmatic and common-or-garden, rather than fanciful or utopian. Of course it is also the case that ideal speech requirements are not met (and it can be argued that they are never met), and his model thus provides an upper limit rather than a pass-mark for language use; a hypothetical horizon, the distance from which indicates the presence, nature and extent of distortion, and a guide to remedial action towards conditions of rationality and consensus.

The ideal speech situation that is implicit in all communication, and against which all communication might be assessed, consists of four conditions. All four conditions must be met in an ideal speech situation.

The first is the condition that what is said is capable of being understood; that it is intelligible to the concerned parties; that the meaning of the communication is clear, comprehensible and meaningful to all.

The second criterion is that which is said be "true." Truth in this context is a validity claim made of propositional content. To be true, a proposition must be defensible and warranted through reason (rather than say, through tradition, or power), where reason is established through discourse. Truth is thus a validity claim made within the context of language use, and is subject to contestation and warranty through argument. Truth is in this context not something to be established through direct reference to an objective, independent world, as scientists and positivists might have it, and is not something to be established through formal logic and semantic analysis, as logicians and metaphysicians might have it. Rather, claims to truth have a "pragmatic" quality, and are established by consensus reached by conceding warranted or valid claims in the course of real or potential disputation, in which all pertinent claims may be put forward, and from which all influences except reasoned argument are excluded.

The third condition is that the speaker be justified in speaking, and have the normative authority to say what is said. Like the second condition of truthfulness, the appropriateness of the communicant making any claim at all is one which can only be established, either actually or potentially, through discursive elaboration and reasoned argument.

The fourth condition is that the speaker be sincere in their contributions to discussion; that they are not setting out to trick or deceive, and are genuine in their attempts to reach a rational consensus by making comprehensible statements that are defensible and warranted and are appropriate for them to make. Unlike claims to truth and claims to be justified in speaking, sincerity cannot be discursively redeemed, but can only be demonstrated historically through action.

An example might help at this point. Suppose that a client approaches their builder and asks–"Is it possible for a balcony to be added to the master bedroom?" Suppose that the builder replies–"Yes, it is possible, but because of the difficulties involved, it will be a very expensive variation." What can be said about this in terms of ideal speech? Firstly, according to Habermas, the conditions for ideal speech are already implicit, and a conversation such as the above would not take place at all unless the conditions of an ideal speech situation are presupposed. These presuppositions make a conversation between the client and builder possible, and constitute a set of ideal criteria against which the pragmatic rationality and degree of distortion of rationality may be judged. So, it remains to apply these criteria.

The first criterion is that of meaning, or mutual comprehensibility. Does the builder understand exactly what the client requires by asking for a balcony? Does the client know the meaning of the builder's term "variation"–used here as a technical term with a contractual implication not carried by the ordinary use of the word? It can be seen that this first test is not as easily passed as might be imagined, and an absolute grasp of each communicant's meaning is often not immediately at hand, but nevertheless, might be negotiated and approached among competent language users. Typically, as in this example, further discussion needs to occur before the first condition is satisfied.

The second condition is that both the client and builder are speaking truthfully. The builder must be warranted to claim that the balcony can be built, and that planning regulations, engineering difficulties or some other factor do not make this impossible. The client may accept the builder's proposition as truthful, or may not. In this latter case, where truth is required but not immediately evident, the client might seek elaboration from the builder, or request confirmation from an engineer or planning authority. In this mode, if ideal speech conditions are to prevail, each will raise all relevant arguments and evidence, and conceal nothing relevant, while desisting from power-plays such as threatening to walk away from the job, withholding payments or seeking recourse in anything other than reason.

To meet the third condition, the situation must be one in which it is appropriate for the client to make such requests, and appropriate for the builder to respond to them. This will not be the case if either is not authorised to speak: if say, the builder lacks the expertise to respond with confidence, or if the client has put the proposition without consulting with a spouse. If the speaker's right to speak is called into question, it needs to be established through elaboration and argument, as do claims to truth.

The fourth and final criterion for an ideal speech situation is that each party be sincere in seeking rational consensus. The client's proposition must signal a genuine desire, and not idle mischief, or a ploy to achieve some objective other than obtaining a balcony. Similarly, the builder must not be posturing–"yes, it can be built"–("but not by me").

Where all four criteria are met, and an assertion is judged to be meaningful, true, appropriate and sincere, undistorted communication has occurred in an ideal speech situation.

Of course, there are strong objections one might have to Habermas' construction of the ideal speech situation. How might one allow for all pertinent claims to be made without waiting for the end of history? How might one establish in practice that utterances have the force of reason alone, and are uncontaminated by external factors such as the will to power, or the momentum of tradition? Is "pragmatic truth" an appropriate objective, or is its failure to reference an "objective truth" residing outside of human discourse an expression of a desire for totalitarian consensus? Can and should rationality dissolve all conflict, all politics?

Nevertheless, objections such as these have been met with vigour (Lyytinen & Hirschheim, 1988; Lyytinen & Klein, 1985; Winograd & Flores, 1986), and the theoretical orientation provided by speech act theory addresses the design and use of project management software in a very direct fashion. *KeyBuilding* is, after all, software designed to regulate speech acts. The software sets out to overtly manage communicative action between parties, in a situation that brings together a number of potentially conflictual stakeholders in the pursuit of a common project. It can in this sense be understood as an attempt to crystallise and give effect to an ideal speech situation. Although in this case the software designers are not familiar with Habermas' work, his project is their project.

In this context, perhaps the most useful insight offered by Habermas' conditions is a consideration of the question of comprehensibility. *KeyBuilding* is a machine through which speech acts are to pass, and is positioned in the centre of a communicative process. A building project is an exercise that generates a great deal of "speech." Many participants are involved, a great deal of "conversation" takes place, a great many things need to be agreed, a great number of documents are produced in different places for different purposes, over extended periods of time. Exacerbating the problem of communicative action and sense-making in this situation is the strongly differentiated character of the numerous discourses that constitute the building professions and trades. Architects for example move in a conceptual world of scale, perspectives, units of measure, lines, planes, volumes and surfaces–a world which is not immediately accessible to clients. Builders have their own dialect, and move in a somewhat different language world, as do each of the trades, material suppliers and the building authorities, and of course each discourse has evolved to meet different discursive needs in the context of different histories, objectives and work practices. There is ample opportunity in a situation which produces such a volume of communication, distributed across space and time, and conducted through different linguistic forms, for meaning to be lost, misunderstandings and differences in interpretation to emerge, and mutual comprehension to lapse.

According to Habermas a lack of comprehension is not discursively redeemable: that is, it does little good to seek understanding in more of the same language (through repetition, speaking louder or speaking more slowly); rather, the condition of comprehensibility can only be approached by shifting language forms, or by recontextualising language use. *KeyBuilding* is capable of providing both facilities. Cross-referencing enables a non-native to shift languages–from a floor plan to a scale-model, from a specification to a picture, from a set of accounts to a bottom line; and to shift contexts–from a contractual clause to a written quote, from a health and safety requirement to an educative bulletin. *KeyBuilding* brings all of these communicative acts together in a single repository, when and where-so-ever they might have originated, and no matter what form they might take, and places them ready to hand in the direct company of others, for comparison, contrast and decoding in the context of the corpus as a whole. The system thus supports the hermeneutic process from which comprehensibility is derived.

Of course, it goes without saying that communication is a precondition for comprehension. As currently designed however, *KeyBuilding* gives the builder the power to deny or approve client access to the documentation accumulated or generated on the system. Even without the system's power to withhold information, the builder is ordinarily in possession of information and language forms not available to the client. The builder-client communicative dyad is thus characteristically asymmetrical. Comprehensibility and meaningful communication in these conditions requires that each party acknowledge and address this asymmetry through recursive cycles of communication. A denial of access to documentation and other "speech acts" is a refusal to communicate, maintains asymmetrical relations and is not likely to enhance mutual comprehension. *KeyBuilding's* facility to deny access is thus not consistent with an ideal speech situation.

The condition of truthfulness is required in order to meet Habermas' second criterion for ideal speech, and a number of points might be made in this context. The first is that *KeyBuilding* manages speech that issues directives, constitutes promises and defines change. In this sense the information represents an accumulation of "acts"–of decisions that have been made (in the form of contracts, permits, variations, warranties and so forth). In effect therefore, the system *defines the truth* at a particular point in time. Secondly, the system is capable of providing discursive resources in the event that truth is called into question, by providing access to rational argument in support of those decisions. For example, in the case of controversy about materials used, the system provides recourse to the supplier's technical specifications, warnings, conditions of use, recommendations, fitting and maintenance instructions, and the like, and in a case of disputes about standards and norms, links are provided to information from the Housing Industry Authority, the Builders Guarantee Fund, and Council planning and building authorities.

The system is not able to satisfy Habermas' demanding condition that rational consensus be reached through argument in which all pertinent claims are able to be made, none are suppressed, and no influences other than rational argument intrude. However, the system does make available a broader and more comprehensive set of resources from which pertinent claims might be drawn, and in providing these references implicitly establishes that these argumentative resources are a legitimate basis for consensus, and other resources (such as power, threats) are not. Once again though, the point must be made that this condition can only be met if and when access is provided to all parties to the controversy. If the builder sets *KeyBuilding* to deny the client access to pertinent evidence, conditions for rational consensus are not in place.

Habermas' third condition insists upon the normative appropriateness of the participants to engage in speech action. It is appropriate for some, but not anyone, to make assertions, requests, directives, promises and declarations that might affect change, and in embracing some parties but excluding others, *KeyBuilding* is making a determination on this condition for ideal speech. The system in effect gives some parties a voice in the conversation (suppliers, planning authorities) and denies others a voice (the Carlton Football Club, the Pope). These examples are reasonably clear-cut–there does not seem to be good reason to exclude planning authorities, or to include the Pope–but some decisions are not straightforward. For example, some builders will not think it appropriate that Building Unions speak through the system. Some will not think it appropriate that suppliers are able to speak directly to clients through the system, rather than through the builder. Builders who use the system will determine which voices are able to speak and act through the system. It is not a "public sphere" in Habermas' terms, but a private space able to be controlled and used strategically by builders. System designers are attending to the sensitivities and perceived interests of builders when determining which voices are to be heard, but we may also bear in mind that a condition for reaching rational consensus is that all pertinent claims can be made.

We turn now to Habermas' fourth condition for ideal speech situations. The sincerity of the builder and of the client is something for each to determine as the relationship unfolds through time. The relationship between builder and client is typically one that cycles through many iterations of open discussion, narrowing to options, reaching consensus, making commitments and delivering on commitments.

Sincerity is demonstrated historically through these iterations, and in some cases through iterations of completed jobs (iterations of iterations). All stages of the cycle are performed discursively, except the all important last, and although the system has no direct role in physical actions taken to deliver on commitments, it is in a position to record cycles of discursive action and physical action in a sufficient degree of detail to be able to judge their consistency. That is, in recording what is said, and enabling it to be compared to what is done, the system provides a resource whereby sincerity might be demonstrated historically. Of course, as has been argued before, the system can only contribute to establishing sincerity where there is a symmetry in the communicative relationship—where the system "sits in the middle" and is used as a resource for both builder and the client, and is used to serve and concretise the relationship between the parties, rather than serving one set of interests.

In summary then, Habermas' social theory of ideal speech provides the researcher and the designer with relevant sensitivities, and a set of concepts and accompanying language to explore those sensitivities. In the context of this social theory, certain aspects of *KeyBuilding* are to be commended, and certain warnings present themselves. These warnings and commendations are relevant to the system developers, but in the same theoretical context, are relevant to users and students of society, as the system (and others like it) mediate speech actions and thus our social condition.

Now, what might Foucault say about *KeyBuilding*?

Foucault and KeyBuilding

Michel Foucault's project has been concerned with an analysis of the different modes by which human beings are made subjects, and how "normality" has been achieved and maintained. His studies of hospitals, doctors' surgeries, prisons and courts, schoolrooms and welfare offices were not conducted in order to develop a "grand theory" of the kind represented by Habermas' ideal speech, but instead, has produced an "archaeology" of the places that structure, construct and maintain normalcy—the healthy body, the sane mind, the dutiful father, the happy child, the good worker, the upstanding citizen. Important to his analysis is the notion of the "discourse," understood to be the rules that permit certain things to be said and disallow others, thus creating systems of possibility for knowledge. Unlike Habermas, Foucault is not concerned with truth or rationality *per se*, but like Habermas, he is interested in the rules which enable these claims to be made—rules which for the main part lie in the way knowledge is structured and act "behind the back" of the author. For example, according to Foucault's social theory, architecture is a discourse, and through education and work-practice, architects learn the "language" of architecture. This language enables certain knowledge-claims to be made in the name of architecture, and disallows others; and allows certain people to speak of these things, and disallows others. In so much as it allows and disallows, it is a discipline. So, truth is an output of discourse, but in Foucault's analysis, truth is not established by rational consensus in ideal conditions, but is always already infused with power. Far from a "contamination" to be excluded in favour of reason (as Habermas suggested), power is integral to the production of truth. Moreover, the relation between truth and power is symmetrical–power produces truth, and truth is essential to the exercise of power. In our current society, a conflation of knowledge and power produce discourses that establish and maintain truth, and normalcy, while at the same time these discourses set the rules for the legitimation of knowledge and the exercise of power. Discourses express knowledge and power and thus give structure, shape and direction to knowledge and power, and in this sense discourses discipline, and they are a discipline. Foucault's ideas of power/ knowledge, discourse and discipline are all interrelated, and are referred to collectively as "the order of things." It is regrettable that Foucault did not turn his attention directly to information technologies and their position in the order of things; however, the concepts and language associated with discourse, the knowledge/power conflation and discipline have been influential in socio-technical research (e.g., Barney, 2000; Poster, 1995). It is equally regrettable that few IS designers have made use of Foucault's work, a notable exception being Orlikowski (e.g., 1991). Some of Foucault's ideas will be taken up in so much as they may be relevant to a discussion of the design of project management and coordination systems. Firstly though, let me continue the theme of power/knowledge.

For Foucault, power is inextricably embedded in knowledge and truth at two levels. Firstly, power regulates truth by defining normalcy–for example, a true and correct set of accounts is defined by accounting, and an appropriately dimensioned beam is defined by engineering. This power to define standards–the normal, the appropriate, the desirable–is maintained through institutions (such as universities, regulators and professional associations), and is exercised through authorised individuals (such as accountants and engineers), who are authorised because they can and do produce this truth. That is, they have the power because they have knowledge of the discourse, and because they have knowledge of the discourse, they are authorised to exercise power. Secondly, over long historical periods, institutions and individuals exercise particular conflations of knowledge/power as a result of violent struggles to lay claim to "eternal" truth (such as that between positivists and constructionists, modernists and postmodernists). In the current order of things, Science is dominant in its claims to eternal truth, but in other epistemes God and Nature have been able to make the claim, and empower institutions (such as the Church and the Monarchy) and individuals (such as the Priest and the Aristocrat), accordingly.

In terms of power/knowledge at the first level mentioned above (normalcy, standards), *KeyBuilding* is authorised to represent truth. In a direct sense, the system *defines* the truth of the matter in relation to the building project, and because it is able to represent the claim to truth, it exercises power simultaneously. *KeyBuilding* allows certain things to be said and does not allow others. It is a database of heterogeneous information resources, and like all databases, it provides a structured space into which or through which language must pass. It provides what Foucault called "grids of specification" which systematically "form the objects of which it speaks" (Poster, 1995, p. 88-89, quoting Foucault, 1973). It insists that certain things be said about the job, in a certain order, in a certain language. *KeyBuilding* thereby has what Foucault called "author status"–the capacity to discursively constitute (rather than connote) a reality. But this is not an arbitrary arrangement which comes about by fiat, or because the system designer has any particular authority in the building industry. Rather, *KeyBuilding* has author status only in so much as it draws upon the authoritative discourses of our day. The discourses of the law have contributed contracts and warranties; the discourses of management, accounting, engineering, drafting, planning, surveying, tiling, wiring, concreting, landscaping, decorating and so forth, are all called upon to make contributions to the system's function. The authority of the system is thus derived from the authority of the discourses that constitute the order of things in the current episteme.

But in terms of the power/knowledge conflation at the second "historical" level, the system makes its own claims to authority. At this time, in this culture, computer-based information systems exercise their power to generate knowledge claims in many domains (e.g., banking and finance), but not all (e.g., legal documentation and art). In the building industry, while all engineers and many architects have situated the computer centrally in their discourses of professional practice, some architects have not, and many builders and many trades have not. It is not yet central to the order of things in building, and is not positioned to exercise power in the production of truth. KeyVision intends to alter this condition, and place *KeyBuilding* in the order of things. From there, *KeyBuilding* will exercise its power to discipline.

For Foucault, "discipline" has two meanings brought together by the concept of power/knowledge. On the one hand discipline is a mechanism of control and coercion, and on the other hand discipline is enabling–it is a set of skills, methods and knowledge that constitute a discourse, and need to be mastered to succeed in engineering, accounting, music, etc. Foucault traced the archaeology of discipline through the 18th and 19th centuries, when the system of public order changed from one based on monarchical decree enforced ultimately through torture and public execution, to one based on law enforced through the prison. Foucault considered the prison to be an archetypal institution in the constitution of the current order of things, and used Jeremy Bentham's 18th-century model of the "Panopticon" prison-design as a central icon in his analysis. The Panopticon was a design for prisons whereby guards could at any time observe any prisoner, who would at no time know whether he or she was observed or not. Bentham considered that in these circumstances prisoners would at all times behave as though they were being observed, whether they were or not, and would in effect discipline themselves. This shift from punishment to discipline and thus self-discipline did not occur out of new-found human empathy or squeamishness about execution and torture, but in Foucault's analysis, is associated with a move from a feudal society to an increasingly urban, industrialised, trade-based society, in which personal agency and the autonomous self-discipline of the worker, the tradesman and the merchant, becomes important. Discipline therefore is not just an alternative form of punishment for lawbreakers, but is important to the agency and conduct of all citizens, most importantly the law-abiding, and is important in the capitalist social condition that emerged through those centuries. Discipline created a new "subject"–a new normalcy for what it is to be a human being. This was so, and still is so, in the two senses of the term discipline mentioned above. In the first sense, discipline is the control we exercise over ourselves and others. In the second sense, a discipline is a set of skills and knowledge that enables us to act effectively in the world. The engineer, accountant and builder derive their authority and power from their disciplines as knowledge domains, and from their self-discipline as subjects.

KeyBuilding is disciplinary in both senses. Indeed, discipline is central to the system. It indicates what must be done in the course of the building job, and thus exercises a coercive function in the coordination of participants. The system seeks to assert itself over the sometimes disorganised or even shambolic work practices of builders. The system disciplines by presenting and suggesting guidelines, timelines, standard documents, regulatory requirements and the like, in the process of each building job. On the other hand the system also works within the various knowledge/power disciplines associated with current building practices, by directly drawing upon them.

As Bentham's Panopticon suggests, for discipline to take its important place in the current order of things, surveillance is necessary. There was a time in history when the more powerful and privileged an individual was, the more likely they were to be the subject of surveillance and close monitoring. Now, in a process Foucault called "descending individualism," the opposite applies. The weaker and less privileged (the patient, the student, the worker) are surveilled by the powerful (the doctor, the teacher, the supervisor). This is also reflected in *KeyBuilding*, where subcontractors and trades are individuated, and are subject to monitoring and discipline by the builder according to a framework set down by powerful players in the building industry. But the builder is also subject to surveillance, not in the same way as Bentham's Panopticon, but in parallel ways. Firstly, the system has the capacity to subject the builder to the gaze of the client, and perhaps to the gaze of other parties also. It is possible for the client to observe the actual job and to compare it to project management timelines, to warranties and guarantees of workmanship, to advice from third parties, to plans and drawings, to advice from product and material suppliers specifying the appropriate usage and fitting and details of workmanship. The client may not access this information, but if they can, it will be assumed by the builder that they will, and being subject to this surveillance the builder, like the prisoner, will be inclined to exercise discipline over the conduct of the job. And this is important to Foucault's point–we are surveilled by ourselves– not by guards. The builder is thus in a position to assure the discipline of those associated with the job–in both senses of the term discipline. In one sense the system integrates and co-ordinates the work of the many people involved in the building project. It helps ensure that everyone marches to the beat of the same drum. In the other sense, by providing a mechanism through which building discourses are made available, it holds them accountable to the norms and standards defined by those discourses, and therefore to the various disciplines that come together to complete a building project.

So, Foucault's social theory provides us with perspectives from which *KeyBuilding* might be interpreted. *KeyBuilding* is a system of discipline, through which knowledge and therefore power flows and circulates. The knowledge/power that flows from and through the variety of discourses and disciplines associated with building, is channelled by the system and is thus channelled from and through the builder. In taking its place among these discourses, and in relation to knowledge/power, surveillance and discipline, *KeyBuilding* takes its place in constructing the order of things, as well as constructing houses.

Latour and KeyBuilding

Bruno Latour is a French intellectual, who, along with Michel Callon, John Law and others, is closely associated with a theory called actor network theory (ANT). Like the ideas of Habermas and Foucault, the theory associated with ANT offers leverage in an analysis of software such as *KeyBuilding*.

Perhaps the most pertinent of these ideas is the notion that the people at KeyVision are not inventing a software application as such, but are assembling a system, or a network. In making this claim, ANT is stressing the very important assertion that any given entity is not a thing in itself, but is only comprehensible as a thing in relation. When ANT refers to *KeyBuilding* as a network, or a thing in relation, it is not simply referring to a computer network and software system as a technical system–an assemblage of hardware and software, data-flows and business processes (with social implications)–nor is it referring to a social system or network–a set of social, cultural and economic activities (expressed as technology). Rather, it is referring to a socio-technical network that places in relation, machines, people, software, institutions, protocols, bureaucracies and all manner of other things, without differentiating analytically between people and machines, or the social and the technical, in terms of agency or primacy. All are active agents (or "actors") that must be induced to join the network and work cooperatively with the network. And thus Thomas Edison, for example, is not someone who laboured with purely technical problems to invent a thing-in-itself such as a light bulb. He was a heterogeneous engineer who worked to assemble copper, glass, wire-fila-ments, generators, meters, transformers, electricians, laws of nature, math-ematical formulae, engineers, politicians, investors, bankers, labourers, local councils, regulatory authorities and others, into a network (or assemblage, imbroglio or quasi-machine) that produced light for householders, profits for investors, work for coal miners, electrocution for the convicted, pollution for the air, unemployment for gaslight-fitters and so forth. Edison recruited these actors to his network, and was symmetrically recruited to theirs. Edison's electric light was a socio-technical system which derived its structure and functions according to the relations of the actors that are assembled together, and according to its relations to financial systems, political systems, regulatory systems, domestic systems and other socio-technical networks with which it is articulated.

In this analysis *KeyBuilding* is not a thing-in-itself–a discrete object on a web-server–it is a socio-technical network of the kind identified by actor network theory. Its components are a heterogeneous assemblage of servers, disk-drives, code, builders, Internet service providers, clients, bureaucracies, product managers, investment advisors, marketing managers, documents, contracts, forms and dia-grams. KeyVision and the builders that employ their system need to mobilise all of these actors (some of which will resist recruitment), win their cooperation and then hold them together in a stable relation. KeyVision is not writing software; they are trying to stitch these actors together to form coherent, cohesive and stable network.

From the actor network view, the system achieves connection between the actors in the network through a circulation of "translations." By "translation" Latour refers to the transformations resulting from negotiation, calculation, persuasion and violence, whereby an actor's interests are articulated in a modified form in order that they be aligned with those with which the actor is connected. So, the architect translates the client's needs and desires into CAD files or ink on paper. The architect's translations will then be taken up and translated into details, cross-sections and images by engineers and drafts-people. Meanwhile, materials-suppliers are also engaged in translating specifications into concrete, glass, timber and bricks. Through another series of techniques and performances, building supervisors translate the ink on paper, the details and cross-sections, the materials specifications and the concrete, glass, timber and bricks, into a work-schedule and directions to the trades. The trades bring these directions together with the ink (and other actors), and translate by placing one brick in relation to another, tiles in relation to a wall, timber in relation to a joist, a door in relation to a wall. Each translation is in part faithful and in part unfaithful to the attributes of that which is translated. Each translation circulates power and manifests a network of relations. *KeyBuilding* constructs a network of actors in relation, and relations are composed of these translations.

CONCLUSION

Information and communications systems are machines that are situated in the midst of social conditions, to mediate structures and performances in those conditions, for good and for ill. Positivists and interpretivists can agree on this. As such, IS researchers have something to gain from theory that focuses in particular on those social conditions. IS designers and socio-technical re-searchers can see from Habermas that creating ideal conditions for "speech" is not a simple matter of installing high-bandwidth communications systems, but requires consideration of the system's mediations in terms of comprehensibility, truth, appropriate speech and sincerity. From Foucault we see that the project is not a simple matter of configuring databases and scheduling systems, but is a matter which is infused with the exercise of power, and discipline, through discourse. And from Latour, building networks is not a simple matter of cabling servers and clients, but is a matter of assembling a large and heterogeneous network of mutually configuring actors, each of which expresses agency, and of translating circulations of relexive action in order to maintain the shape and direction of the system as a whole.

This story of the socio-technical has been told through *KeyBuilding*, but the conceptual tools and language of social theory–ideal speech, discourse, discipline, networks, translation and others–may be used profitably in an analysis of any socio-technical system. And just as IS designers may profit from social theory, students of society cannot ignore the work of information system designers, or treat information systems as passive objects in the background–as dependent variables incapable of social agency. Digital systems are very much part of the social action.

REFERENCES

Ackoff, R. (1971). Towards a system of system concepts. *Management Science*, *17*, 661-671.

Ang, S. (1996). A comment on the intellectual structures of information systems development. *Accounting, Management and Information Technology*, *6*(1/2), 65-69.

Auramaki, E., Hirschheim, R. and Lyytinen, K. (1992). Modelling offices through discourse analysis. *The Computer Journal*, *35*(4), 342-352.

Barney, D. (2000). *Prometheus Wired: The Hope for Democracy in the Age of Network Technology*. Vancouver: The University of Chicago Press.

Berg, M. (1998). The politics of technology: On bringing social theory into technological design science. *Technology and Human Values*, *23*(4), 456-490.

Boland, R. J. and Day, W. F. (1989). The experience of system design: A hermeneutic of organizational action. *Scandinavian Journal of Management*, *5*(2), 87-104.

Checkland, P. (1981). *Systems Thinking, Systems Practice*. Chichester: John Wiley & Sons.

Checkland, P. and Scholes, J. (1990). *Soft Systems Methodology in Action*. Chichester: John Wiley & Sons.

Danaher, G., Schirato, T. and Webb, J. (2000). *Understanding Foucault*. Sydney: Allen & Unwin.

Dewan, S. and Kraemer, K. L. (2000). Information technology and productivity: Evidence from country-level data. *Management Science*, *46*(4), 548-562.

Foucault, M. (1973). *The Order of Things: An Archaeology of the Human Sciences*. New York: Vintage Books.

Giddens, A. (1984). *The Constitution of Society: Outline of the Theory of Structure*. Berkeley, CA: University of California Press.

Gimlin, D., Rule, J. and Sievers, S. (2000). The uneconomic growth of computing. *Sociological Forum*, *15*(3), 485-510.

Habermas. (1998). *On the Pragmatics of Communication*. Cambridge, MA: The MIT Press.

Hirschheim, R., Klein, H. K. and Lyytinen, K. (1996). Exploring the intellectual structures of information systems development: A social action theoretic analysis. *Accounting, Management and Information Technology*, *6*(1/2), 1-64.

Iivari, J., Hirschheim, R. and Klein, H. K. (1998). A paradigmatic analysis contrasting information systems development approaches and methodologies. *Information Systems Research*, *9*(2), 164-193.

Introna, L. D. and Whitley, E. A. (1997). Against method-ism. *Information Technology & People, 10*(1), 31-45.

Janson, M. A., Woo, C. C. and Smith, L. D. (1993). Information systems development and communicative action theory. *Information & Management, 24*, 59-72.

Johannesson, P. (1995). Representation and communication–A speech act-based approach to information system design. *Information Systems, 20*(4), 291-303.

Klein, H. K. and Myers, M. D. (1999). A set of principles for conducting and evaluating interpretive field studies in information systems. *MIS Quarterly, 23*(1), 67-93.

Klein, H. K. and Truex, D. (1995). Discourse analysis: A semiotic approach to the investigation of organizational emergence. In Anderson, P. B. and Holmqvist, B. (Eds.), *The Semiotics of the Workplace*. Berlin: Walter DeGruyter.

Landauer, T. K. (1997). *The Trouble with Computers: Usefulness, Usability, and Productivity*. Cambridge, MA: A Bradford Book, The MIT Press.

Law, J. (1991). *A Sociology of Monsters: Essays on Power, Technology, and Domination*. New York and London: Routledge.

Law, J. and Hassard, J. (1999). *Actor Network Theory and After*. Oxford: Blackwell.

Lee, A. S. (1994). Electronic mail as a medium for rich communication. An empirical investigation using hermeneutic interpretation. *MIS Quarterly, 18*(2), 143.

Lee, A. S. (1999). Rigor and relevance in MIS research: Beyond the approach of positivism alone. *MIS Quarterly, 23*(1), 29-33.

Lucas, H. C. J. and Adenso-Diaz, B. (2000). Information technology and the productivity paradox: Assessing the value of investing in IT. *Interfaces, 30*(2), 117-118.

Lyytinen, K. (1991). A taxonomic perspective of information systems development: Theoretical constructs and recommendations. In R. J. B. Jr. and Hirschheim, R. A. (Eds.), *Critical Issues in Information Systems Research*. Chichester: John Wiley & Sons.

Lyytinen, K. and Hirschheim, R. (1988). Information systems as rational discourse: An application of Habermas' theory of communicative action. *Sandinavian Journal of Management, 4*(1/2), 19-30.

Lyytinen, K. and Klein, H. (1985). The critical theory of Jurgen Habermas as a basis for a theory of information systems. In Mumford, E., Hirschheim, R., Fitzgerald, G. and Wood-Harper, A. T. (Eds.), *Research Methods in Information Systems*, 219-236. Amsterdam: Elsevier Science Publishers B.V. (North-Holland).

Mahmood, M. A. and Mann, G. J. (2000). Special issue: Impacts of information technology investment on organizational performance. *Journal of Management Information Systems, 16*(4), 3-10.

Mingers, J. (1984). Subjectivism and soft systems methodology–A critique. *Journal of Applied Systems Analysis, 11*, 85-103.

Orlikowski, W. and Baroudi, J. J. (1991). Studying information technology in organisations: Research approaches and assumptions. *Information Systems Research, 2*(1), 1-28.

Orlikowski, W. J. (1991). Integrated information environment or matrix of control? The contradictory implications of information technology. *Accounting, Management and Information Technologies, 1*(1), 9-42.

Orlikowski, W. J. (1992). The duality of technology: Rethinking the concept of technology in organizations. *Organization Science, 3*(3), 398-427.

Orlikowski, W. J. and Robey, D. (1991). Information technology and the structuring of organizations. *Information Systems Research, 2*(2), 143-169.

Poster, M. (1995). *The Second Media Age.* Cambridge, MA: Polity Press.

Preston, A. M. (1991). The 'problem' in and of management information systems. *Accounting, Management and Information Technologies, 1*(1), 43-69.

Schneiderman, B. and Carroll, J. M. (1988). Ecological studies of professional programmers: Guest editors' introduction. *Communications of the ACM, 32*(11), 1256-1258.

Sheridan, J. (2000). Productivity payoff? *Industry Weekly, 248*(13), 22-26.

Skinner Q. (1985). *The Return of Grand Theory in the Human Sciences.* Cambridge, MA: Cambridge University Press.

Suchman, L. (1987). *Plans and Situated Actions: The Problem of Human-Machine Communication.* Cambridge, MA: Cambridge University Press.

Tsoukas, H. (1992). Panoptic reason and the search for totality: A critical assessment of the critical systems perspective. *Human Relations, 45*(7), 637-657.

Ullman, E. (1995). Out of time: Reflections on the programming life. In Brook, J. and Boal, I. (Eds.), *Resiting the Virtual Life,* 131-143. San Franciso, CA: City Lights.

Vickers, M. H. (1999). Information technology development methodologies: Towards a non-positivist, developmental paradigm. *The Journal of Management, 18*(3), 255-272.

Walsham, G. (1995). The emergence of interpretivism in IS research. *Information Systems Research, 6*(4), 376-394.

Walsham, G. (1995). Interpretive case studies in IS research: Nature and method. *European Journal of Information Systems, 4*, 74-81.

Wilson, F. (1999). Flogging a dead horse: The implications of epistemological relativism within information systems methodological practice. *European Journal of Information Systems, 8,* 161-169.

Wilson, F. A. (1997). The truth is out there: The search for emancipatory principles in information systems design. *Information Technology & People, 10*(3), 187-204.

Winograd, T. and Flores, F. (1986). *Understanding Computers and Cognition.* Norwood: Ablex Publishing.

Zuboff, S. (1988). *In the Age of the Smart Machine.* New York: Basic Books.

Chapter XII

A Social Perspective on Information Security: Theoretically Grounding the Domain

Steve Clarke
University of Luton, UK

Paul Drake
GlaxoSmithKline PLC, UK

ABSTRACT

Information security has become a largely rule-based domain, substantially focusing on issues of confidentiality. But the standards developed to achieve this, both in the U.S. and in the UK, have not been adopted as widely as had been hoped.

By casting information security as a human-centred domain, this chapter, by means of a critique fom a social theoretical perspective, seeks to offer a way forward to a more widely acceptable approach. Social philosophy, social theory, and empirical evidence all suggest a basis in critical social theory as a potential way forward, and an initial framework based on this, is developed within this study.

All of this is seen to point toward information security seen as human action, mediated through subjective understanding, and this research is now focusing on the operationalisation of these concepts.

INTRODUCTION

Information security is a relatively new domain, and one of its strengths is that it was conceived and has been developed in accordance with the practical experience of some major international organisations. However, one outcome of this is that its primary focus on practice has left relevant theoretical underpinning to the domain substantially unexplored.

While many would argue information to be a valuable asset, the information security standards which have resulted from the activity alluded to above have not been widely accepted. In this chapter it is argued that this is not so much to do with the quality of the standard and how it is maintained, but rather that the current approach to information security is in itself flawed as a concept, and has much to learn from the domain of social theory. A key issue to emerge within this research project has been the extent to which information security has been approached from a perspective of confidentiality or secrecy, rather than one of improved sharing of information: an issue which is explored within this chapter.

The chapter firstly presents an outline of the current theory and practice of information security. This is seen to point to the value of viewing the domain through social theory, and in particular critical social theory. In the remainder of the chapter, this theme is further developed, and is used to propose a future direction for information security which is very different from the currently favoured view.

INFORMATION SECURITY: CURRENT THEORY AND PRACTICE

Over the past 10 years, there has been increasing interest in the subject of information security (see, for example, Drake, 1998), with particular emphasis on information technology or computer security (e.g., Langford, 1995; Neumann, 1995; Gollman, 1999).

An early and still considered seminal work on information security is the Department of Defense Computer System Evaluation Criteria (the so-called 'Orange Book': DoD, 1987). Although constructed around the security of computer systems to be procured for the U.S. Department of Defense, the document established many of the basic information security principles practised today, and was followed by the European Information Technology Security Evaluation Criteria (EC, 1991). It is in this latter document that the ubiquitous confidentiality, integrity and availability (CIA) principles of information security were first widely documented. CIA embraces the main principles of information security as practised by the industry, the implication of which is that there exists a primary need to prevent access to information by those not entitled to have it, keep it accurate and up to date, and make sure authorised users have access when they need it.

In the early to mid-1990s, a group of representatives from some of the largest organisations in the UK decided to collaborate to formalise information security standards. They established a committee under the stewardship of the Department of Trade and Industry and the British Standards Institute to create a British Standard (BSI, 1999a; 1999b). Each of these organisations (and others) had been working to establish frameworks to adequately secure the information systems within their organisations, and the British Standard had the simple aim of standardising these frameworks into a model that could be applied to any organisation. Those organisations using this model could therefore have some confidence in the security practices of any potential business partner who also follows the standard, thereby reducing the need to invest resources in independent checks.

There is little doubt that fewer organisations than were expected have embraced the standard and implemented the model. Typically, the fastest 'movers' have been those originally involved in its development and maintenance (e.g., Shell, Unilever, Cambridgeshire County Council and Logica); and those that have been the subject of adverse external audit reports due to potentially inaccurate information systems or information security incidents such as sabotage and malpractice. Although reliable and auditable information on this latter category is generally not in the public domain, there is considerable evidence to suggest that the trend in the frequency of such incidents is upwards (for example, Commission, 1998; NCC, 1998; Symonds, 1999).

The beginnings of a less rule-based approach to information security are to be found in Russell (1991), who makes an early mention of the CIA, but, recognising the common perception that security equates to secrecy (confidentiality), goes on to raise the possibility that integrity and availability may be more important in some environments. This provides the basis for the direction taken within this study, one of the tenets of which is to emphasise the importance of sharing information rather than restricting access to it. To some extent, the aims of confidentiality and of availability may be seen to pull against each other: the more confidential a set of information, the less available it will be. This has raised the question of 'available to whom?' and has led to a consideration of information as a human issue, rather than as an issue concerned with information technology or computer security.

There is, then, a well-established practical basis for information security, but one which has not been adopted as widely as might have been expected. The aim of this chapter is to look for reasons why this might be so, and possible alternative approaches which might serve the domain more satisfactorily. Investigations to date suggest poor theoretical grounding for information security as a discipline. That literature which is available casts the domain as one focusing on secrecy and restriction, in which a rule-based approach is seen to be relevant. To mount a critique of this position, this research programme began by viewing it from an alternative perspective, and since the prevailing view may be seen as instrumental and objective, the alternative chosen was one informed from a subjective stand-point. In theoretical terms, the subjective/objective debate is firmly set in social theory, so it is here that we began our critique.

INFORMATION SECURITY AND SOCIAL THEORY

A still seminal work in the classification of social theory, and one which is useful in helping to think about the issues involved, is Burrell and Morgan's (1979) typology. Figure 1 summarises this position through an expansion of the Burrell and Morgan grid (Clarke, 2000: after Oliga, 1991).

Figure 1: The social validity of hard, soft and critical approaches

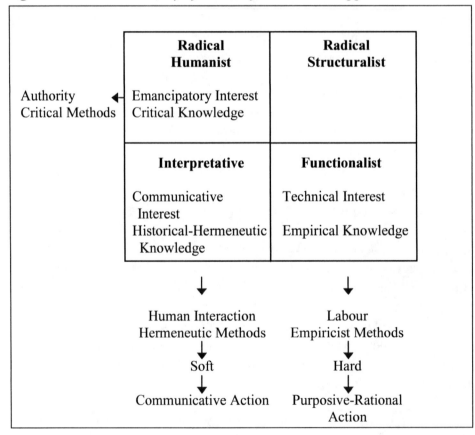

Burrell and Morgan argue that all social theories can be categorised within this framework. In terms of business organisations, they see a concentration mostly on functionalism, following an instrumental rationality based on the methods of the natural sciences. There is some evidence of interpretivistic work in organisational analysis, to the extent that investigation may proceed according to the differing viewpoints of those involved rather than by a search for 'the facts.'

From this social theoretical perspective, information security appears as mostly functionalist, with little explicit recognition of influence from the interpretative paradigm. The rule-based methods, developed as part of the information security standard, firmly locate the work to date in a functionalist world, in which there is seen to be an objective reality independent of human interpretation.

In looking for a way out of this dilemma, social theory therefore points first to the interpretative paradigm, where human interaction is privileged within a subjective, communicative rationality. However, social theory also suggests *problems* with interpretivism, in that the kind of open debate necessary for human viewpoints to be recognised and acted upon may be suppressed or distorted by power structures within a social, and particularly organisational, context.

It is the radical humanist paradigm, focusing on critical social theory, in which the potential to address these issues is to be found, giving rise to a subjective approach with radical intent. Much work has been carried out to assess the relevance of and apply this within the domain of information systems in general (see, for example, Hirschheim & Klein, 1989; Hirschheim, Klein et al., 1991; Clarke & Lehaney, 1999a; 1999b). This research study has pursued this theme within information security, and the findings to date are presented in the following sections.

INFORMATION SECURITY AND CRITICAL THEORY

The dominant approach to information security, then, has been pragmatic, based on an instrumental, step-by-step method, rooted in scientific thinking (reductionist, step-wise and seeking 'solutions' to 'problems'). In looking to critical theory for a critique of this position, the search for a basis on which to ground information security may be seen as beginning with the Enlightenment, during which scientific advancement caused instrumental reason, through scientific method, to be privileged ahead of the then dominant mystical and religious dogmas. Underpinning all of this was humankind's confidence in the power which this new scientific philosophy conferred over nature.

The outcome of this in terms of how it affects current thinking is that scientific functionalism gained precedence, during the 17th century and beyond, not only over existing religious dogmas, but over *all forms of reason*. Kant (1787) argued that essentially this could be interpreted as 'man' having forgotten how to think unless given rules by which to do so. Kant made a distinction between instrumental and practical reason: scientific method applies only instrumental logic toward truth claims, with the purpose of uncovering objective truths–however many current scientists deny this, their actions and words betray their real beliefs (so, for instance, we have the ongoing aim to 'unify physics,' which implicitly depends on there being a single objective reality underlying the workings of the Universe, to which we both have access and are expected ultimately to be able to explain). Kant argued that we had become trapped in a position where we could think only instrumentally, within laws or rules laid down for us–dialectic or practical thinking was being ignored.

The Kantian strand in critical theory leads to the idea that, in a dialectic, reason becomes redefined: it is no longer represented by a vertical process of thought, leading instrumentally to the confirmation or denial of objective truths, but reason is rather concerned with *normative validity*. In the former, "formal-logical reasoning proceeds in a linear and unreflective manner," while in the latter, "dialectical reasoning breaks through the given premises, and frees us to overcome our fixed patterns of thinking–and our being contented with them" (Ulrich, 1983b, p. 220). From this can be traced Kant's view that *practical* meant that which is possible through freedom, explicitly challenging coercion, so that participants (the involved and affected) may be free to meaningfully participate.

All of this points to critical theory being of value as an alternative view in a predominantly instrumental domain such as information security. This critical stream has been taken forward, since the 1920s, by first the Frankfurt School, and latterly Foucault and Habermas (for an outline, see Brocklesby and Cummings, 1996). In the UK, it has been used as a basis by critical thinkers within the systems movement (see, for example, Flood & Jackson, 1991; Mingers, 1997; Clarke & Lehaney, 2000; Jackson, 2000).

Information security, then, may be seen as having been approached to date as a pseudo-scientific domain, but one which lacks a convincing theoretical base. The tenets of scientific method are to be found in its reliance on an instrumental approach, but this appears as an impoverished view, privileging confidentiality rather than openness and information sharing. The early stages of this ongoing research, by drawing on theoretical and practical work within critical theory, take the first steps in developing an alternative theoretical framework for information security.

CRITICAL THEORY AS A BASIS FOR INFORMATION SECURITY

Information security may be interpreted as grounded in the philosophy of science: it is substantially rule-based and instrumental: in the U.K., for example, BS7799 is intended to be auditable, and must be specific; the process of certification is based around compliance or non-compliance.

The relevance of the domain of critical theory to information *systems* has been discussed extensively (for example Hirschheim & Klein, 1989; Gregory, 1993; Clarke, 1997, 2000). This chapter seeks to pursue the critical strand and relate it more directly to the study of information security. To this end, Figure 2 interprets information security through Burrell and Morgan's typology. In an ideal world, the rule-based approach of functionalist information security and the discursive methods of interpretivism should be sufficient grounding for the domain, but power, a key focus of the radical humanist and radical structuralist paradigms, distorts these.

A radical restructuring of the domain ('radical structuralism'), while appealing to some, is not available as a remedy, implying as it does a dimension of direct political action which lies beyond the scope of this study. This leaves radical humanism as a potential way forward. Within this, critical theory points to certain key issues to be addressed, and these are the subject of the following section.

Figure 2: A reconstruction of information security based on Burrell and Morgan

Radical Humanism	Radical Structuralism
• Means to overcome coercive constraints in use and distribution of information • Equal availability of information to all • Consideration of who ought to have access rather than who does	• Restructured position in which there are no constraints on flow and use of information as it is owned by all • Concepts such as 'confidentiality' have no meaning
Interpretivism	Functionalism
• Availability of information through discourse • Bias to share information favoured over need to conceal	• Implementation based on own previous experience and empirical knowledge of others • Rigid adherence to controls and compliance with them • Rules governing who has access

TOWARD A 'CRITICALLY NORMATIVE' MODEL OF INFORMATION SECURITY

As shown in Figure 2, critical theory, being grounded in the radical humanist paradigm, follows a humanistic approach to surfacing and addressing the distortions caused by power. Fundamental to this is the concept of a dialectic to surface how participants see a given context 'ought' to be perceived (the normative position), rather than how it 'is' (the instrumental position). A key to applying this concept, and one which has been applied within information security, is boundary critique.

Critical Assessment of the System Boundary

To intervene within any problem context requires that the scope of that context be defined. In systems terms this requires determining the boundary of the system, but frequently this is done in an arbitrary and uncritical way. Ulrich (1983b, 1988, 1996) and Midgley (1992) argue that we should critically challenge what should or should not be considered part of any system.

Ulrich calls for a "critically normative understanding of boundary judgments ... systems thinking that is not critically normative in this sense will evade all significant problems of practical reason and thereby fail to be either practical or scientific" (Ulrich, 1983a, p. 25). Midgley's approach is to begin with a boundary definition which is accepted as arbitrary, and progress by " ... looking for grey areas in which marginal elements lie that are neither fully included in, nor excluded from, the system definition." The critical choices made at the boundary are of truth (represented by questions of what is) and rightness (represented by questions of what ought to be). An example of boundary critique based on these approaches, and drawn from the outcomes of an empirical investigation undertaken as part of this research, is represented by Figure 3 and Table 1.

Critical assessment of the system boundary should be undertaken by a representative sample of participants in the system. Starting with the arbitrary boundary definition (Figure 3), critical systems heuristics (CSH: Ulrich, 1983a) can be used to enhance the perception of the 'system of information security,' at all times maintaining the distinction between theoretical reason, applied instrumentality to determine truth claims and practical reason, concerned with the normative validity of practical propositions.

The primary approach to boundary critique in this research was undertaken using CSH. Systems designers and managers were first asked the 'is' questions in the left-hand column of Table 1. These results were then presented to a wider participant group (also including some systems designers and managers) to address the questions in the right-hand column.

Figure 3: Critique of the system boundary (after Midgley, 1992)

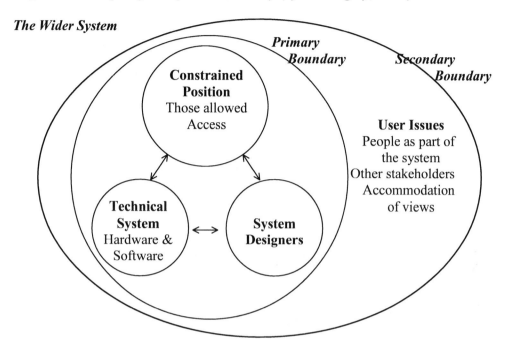

As Table 1 indicates, the participants' perceptions of the system of concern differed considerably from the then current view of the organisation. In this intervention these differences were valuable in reconceptualising a system, which became no longer perceived as a clearly defined technical or organisational problem to which a solution was to be found, but as a complex interaction of all the issues involved in information security. This changed the focus from technology or organisational functions to the views and ideals of the stakeholder groups involved in the system. The task became not one of how to engineer a solution to a known and agreed problem, but how to study and improve a problem situation made up of complex interacting issues. People were not *part* of the system, they were the *primary focus of study*. In terms of Figure 3, the user issues, which were initially marginalised, became core to the whole system of information security.

The theoretical and empirical research so far undertaken has led to a position whereby critical social theory has been successfully argued as a viable future direction for information security. In the next section we report the early stages of the next part of this research project, the aim of which is to further operationalise these concepts.

Table 1: Critically heuristic boundary questions for information security

Motivation

Whose interests *are* served?	Whose interests *ought to be* served?
As represented in the primary boundary of Figure 3, the perception on which system development has hitherto been based has been that of a technological system, required to meet the needs of confidentiality, integrity and availability.	The introduction of the needs of 'user groups' added these as part of the primary system, rather than seeing them marginalised between the primary and secondary boundaries. This largely retained an 'internal' focus in the minds of the participants, bringing in other groups within the organisation, but still excluding those affected in the wider community.
What is the plan's purpose? Including actual and potential consequences, and unintended or unforeseen side effects.	**What ought to be the plan's purpose?**
To prevent unauthorised access and allow authorised access, while maintaining the integrity of the system.	What surfaced in this part of the study was that, if the purpose of the system was seen to be support of the activity of participants in the system, the objectives of the development would be easier to achieve, since the latter is dependent on the former. In other words, the purpose should be seen as greater availability of information to a wider community.
What is the plan's built-in measure of improvement?	**What ought to be the underlying measure of improvement?**
Zero breaches of security.	Improved dissemination of information.

Basis of Knowledge

Who is involved?	Who ought to be involved?
System developers and management.	All those involved in and affected by the system.
On what expertise does the plan rely?	**What expertise ought to be brought in?**
The knowledge held by information security professionals.	The system does not rely on expert knowledge as such. It is necessary to utilise experts in design and development once the overall plan is determined, but such design issues should not drive the intervention. Expertise in this system rests with those who participate in it.
On what is assessment of improvement based? For example: consensus among experts, involvement, experience of those involved?	**On what ought assessment of improvement to be based? For example: consensus among experts, involvement, experience of those involved?**
The number of security breaches.	The extent to which the operational activities and strategic development of information security are enhanced through participation in the system.

CRITICALLY NORMATIVE INFORMATION SECURITY: WHERE NEXT?

To date in this research project, while the value of pursuing a critically normative approach to information security has been demonstrated, a fully developed critically normative operational model remains to be derived. As a first attempt at developing such a model, a return to, and critique of, the principles of critical theory was pursued, and has yielded the initial results outlined below.

Critical Theory Revisited: A Revised Basis for Information Security

The ability to communicate by use of language is something that human beings bring to the world by nature of their existence: that is to say, it is not developed empirically, but is *a priori*. To the extent that any theoretical position can be grounded on such an *a priori* ability, then such a position may be seen as fundamental to us as communicative human actors.

In so far as communication, at least partially, may be oriented toward mutual understanding, it might be argued as the foundation of knowledge creation and sharing. In these terms, knowledge is not reducible (as is so often seen in scientific or pseudo-scientific study) to the properties of an objective world, but can be defined *both* objectively *and* according to the *a priori* concepts that the knowing subject brings to the act of perception. This knowing subject, being social, mediates all knowledge through social action and experience: subject and object are linked in the acts of cognition and social interaction, and the so-called subjective and objective 'paradigms' may be represented as just a convenient tool for understanding, which has been accorded too much primacy as a form of reality.

Rather, then, than relying on the concept of paradigms, this concept, and particularly the idea of paradigm incommensurability, should be opened up to challenge. Consider the so-called subjective/objective dichotomy. According to the paradigm argument, viewed (say) from an epistemological perspective, one who sees a problem context as positivistic, and seeks, for example, a technological solution, will be unable to communicate and share knowledge with another who views the same problem context as existing in the views and opinions of those participants involved in and affected by the system of concern. There are at least two fundamental difficulties with this:

1. It contradicts common human practice, and, dare it be suggested, common sense. Human participants in social groups commonly combine technical ('positivistic') and interpretative ('anti-positivistic') activity, seemingly denying the paradigm incommensurability thesis from an epistemological standpoint.

2. Theoretically, the paradigm incommensurability view seems to have dubious support. At its most basic level, it derives from the idea that technical, scientific, functionalist activity cannot be conducted together with interpretivistic, subjective activity. But if, theoretically, subjective and objective are inseparable, paradigm incommensurability becomes much less compelling.

In essence, then, it can be argued that these difficulties disappear once a scientific basis for our thinking is denied. For example, suppose science (as is suggested by Kant) is seen as just one form of knowledge, which in any case is simply a convenient human perception of how the world works. Now, all human endeavour becomes mediated through subjective understanding, and the paradigms as impenetrable barriers disappear. So, the problem of the paradigm thesis being no longer defensible is resolved, since it is no longer being relied on. However, this problem has been replaced with another, which may be stated as follows:

1. Accepting all human actions as mediated through subjective understanding leads to the possibility of a basis for information security in the universal characteristics of language.
2. The dichotomy between subject and object has gone, and with it, the paradigm problem.
3. Information security is recast as an entirely communicative issue. For example, technological issues become instead a question of how technology may further enable human interaction, all within a framework of human intercommunication.
4. The difficulty which now arises is essentially a practical one, of how to incorporate these ideas into management, and information security practice.

Work by Habermas (1976, 1987) on communicative action presents a universal theory of language which suggests that all language is oriented toward three fundamental validity claims: truth, rightness and sincerity. What is most compelling about this theory, however, is that all three validity claims are *communicatively mediated*. This viewpoint is most radically seen in respect of the truth claim, where it is proposed that such a claim results not from the content of descriptive statements, but from the Wittgenstinian approach casting them as arising in language games which are linked to culture: truth claims are *socially contextual*.

'Truth,' can therefore be assessed by reference to communication: truth is what statements, when true, state! Rightness is about norms of behaviour, which are culturally relevant, and are therefore to be determined by reference to that which is acceptable to those involved and affected in the system of concern as a cultural group. Finally, sincerity is about the speaker's internal world: his/her internal subjectivity.

These ideas can now be taken forward to provide an information security approach, or set of approaches, which are theoretically grounded, and closer to that which is experienced in action. The next section begins this process.

A FIRST CRITICALLY NORMATIVE FRAMEWORK FOR INFORMATION SECURITY

All of this indicates the potential for an approach explicitly grounded in critical social theory, but raises questions about the success of such a project. The arguments of this chapter point to a possible future direction, and, while the position taken here is embryonic and presents many challenges which have not as yet been addressed, it does offer a way forward for information security, which should be:

- Grounded in communicative action.
- Explicitly based on participation.
- Critically informed.

This critically normative approach to information security (Table 2) presents a very different picture of the future of the domain to the one currently favoured.

While significant progress has been made toward a new 'critically normative' approach to information security, the work would not be complete, even at this stage, without an overall critical reflection on the arguments to date. This is therefore undertaken below, before drawing some initial conclusions from the study.

CRITICAL REFLECTION

The real issue here is that we have moved information security from instrumental to normative: we are concerned less with questions of 'what is' and more by those of 'what ought to be.' But this brings with it some significant problems. The first of these, addressing the scope of an information security system and developing an improved, richer understanding of it, we have to some extent achieved through critical boundary judgments, but other difficulties remain.

Table 2: An alternative future for information security

The Instrumental View	The Critically Normative View
Confidentiality/Restriction	Availability/De-Restriction/Sharing
Information Restriction	Information Sharing
Pragmatic	Theoretical/Empirical
Technological/Computer Systems	Human Activity Systems

Instrumental	'Practical'
	Critically Normative. Apply Critique to:
	    Normative Content
	    Norms
	    Boundary Judgments
	    'System'

Pseudo-Scientific	Social
Rule-Based	Challenge the Rules
Truth	Normative Validity
Formal-Logical: Unreflective	Dialectical: Free to Think
'Is'	'Ought'
Functional	Radical
Accept the 'Material Conditions'	Critique of 'Material Conditions'
Rational equals Seeking the 'Truth'	Rational equals a dialectic between the 'involved and affected,' all of whom are free to contribute

This new perspective recasts information security, not as instrumental decision making according to a certain set of norms, but instead as 'rational' if those involved in and affected by the system of concern "make transparent to themselves and to each other the normative content" (after Ulrich, 1983a). The critical thrust of this approach requires that the interventionist apply critique both within a set of norms, and against the norms themselves, making the critique self-reflective or 'practical' in Kantian terminology. This involves surfacing the values or norms that underlie the position taken or judgments made. A dialectical approach is seen to be essential here, the purpose of the dialectic (Ulrich, 1983a, p. 289) being to bring together all participants in the process through a discourse which surfaces their normative positions.

Within this research, as evidenced by the first question of Table 1, much of the focus has been on the *content* of an information security system, while the *material conditions* of that system have, it could be argued, been opened up to insufficient challenge. In other words, *context,* and particularly the need and potential to challenge that context, has not been given enough attention. This may ultimately prove to be our greatest difficulty in undertaking this work, but it is one which we see as essential to the success of the project.

CONCLUSIONS

A Kantian approach, together with the interpretations of it by critical thinkers, has led to our questioning the basis for a theory and practice of information security. Instrumental or theoretical reason, by focusing on producing *objective knowledge,* seems an impoverished view when compared with the insights generated through practical reason. Practical reason, with its critically informed search for that which *ought* to govern our social world, has the potential to free us from the rule-based traps we have fallen into.

It is proposed, therefore, that a critically normative approach to information security be developed, based on relevant social theoretical constructs, and focusing primarily on critical theory. The aim must be to build a system of information security based on a critically informed dialectic, where the normative content of the system, its boundaries and the material conditions within which it is presently perceived, are all open to challenge and debate. All those involved in and affected by the system of concern should participate, with an emphasis on information sharing rather than restricted access to information, and with the overall objective of determining what the system *ought to be*, not what it *is*.

This proposed journey from instrumental to practical reason as a basis for information security will be a long one, but our research has, we believe, demonstrated it to be worthy of further development. For our part, with the first phase of theoretical analysis now substantially complete, the immediate future will concentrate on designing a framework for information security, for use in empirical application. In terms of how this is to be achieved, the aim here is not to develop some new methodology, but rather to offer strategies and guidelines for the use of existing methodologies, methods and techniques. The next part of this project is therefore to apply these ideas to a range of methodologies, and from this develop critically informed guidelines for action.

REFERENCES

Brocklesby, J. and Cummings, S. (1996). Foucault plays Habermas: An alternative philosophical underpinning for critical systems thinking. *Journal of the Operational Research Society*, *47*(6), 741-754.

BSI. (1999a). *Code of Practice for Information Security Management: BS7799 Part 1*. London: British Standards Institute.

BSI. (1999b). *Specification for Information Security Management Systems: BS7799 Part 2*. London: British Standards Institute.

Burrell, G. and Morgan, G. (1979). *Sociological Paradigms and Organisational Analysis*. London: Heinemann.

Clarke, S. A. (1997). Critical complementarism and information systems: A total systems approach to computer-based information systems strategy and development. *Information Systems and Computing*. Uxbridge: Brunel.

Clarke, S. A. (2000). From socio-technical to critical complementarist: A new direction for information systems development. In Coakes, E., Lloyd-Jones, R. and Willis, D. (Eds.), *The New SocioTech: Graffiti on the Long Wall*, 61-72. London: Springer.

Clarke, S. A. and Lehaney, B. (1999a). Human centered research and practice in information systems. *Journal of End User Computing*, *11*(4), 3-4.

Clarke, S. A. and Lehaney, B. (1999b). Human-centred methods in information systems development: Is there a better way forward? *Managing Information Technology Resources in Organisations in the Next Millennium*. Hershey, PA: Idea Group Publishing.

Clarke, S. A. and Lehaney, B. (2000). Mixing methodologies for information systems development and strategy: A higher education case study. *Journal of the Operational Research Society*, *51*(5), 542-556.

Commission, A. (1998). *Ghost in the Machine: An Analysis of IT Fraud and Abuse*. London: Audit Commission.

DoD. (1987). *US Department of Defense Trusted Computer System Evaluation Criteria (The Orange Book)*. Washington DC, US Department of Defence.

Drake, P. (1998). *The Use of Information Security: Theory in Practice.* Cambridge: Anglia Business School.

EC. (1991). *Commission of the European Communities, European Information Technology Security Evaluation Criteria (ITSEC),* European Commission.

Flood, R. L. and Jackson, M. C. (Eds.). (1991). *Critical Systems Thinking: Directed Readings.* Chichester: John Wiley & Sons.

Gollman, D. (1999). *Computer Security.* Chichester: John Wiley & Sons.

Gregory, F. H. (1993). Soft systems methodology to information systems: A Wittgensteinian approach. *Journal of Information Systems, 3,* 149-168.

Habermas, J. (1976). On systematically distorted communication. *Inquiry, 13,* 205-218.

Habermas, J. (1987). *Lifeworld and System: A Critique of Functionalist Reason.* Boston, MA: Beacon Press.

Hirschheim, R. and Klein, H. K. (1989). Four paradigms of information systems development. *Communications of the ACM, 32*(10), 1199-1216.

Hirschheim, R. and Klein, H. K. (1991). Information systems development as social action: Theoretical perspective and practice. *Omega, 19*(6), 587-608.

Jackson, M. C. (2000). *Systems Approaches to Management.* New York, Kluwer/Plenum.

Kant, I. (1787). *Critique of Pure Reason.* London (1929): Macmillan.

Langford, D. (1995). *Practical Computer Ethics.* New York: McGraw-Hill.

Midgley, G. (1992). The sacred and profane in critical systems thinking. *Systems Practice, 5*(1), 5-16.

Mingers, J. (1997). Towards critical pluralism. In Mingers, J. and Gill, A. (Eds.), *Multimethodology: Towards Theory and Practice of Integrating Methodologies.* Chichester: John Wiley & Sons.

NCC. (1998). *NCC IT Security Breaches Survey.* London: National Computer Centre & Department of Trade & Industry.

Neumann, P. (1995). *Computer-Related Risks.* Reading, MA: Addison-Wesley.

Oliga, J. C. (1991). Methodological foundations of systems methodologies. In Flood, R. L. and Jackson, M. C. (Eds.), *Critical Systems Thinking: Directed Readings,* 159-184. Chichester: John Wiley & Sons.

Russell, D. G. (1991). *Computer Security Basics.* O'Reilley & Associates Inc.

Symonds, M. (1999). A survey of business and the Internet. *The Economist, Q1,* 240.

Ulrich, W. (1983a). *Critical Heuristics of Social Planning: A New Approach to Practical Philosophy.* Berne: Haupt.

Ulrich, W. (1983b). *The Itinerary of a Critical Approach*. Berne: Haupt.

Ulrich, W. (1988). Systems thinking, systems practice, and practical philosophy: A program of research. *Systems Practice, 1*(2), 137-163.

Ulrich, W. (1996). A primer to critical systems heuristics for action researchers. *Forum One: Action Research and Critical Systems Thinking*. Hull: University of Hull, Centre for Systems Studies.

Chapter XIII

Actor-Network Theory as a Socio-Technical Approach to Information Systems Research

Arthur Tatnall
Victoria University in Melbourne, Australia

ABSTRACT

An information system is a socio-technical discipline involving both human and non-human entities. Much of the research done in an information system context investigates changes caused by the introduction of new business or organisational system, or changes made to an existing system, and so can be regarded as research into aspects of technological innovation. Information systems are complex entities and their development is a complex undertaking. Research in information systems needs to take account of the complexity of information systems development rather than take steps to hide this. An approach to information systems research, based on actor-network theory, offers a good means of allowing impartial treatment of the contributions of both human and non-human actors, and of handling the complexities involved. This chapter outlines such an approach.

INTRODUCTION: INFORMATION SYSTEMS AS A SOCIO-TECHNICAL DISCIPLINE

In systems theory, a system is defined as a group of elements that are integrated with the purpose of achieving some common objective (Emery, 1969; Kendall & Kendall, 1992). An information system is a complex entity comprising computer hardware, software, people, procedures and data, integrated with the purpose of collecting, storing, processing, transmitting and displaying information (Tatnall, Davey, Burgess, Davison & Fisher, 2000). The dictionary defines something that is 'complex' as being characterised by a combination of interconnected parts, many of which may not be easily separable (Macquarie Library, 1981) and an information system certainly fits this definition (Bonnici & Warkentin, 1995; Agarwal, Krudys & Tanniru, 1997). Building an information system is a difficult task, partly due to the problem of ascertaining the requirements of the intended users, but also because of the complexity of the large number of human-machine interactions (Banville, 1991). This complexity is reflected in the difficulty of building these systems to operate free from error and to perform as intended (Thomsett, 1993).

The implementation of new information systems, or rebuilding of existing systems, should be considered as a process of innovation and seen through the lens of innovation theory. The dictionary defines innovation as "the alteration of what is established; something newly introduced" (Oxford, 1973), and "introducing new things or methods" (Macquarie Library, 1981). The word 'innovation' is considered to be synonymous with 'newness' and 'change' (Dutch, 1962), and an innovation can also be described as an idea that is perceived to be new to a particular person or group of people (Rogers, 1995). As the introduction or improvement of an information system in an organisation *necessarily* involves change, and as the system will always be seen as new by at least some of its users, whether it is acknowledged or not, information systems research often involves research into technological innovation.

The discipline of information systems (IS) is concerned with the ways people build and use computer-based systems to produce useful information, and so has to deal with issues involving both people and machines, and with the multitude of human and non-human entities that comprise an information system (Checkland, 1981). Information systems is neither merely a technical discipline nor a social one, but one that is truly socio-technical. Researchers in information systems face the problem of how to handle complexities due to interconnected combinations of computers, peripherals, procedures, operating systems, programming languages, software, data and many other inanimate objects–how they all relate to humans and human organisations, and how humans relate to them (Davis, Gorgone, Cougar, Feinstein & Longnecker, 1997).

This chapter will outline a socio-technical approach, based on actor-network theory (ANT), to researching how people interact with and use information systems. In actor-network theory the key is in using an approach that is neither purely social nor purely technical, but socio-technical.

QUALITATIVE RESEARCH TRADITIONS IN INFORMATION SYSTEMS

Each field of academic inquiry is characterised by its own preferred and commonly used research approaches and traditions. In information systems research Myers (1997) outlines four qualitative traditions as being particularly significant: case study research, ethnography, grounded theory and action research.

Case study research is, as Orlikowski and Baroudi (1991) point out, the most commonly used qualitative approach in information systems. As IS research topics commonly involve the study of organisational systems, they contend that a case study approach is often quite appropriate. Many case study researchers in information systems takes a positivist perspective (Benbasat, Goldstein & Mead, 1987; Lee, 1989; Yin, 1994), but some instead adopt an interpretive stance (Walsham, 1993, 1995) while others, like Kaplan (1988), advocate a middle course involving a combination of qualitative and quantitative methods.

Ethnography has grown in prominence as a suitable approach to information systems research after work such as that undertaken by Suchman (1987) and Zuboff (1988). It has been used especially in research where the emphasis is upon design, computer-supported cooperative work, studies of Internet and virtual communities, and information-related policies (Star, 1995).

Grounded theory is "an inductive, theory discovery methodology" (Martin & Turner, 1986) which seeks to develop theory that is grounded in data that is systematically gathered and analysed and involves "continuous interplay" between data and analysis (Myers, 1997). Orlikowski (1993) argues that in information systems research situations involving organisational change, a grounded theory approach can be useful as it allows a focus on "contextual and processual" elements as well as on the actions of key players.

Action research (Lewin, 1946) has been described as proceeding in a spiral of steps where each step consists of planning, action and evaluation of the result of the action. It is seen as aiming "... to contribute both to the practical concerns of people in an immediate problematic situation and to the goals of social science by joint collaboration within a mutually acceptable ethical framework" (Rapoport, 1970, p. 499). While action research has long been embraced in fields like organisational development and education (Kemmis & McTaggart, 1988), apart from a few notable exceptions in the work of scholars like Checkland and Scholes (1991) and Baskerville and Wood-Harper (1998), it has had less application in Information Systems (Myers, 1997). A variant of action research that is, however, slowly gaining acceptance in information systems is soft systems methodology.

Soft systems methodology (SSM), developed by Peter Checkland (1981, 1988; Checkland & Scholes, 1991) and his colleagues from Lancaster University, attempts to give due recognition to both the human and technological aspects of a system, and is claimed to be useful for the analysis of systems where technological processes and human activities are highly interdependent (Finegan, 1994). SSM acknowledges both human and non-human aspects of information systems, but considers these to be entirely separate types of entities. Although originally intended for the analysis of information systems, Rose (1997) contends that SSM has application as a social research tool, especially in situations where the focus is on organisational decision making. SSM has been explicitly identified by Checkland (1991) as an action research methodology. The basis of soft systems methodology is a comparison between the world as it is, and some models of the world as it might be (Dick, 1998). It attempts to keep these two worlds separate while ensuring an appropriate mapping between them (Wood-Harper, Corder, Wood & Watson, 1996). Although taking complex systems as its unit of analysis, its aim is to simplify these systems to a level where the 'essential ingredients' (Checkland, 1988) stand out and the less relevant details are removed or concealed.

PROBLEMS CAUSED BY ESSENTIALIST APPROACHES TO IS RESEARCH

A research approach often used in investigating innovations and new developments in information systems is to focus on the technical aspects of the change, and to treat 'the social' as the context in which its development and adoption take place (Tatnall & Gilding, 1999). Approaches of this type assume that outcomes of technological change are attributable to the 'technological' rather than the 'social' (Grint & Woolgar, 1997). At the other extreme, social determinism holds that relatively stable social categories can be used to explain technological change (Law & Callon, 1988) and concentrates on the investigation of social interactions, relegating the technology to context–to something that can be bundled up and forgotten.

This bundling means that fixed and unproblematic properties or 'essences' can then be assigned to the technology and used in any explanation of change. While initially appealing, the problem with an approach like this is that it can lead to a simplistic explanation that fails to reveal the true complexities of the situation under investigation. For instance, suppose that an IS researcher was investigating the uptake of a business-to-business eCommerce Portal developed by a local government authority for use by local businesses within a regional area. Using an essentialist approach to the research, the researcher may begin by outlining all the characteristics of eCommerce portals and all the advantages and problems with their use, and then go on to suggest that the adoption, or rejection, of this technology by the local businesses was due largely to these characteristics. While this is likely to be partially true, it is unlikely to provide the complete explanation. The nature and size of each local business, the inter-business interactions they currently engage in, the vigour and persuasiveness with which the local government authority advocated the portal, and the backgrounds and interests of particular individuals in many of the local businesses are also likely to have had an important affect that would, most likely, be ignored by the essentialist approach.

Anti-essentialism, which Chagani (1998) names as a characteristic of postmodern scholarship, rejects the idea of categorisations like 'human nature' and denies the existence in human beings of essences, natures or any other universals that "place a grounded and constant meaning on existence" (Chagani, 1998, p. 2). An essentialist position, according to Haslam (1998), would have it that forms of human diversity–'human kinds' or 'social categories'–can be understood in ways that relate to the natural domain. In a rather biological way, different 'kinds of people' are then taken to have inherent, fixed, identity-determining essences, a view that few scholars now accept in relation to *humans*. Most of the essentialist versus anti-essentialist debate has been about the presence, or otherwise of essences in humans, but this debate has also been extended to *non-humans*. Grint and Woolgar (1997, p. 9) contend that most views of technology attribute an "essential inner core of technical characteristics" to the non-human elements, while portraying the human elements as secondary and transitory. Arguing for a social constructivist approach in which technology is attributed no influence that can be gauged independent of human explanation, they maintain that technology is best thought of as being constructed entirely through human interpretation.

Bromley (1997) argues that as long as 'technology' is seen as a distinct type of entity which is separate from 'society,' the question will always need to be asked "Does technology affect society or not?" One answer to this question is that it does, but this leads us to the technological determinist position of viewing technology as autonomous and as having some essential attributes that act externally to society. The other answer, that it does not, means that technology must be neutral and that individual humans must assign it their own values and decide on their own account how to use it.

ACTOR-NETWORK THEORY, A SOCIO-TECHNICAL RESEARCH APPROACH

Actor-network theory (ANT) considers both social and technical determinism to be flawed and proposes instead a socio-technical account (Callon & Latour, 1981, 1986; Law & Callon, 1988) in which neither social nor technical positions are privileged. In this socio-technical order nothing is purely social and nothing is purely technical (Law, 1991). What seems, on the surface, to be social is partly technical, and what may appear to be only technical is partly social. ANT deals with the social-technical divide by denying that purely technical or purely social relations are possible.

ANT asserts that the world is full of hybrid entities (Latour, 1993) containing both human and non-human elements. One could question, for instance, which of the contributions to a piece of software are due to some aspect of the computer hardware or the compiler and programming language tools, and which are the result of human interactions and the particular likes and preferences of the human programmer. Actor-network theory developed around problems associated with attempts to handle socio-technical 'imbroglios' (Latour, 1993) like electric cars (Callon, 1986a), scallop fishing (Callon, 1986b), Portuguese navigation (Law, 1987) and supersonic aircraft (Law & Callon, 1988) by regarding the world as heterogeneous (Chagani, 1998). ANT offers the notion of heterogeneity to describe projects such as the one described earlier in which a local government authority has engaged an Internet service provider (ISP) and a software company to build a business-to-business eCommerce portal for use by local businesses within a regional area. The project will involve not just these entities, but also non-human entities such as computers, computer programs, data storage devices, modems and telephone lines, and human entities including local business proprietors from small and large businesses, customers, programmers and local council staff. The utilisation of heterogeneous entities (Bijker, Hughes & Pinch, 1987) then avoids questions of: "Is it social?" or "Is it technical?" as missing the point, which should be: "Is this association stronger or weaker than that one?" (Latour, 1988, p. 27).

Latour contends that a major difficulty in considering how technology and society interact is the lack of suitable words, as long as we consider the two as acting separately. He argues that this dividing line should be abandoned in our consideration of the contributions of human and non-human actors. "Contrary to the claims of those who want to hold either the state of technology or that of society constant, it is possible to consider a path of an innovation in which *all the actors* co-evolve" (Latour, 1991, p. 117).

Information systems researchers using an ANT approach would concentrate on issues of network formation, investigating the human and non-human alliances and networks built up by the actors involved. They would concentrate on the negotiations that allow the network to be configured by the enrollment of both human and non-human allies, and would consider any supposed characteristics of the system only as network effects resulting from association. In actor-network theory interactions and associations between actors and networks are all important, and actors are seen simply as the sum of their interactions with other actors and networks.

In the case of the business-to-business portal, an actor-network researcher would begin by identifying some of the important actors, starting perhaps with the local government portal project manager. An interview with the project manager would reveal why the project was instigated and identify some of the other actors. The main advice on method suggested by the proponents of actor-network theory is to "follow the actors" (Callon, 1986a; Latour, 1996) and let them set the framework and limits of the study themselves, and one line of inquiry resulting from the interview with the project manager might be to approach the portal software designer and programmers. Another set of actors is the proprietors of the local businesses themselves, and the project manager may suggest some 'business champions' to interview first. At least some of these business people might then point to the influence exerted by the computer hardware or software as a significant factor, so identifying some non-human actors. From this point on the key is to follow the actors, both human and non-human, searching out interactions, negotiations, alliances and networks. Negotiations between actors must be carefully investigated. Apart from the obvious human-to-human kind of negotiation, human-to-non-human interactions must also be included such as the business people trying to work out how the portal operates, and how to adapt this technology to be most suitable for their own business purposes. The process of adopting and implementing the portal can now be seen as the complex set of interactions that it is, and not just the inevitable result of the innate characteristics of this technology.

HOW ACTOR-NETWORK THEORY HANDLES COMPLEXITY

Longenecker et al. (1994, p. 175) suggest that computer-based information systems should be regarded as complex socio-technical entities, begging the question of how this complexity should be handled. A common method of handling complexity in all subject areas lies in simplification, but the danger with simplification is that it runs the risk of removing just those things that constitute a useful description of the phenomenon under investigation by concealing the parts played by many of the actors (Suchman, 1987). Of course some simplification is necessary in order to represent the infinite possibilities of any complex situation, and all research methodologies offer ways of simplifying complex social phenomena. The question here is which details to include and which to leave out, and who is to decide. In this respect, an appropriate research approach needs to ensure that complexities are not lost "in the process of labelling" (Law, 1999, p. 9).

In actor-network theory the extent of a network is determined by actors that are able to make their presence *individually felt* (Law, 1987) by other actors. The definition of an actor requires this and means that, in practice, actors limit their associations to affect only a relatively small number of entities whose attributes are well defined within the network (Callon, 1987). This simplification is only possible if no new entities appear to complicate things, as the actor-network is the context in which the significance and limitations of each simplified entity is defined (Callon, 1986a). If a new element is added, or if one is removed, then some of the other associations may be changed as it is the juxtaposition of actors within the network that is all-important.

An actor is not just a 'point object' but an association of heterogeneous elements, themselves constituting a network. Each actor is thus also a simplified network (Law, 1992). In an object-oriented programming environment, each component of the computer program can be considered as an object (Parsons & Wand, 1997) with its own properties, methods and actions. In common with the encapsulation of objects in object-oriented environments, the actors, or 'heterogeneous entities' (Bijker, Hughes et al., 1987), encountered in actor-network theory have attributes and methods and may themselves be composed of other objects or actors. So, when looked into carefully, an actor itself consists of a network of interactions and associations.

An actor can, however, in many ways also be considered as a 'black box' (Callon, 1986a), and when we open the lid of the box to look inside, it will be seen to constitute a whole network of other, perhaps complex, associations. In many cases details of what constitutes an actor–details of its network–are a complication we can avoid having to deal with all the time. We can usually consider the entity just as an actor, but when doing this it must be remembered that behind each actor there hide other actors that it has, more or less effectively, drawn together, or 'black-boxed' (Callon, 1987). This means that any changes affect not just this actor, but also the networks it simplifies.

In the same way a network may be simplified or 'punctualised' (Law, 1992) to look like a single point actor. Law notes that if a network is punctualised in this way to be seen as a single block, it disappears and is replaced by the action itself and the "seemingly simple author of that action" (Law, 1992, p. 385). The entry of new actors, desertion of existing actors or changes in alliances can cause the black boxes of networked actors to be opened and their contents reconsidered. A network relies on the maintenance of its simplifications for its continued existence. These simplifications are under constant challenge and if they break down the network will collapse, perhaps to re-form in a different configuration as a different network.

When investigating the eCommerce portal it might be convenient, most of the time, to consider both the ISP and the portal software to constitute a black box. This would mean that this aspect of the technology could then be considered as just a single actor–the portal, and its interactions with other actors investigated on this basis. At other times it might be necessary to lift the lid of the black box and investigate the enclosed network of the ISP, telephone lines, computers, data storage, programmers and interface designers it contains. The advantage of black-boxing though is that most of the time, however, the portal can be regarded as just another actor.

The important thing to note about the use of black-boxing for simplification is that the complexity is not just put into the black box and lost, as it is always possible, and indeed necessary, to periodically reopen the black box to investigate its contents. The complexity is punctualised (Law, 1992, p. 385), but not lost. It is often useful to simplify a network that acts as a 'single block' and view it as an actor. This makes it easier to deal with. An actor then: "... can be compared to a black-box that contains a network of black-boxes that depend on one another both for their proper functioning and for the proper functioning of the network" (Callon, 1987, p. 95).

USING ACTOR-NETWORK THEORY IN INFORMATION SYSTEMS RESEARCH

The next section will look at examples of how actor-network theory can be used in the analysis of situations involving the use of information systems and technology in a social context.

Structured Systems Analysis and Design in a UK City Council

A study by Kautz and McMaster (1994) deals with the failure of a City Council in the UK to adopt a structured approach as its systems development methodology (SSADM). The City Council investigated was a large organisation with more than 35,000 staff. The case study concerned only the Development Section of the Council's IT Unit, headed by a Chief Development Officer (CDO). In the Development Section the staff were organised into teams responsible for the development and maintenance of their client department's systems. These teams were typically led by a systems analyst and were made up of senior and junior programmers.

In 1988, partly in response to dissatisfaction with the services provided by the Development Section, the CDO decided that the Unit would adopt SSADM. She promoted this to all the Chief Officers and other key figures from client departments as the answer to all of their problems. The Unit undertook the necessary training and procured a CASE tool ready for the initial pilot implementation. Unfortunately nothing went right after this time, and considerable problems were experienced with the introduction of SSADM. In particular, the development staff resisted this innovation which eventually had to be abandoned.

The key to technology transfer from the ANT viewpoint is the creation of a powerful enough consortium of actors' interests to carry through the innovation. The problem here can thus be attributed to the failure of the CDO to create a strong and stable enough network of alliances to carry it through.

The key actors in the implementation were users, IT development staff and IT projects. In relation to the non-human IT projects, ANT suggests that it does not really matter whether we look at these non-human actors or at the people involved in them since these constitute an inseparable 'socio-technical imbroglio' (Latour, 1993). The CDO attempted to gain the support of users, and draw them into the network, by arguing that the new methodology would overcome problems of late delivery and low quality. She attempted to gain the support of the developers by arguing that SSADM would help them cope with applications backlog by increasing productivity. The non-human projects were enlisted with the argument that SSADM offers a way of improving project management and documentation quality. The project failed because the Chief Development Officer did not manage to get the cooperation of each of these groups, and in particular the developers, who resisted the idea that SSADM was the answer to their problems.

Adoption of a Film Slide Scanner by a Small Publishing Company

DP Pty Ltd is a small publishing company where four people work on the publication of information systems textbooks, doing much of the writing themselves, and all of the work involved in publication of their books (Tatnall, 2002). Most of DP's print runs are quite small and so the company makes use of a printer with access to Xerox printing technology rather than offset printing. Several years ago DP decided to improve the appearance of its textbook covers, and a number of options were considered until someone thought of using a photograph as the cover background. Company expertise in computer graphics was not high, so the brother of one of the directors, who was a professional landscape photographer, was asked to assist by supplying a photograph. The photograph chosen for the new book was supplied in printed form and a problem arose in trying to work out how to convert it into a suitable format for the cover so that it could incorporate the cover text. A digital image seemed to be the answer, and the photograph was scanned using a flat-bed scanner and the image imported into a PDF file ready for printing.

Today the company makes use of a Nikon LS-2000 slide and negative scanner, considerably improving the quality of the book covers, but also making the process of producing them much simpler. The question that must now be asked is "Why did DP decide to adopt this particular item of technology?" A simple explanation might suggest that the directors of the company examined the characteristics of slide and negative scanners and selected the Nikon as the best suited to their requirements. While this explanation is not incorrect, interviews with the directors show that it reveals only a part of the story.

An actor-network analysis (Tatnall, 2002) of this acquisition provides much more insight into why the slide and negative scanner was adopted. The ANT analysis sees the existence of a socio-technical network consisting of the publishing company personnel, their families, their computers and their books, and how this was destabilised by the need to find a new way of producing book covers. The addition of a new actor, the landscape photographer, introduced new possibilities that worked to further destabilise this network. The slide scanner, also seen as an actor seeking to enter the network, offered new possibilities in which existing and future slides and negatives could easily be turned into digital images. It was also apparent that *any* of the directors' old slides and negatives could easily be turned into digital images, not just those required for book covers. As well as producing book covers, both directors quickly saw advantages in a device that could also easily convert the old slides and negatives they had, over the years, each taken of their children and of their holidays, into digital format. The latter reason was the decisive one, and thus it was a combination of factors, some business-related but others rather more personal, that led to the adoption of this technology.

Adoption of Visual Basic in the Curriculum of an Australian University

An actor-network analysis of how an Australian university incorporated the programming language Visual Basic into its information systems curriculum (Tatnall, 2000; Tatnall & Davey, 2001) uncovered a complex web of human and non-human interactions. It might appear that the adoption of a programming language into a university curriculum would be a simple process of university academics evaluating possible candidate languages on behalf of the IS Department, and then choosing the one that best fit the requirements of the course. The situation in the university studied, however, turned out to be much more complex.

The story begins with the intersection of two networks: a consulting network and a university curriculum network. Fred, an academic at the university, had been working with his son on a small consulting job involving graphics programming, and had discovered that Visual Basic (VB) proved to be an ideal tool for this job. Back at the university Fred now sought to incorporate VB into one of the subjects he taught. What he needed was a screen prototyping tool, not a programming language. It was by using *only some features* of VB, what ANT calls 'translation' (Callon, 1986b), that he was able to fit it to his needs. By undergoing another translation VB was also able to be used in an elective operating systems programming subject.

Before Visual Basic could move further into the curriculum mainstream, however, there had to be negotiations with two programming languages that already had established places. One of these languages was Pick Basic that had been used as the main vehicle for the teaching of introductory programming for some years. In ANT terms Visual Basic needed to negotiate with Pick Basic for its place in the curriculum. In other terms this could be seen as VB's proponents negotiating with the advocates of Pick Basic, but it is really rather more than this. Inside Pick Basic's black box, its network includes not just Pick Basic itself and its human advocates, but also its industry supporters and the companies that employ the university's graduates in Pick positions. The true complexity of the situation now begins to become apparent as a new actor, Visual Basic, engages with an existing actor, Pick Basic, to fight for a place in the curriculum.

LIMITATIONS AND CRITICISMS OF ACTOR-NETWORK THEORY

There are several main criticisms of actor-network theory. To begin, there is the criticism (Grint & Woolgar, 1997) that it is not always sufficiently clear where the boundaries of a network lie or whose account of a network is to be taken as definitive. Grint and Woolgar (1997) note that the analyst's story seems to depend on a description of the 'actual' network as if this was objectively available. Radder (1992) expresses some concern with what he sees as the goal orientation of ANT: its tendency to look towards stabilisation, black-boxing, and control. He asks of the nature of the stabilisation process, and questions from whose point of view it is seen, pointing out a tendency in ANT to look at things from the viewpoint of the 'winners'–the successful actors. He argues that a bias to do this is built into ANT's definition of an actor as: "... any element which bends space around itself, makes other elements dependent upon itself and translates their will into a language of its own" (Callon & Latour, 1981, p. 283, quoted from Radder, 1992, p. 181). Under this definition, Radder contends, there are only winning actors.

A second criticism relates to ANT's treatment of non-human actors. A critique by Collins and Yearley (1992) claims that in giving an autonomous voice to 'things,'

ANT concedes too much to realist and technical accounts. In reply, Callon and Latour (1992) claim that technological artefacts are implicated in the very fabric of the social and are "social relations viewed in their durability and cohesion" (Singleton & Michael, 1993, p. 231). Also in relation to its treatment of human and non-human actors, Lee and Brown (1994) propose that actor-network theory's very liberalism and democracy mean that it has no 'Other.' Whereas much of sociology has put anything non-human or non-social outside its disciplinary boundaries and made it 'Other,' ANT has not. They assert that ANT's success in challenging the human/non-human dualism puts it at risk of: "... stretching the Nietzschean world view and the discourse of liberal democracy to cover every-thing" (Lee & Brown, 1994, p. 774), and in doing so risk the production of "yet another ahistorical grand narrative and the concomitant right to speak for all" (Lee & Brown, 1994, p. 774).

Thirdly, Grint and Woolgar (1997) argue that ANT retains a degree of residual technicism in its need to sometimes refer to 'actual' technical capacities of a technology. They quote Callon's (1986a) analysis of the attempts at building a French electric car, in which they claim that he makes reference to the 'unfortunate tendency' of the catalysts to become quickly contaminated. They note that the anti-essentialist approach of actor-network theory would point to this 'actual property' being treated as a construction. Despite these minor reservations, however, Grint and Woolgar note that actor-network theory points to the possibility of an understanding of technology that does not rely on the presence of a "god within the machine."

CONCLUSION

In this chapter I have argued that information systems is a socio-technical discipline involving both human and non-human entities, and that information systems implementations are complex activities almost inevitably involving some form of technological innovation. I have also argued that simplistic views of how information systems are built, implemented and used often conceal important interactions between human and non-human actors and so give a less than complete picture of what has happened.

A simplistic view of the eCommerce portal would have it that businesses made the adoption primarily because of the portal's characteristics, and would miss other influences due to inter-business interactions and the backgrounds of the people involved. In the case of the UK City Council, it would be difficult to see why SSADM, a methodology that seemed perfectly suitable to their needs, had failed. It is only when an ANT study of all the entities involved is undertaken that the failure of the CDO to build a durable network of associations becomes apparent. The reasons behind the publishing company's acquisition of a slide and negative scanner become clear when an ANT analysis identifies all the actors, and shows that an important reason for the adoption had nothing to do with the business itself. It only became apparent when the black box representing the directors' personal lives was opened. Finally, the ANT study into the incorporation of Visual Basic into a university curriculum illustrated this to be an extremely complex process of negotiations between academics and non-human actors such as programming languages, and one in which Visual Basic was adopted not in its original form, but after being translated into several different forms that proved suitable for the subjects where it was used.

An actor-network approach avoids the need to consider the social and the technical, and thus human and non-human actors, in different ways. I contend that highlighting how the human and non-human actors involved in socio-technical situations, such as the building and use of information systems, interact with each other is an important benefit of adopting an ANT research framework. In showing how these interactions may lead to the formations of stable networks, actor-network theory offers a useful way to handle the complexity of such studies.

REFERENCES

Agarwal, R., Krudys, G. and Tanniru, M. (1997). Infusing learning into the information systems organization. *European Journal of Information Systems*, 6(1), 25-40.

Banville, C. (1991). A study of legitimacy as a social dimension of organizational information systems. In Nissen, H. E., Klein, H. K. and Hirschheim, R. (Eds.), *Information Systems Research: Contemporary Approaches and Emergent Traditions*, 107-129. Amsterdam: Elsevier Science Publications.

Baskerville, R. L. and Wood-Harper, T. (1998). Diversity in information systems action research methods. *European Journal of Information Systems*, 7(2), 90-107.

Benbasat, I., Goldstein, D. K. and Mead, M. (1987). The case study strategy in studies of information systems. *MIS Quarterly*, 11(3), 369-386.

Bijker, W. E., Hughes, T. P. and Pinch, T. J. (Eds.). (1987). *The Social Construction of Technological Systems: New Directions in the Sociology and History of Technology*. Cambridge, MA: MIT Press.

Bonnici, J. and Warkentin, M. (1995). Revisited: Fabbri and Mann's criticism of the DPMA model curriculum. *Journal of Computer Information Systems*, 35(3), 96-98.

Bromley, H. (1997). The social chicken and the technological egg: Educational computing and the technology/society divide. *Educational Theory*, *47*(1), 51-63.

Callon, M. (1986a). The sociology of an actor-network: The case of the electric vehicle. In Callon, M., Law, J. and Rip, A. (Eds.), *Mapping the Dynamics of Science and Technology*, 19-34. London: Macmillan Press.

Callon, M. (1986b). Some elements of a sociology of translation: Domestication of the scallops and the fishermen of St. Brieuc Bay. In Law, J. (Ed.), *Power, Action & Belief. A New Sociology of Knowledge?* 196-229. London: Routledge & Kegan Paul.

Callon, M. (1987). Society in the making: The study of technology as a tool for sociological analysis. In Bijker, W. E., Hughes, T. P. and Pinch, T. J. (Eds.), *The Social Construction of Technological Systems*, 85-103. Cambridge, MA: The MIT Press.

Callon, M. and Latour, B. (1981). Unscrewing the big leviathan: How actors macro-structure reality and how sociologists help them to do so. In Knorr-Centina, K. and Cicourel, A. V. (Eds.), *Advances in Social Theory and Methodology: Toward an Integration of Micro and Macro-Sociologies*, 277-303. London: Routledge & Kegan Paul.

Callon, M. and Latour, B. (1992). Don't throw the baby out with the bath school: A reply to Collins and Yearley. In Pickering, A. (Ed.), *Science as Practice and Culture*, 343-368. Chicago, IL: Chicago University Press.

Chagani, F. (1998). Postmodernism: Rearranging the furniture of the universe. *Irreverence*, *1*(3), 1-3.

Checkland, P. (1981). *Systems Thinking, Systems Practice*. Chichester: John Wiley & Sons.

Checkland, P. (1991). From framework through experience to learning: The essential nature of action research. In Nissen, H. E., Klein, H. K. and A., H. R. *Information Systems Research: Contemporary Approaches and Emergent Traditions*, 397-403. Amsterdam: North-Holland.

Checkland, P. and Scholes, J. (1991). *Soft Systems Methodology in Action*. Chichester: John Wiley & Sons.

Checkland, P. B. (1988). Soft systems methodology: An overview. *Journal of Applied Systems Analysis*, (15), 27-30.

Collins, H. M. and Yearley, S. (1992). Epistemological chicken. In Pickering, A. (Ed.), *Science as Practice and Culture*, 301-326. Chicago, IL: Chicago University Press.

Davis, G. B., Gorgone, J. T., Cougar, J. D., Feinstein, D. L. and Longnecker, H. E. J. (1997). *IS '97 Model Curriculum and Guidelines for Undergraduate*

Degree Programs in Information Systems. USA, Association for Information Technology Professionals.

Dick, B. (1998). Soft systems methodology. *Action Research and Evaluation on Line*. http://www.scu.edu.au/schools/sawd/areol/areol_session13, October 11.

Dutch, R. A. (Ed.). (1962). *Roget's Thesaurus*. London: Longman.

Emery, F. E. (Ed.). (1969). *Systems Thinking*. Middlesex: Penguin.

Finegan, A. (1994). *Soft Systems Methodology: An Alternative Approach to Knowledge Elicitation in Complex and Poorly Defined Systems*. http://www.csu.edu.au/ci/vol1/Andrew.Finegan/paper.html, November 15, RMIT Centre for Remote Sensing and Land Information.

Grint, K. and Woolgar, S. (1997). *The Machine at Work–Technology, Work and Organisation*. Cambridge, MA: Polity Press.

Haslam, N. O. (1998). Natural kinds, human kinds, and essentialism. *Social Research*, *65*(2), 291-314.

Kaplan, B. and Duchon, D. (1988). Combining qualitative and quantitative methods in information systems research: A case study. *MIS Quarterly*, *12*(4), 571-586.

Kautz, K. and McMaster, T. (1994). Structured methods: An undelivered promise? *Scandinavian Journal of Information Systems*, *6*(2).

Kemmis, S. and McTaggart, R. (1988). *The Action Research Reader*. Geelong: Deakin University Press.

Kendall, K. E. and Kendall, J. E. (1992). *Systems Analysis and Design*. Englewood Cliffs, NJ: Prentice Hall.

Latour, B. (1986). The powers of association. In Law, J. (Ed.), *Power, Action and Belief. A New Sociology of Knowledge? Sociological Review Monograph 32*, 264-280. London: Routledge & Kegan Paul.

Latour, B. (1988). The prince for machines as well as for machinations. In Elliott, B. (Ed.), *Technology and Social Process*, 20-43. Edinburgh, UK: Edinburgh University Press.

Latour, B. (1991). Technology is society made durable. In Law, J. (Ed.), *A Sociology of Monsters. Essays on Power, Technology and Domination*, 103-131. London: Routledge.

Latour, B. (1993). *We Have Never Been Modern*. Hemel Hempstead: Harvester Wheatsheaf.

Latour, B. (1996). *Aramis or the Love of Technology*. Cambridge, MA: Harvard University Press.

Law, J. (1987). Technology and heterogeneous engineering: The case of Portuguese expansion. In Bijker, W. E., Hughes, T. P. and Pinch, T. J. (Eds.), *The Social Construction of Technological Systems: New Directions in the Sociology and History of Technology*, 111-134. Cambridge, MA: MIT Press.

Law, J. (1991). Introduction: Monsters, machines and sociotechnical relations. In Law, J. (Ed.), *A Sociology of Monsters: Essays on Power, Technology and Domination*. London: Routledge.

Law, J. (1992). Notes on the theory of the actor-network: Ordering, strategy and heterogeneity. *Systems Practice, 5*(4), 379-393.

Law, J. (1999). After ANT: Complexity, naming and topology. In Law, J. and Hassard, J. (Eds.), *Actor Network Theory and After*, 1-14. Oxford: Blackwell Publishers.

Law, J. and Callon, M. (1988). Engineering and sociology in a military aircraft project: A network analysis of technological change. *Social Problems, 35*(3), 284-297.

Lee, A. S. (1989). A scientific methodology for MIS case studies. *MIS Quarterly, 13*(1), 33-50.

Lee, N. and Brown, S. (1994). Otherness and the actor network: The undiscovered continent. *American Behavioral Scientist, 37*(6), 772-790.

Lewin, K. (1946). Action research and minority problems. *Journal of Social Issues*, (2), 34-46.

Longenecker, H. E. J., Feinstein, D. L., Couger, J. D., David, G. G. and Gorgone, J. T. (1994). Information systems '95: A summary of the collaborative IS curriculum specification of the Joint DPMA, ACM, AIS Task Force. *Journal of Information Systems Education*, (Winter), 174-186.

Macquarie Library. (1981). *The Macquarie Dictionary*. Sydney: Macquarie Library.

Martin, P. Y. and Turner, B. A. (1986). Grounded theory and organizational research. *The Journal of Applied Behavioral Science, 22*(2), 141-157.

Myers, M. D. (1997). Qualitative research in information systems. http://misq.org /misqd961/isworld/, May 20, *MIS Quarterly*.

Orlikowski, W. J. (1993). CASE tools as organizational change: Investigating incremental and radical changes in systems development. *MIS Quarterly, 17*(3), 1-28.

Orlikowski, W. J. and Baroudi, J. J. (1991). Studying information technology in organizations: Research approaches and assumptions. *Information Systems Research, 2*(1), 1-28.

Oxford. (1973). *The Shorter Oxford English Dictionary*. Oxford: Clarendon Press.

Parsons, J. and Wand, Y. (1997). Using objects for systems analysis. *Communications of the ACM, 40*(12), 104-110.

Radder, H. (1992). Normative reflexions on constructivist approaches to science and technology. *Social Studies of Science, 22*(1), 141-173.

Rapoport, R. N. (1970). Three dilemmas in action research. *Human Relations, 23*(4), 449-513.

Rogers, E. M. (1995). *Diffusion of Innovations*. New York: The Free Press.

Rose, J. (1997). Soft systems methodology as a social science research tool. *Systems Research and Behavioral Science, 14*, 249-258.

Singleton, V. and Michael, M. (1993). Actor-networks and ambivalence: General practitioners in the UK cervical screening programme. *Social Studies of Science, 23*, 227-264.

Star, S. L. (1995). *The Cultures of Computing*. Oxford: Blackwell Publishers.

Suchman, L. A. (1987). *Plans and Situated Actions. The Problem of Human-Machine Communication*. Cambridge, MA: Cambridge University Press.

Tatnall, A. (2000). Innovation and change in the information systems curriculum of an Australian university: A socio-technical perspective. *PhD Thesis*, Education. Rockhampton, Central Queensland University.

Tatnall, A. (2002). Modelling technological change in small business: Two approaches to theorising innovation. In Burgess, S. (Ed.), *Managing Information Technology in Small Business: Challenges and Solutions*. Hershey, PA: Idea Group Publishing.

Tatnall, A. and Davey, B. (2001). *How Visual Basic Entered the Curriculum at an Australian University: An Account Informed by Innovation Translation*. Challenges to Informing Clients: A Transdisciplinary Approach (Informing Science2001), Krakow, Poland.

Tatnall, A., Davey, B., Burgess, S., Davison, A. and Fisher, J. (2000). *Management Information Systems–Concepts, Issues, Tools and Applications*. Melbourne: Data Publishing.

Tatnall, A. and Gilding, A. (1999). Actor-network theory and information systems research. *10th Australasian Conference on Information Systems (ACIS)*, Wellington, Victoria University of Wellington.

Thomsett, R. (1993). *Third Wave Project Management: A Handbook for Managing the Complex Information Systems for the 1990s*. Englewood Cliffs, NJ: Prentice Hall.

Walsham, G. (1993). *Interpreting Information Systems in Organizations*. Chichester: John Wiley & Sons.

Walsham, G. (1995). Interpretive case studies in IS research: Nature and method. *European Journal of Information Systems*, (4), 74-91.

Wood-Harper, A. T., Corder, S., Wood, J. R. G. and Watson, H. (1996). How we profess: The ethical systems analyst. *Communications of the ACM, 39*(3), 69-80.

Yin, R. K. (1994). *Case Study Research, Design and Methods*. Newbury Park, CA: Sage Publications.

Zuboff, S. (1988). *In the Age of the Smart Machine*. New York: Basic Books.

Final Thoughts

It is now almost two years since this book project began, with a meeting of the editors during the May 2000 IRMA Conference in Anchorage, Alaska. The objective has not wavered from the original intent to source a variety of global contributions, which would represent a range of viewpoints on the social, technical and cognitive issues within information management. Whatever success you, as readers, consider to have been achieved is due entirely to the exceptionally high quality of the submissions received, and for this we, as editors, are indebted to all contributors.

In one text, even of 13 chapters, all we can hope is that we have been able to represent some of the key issues currently seen to be important. The final verdict, however, must rest with you, the readers, and we will be happy to receive any comments which you feel may help in furthering our understanding of the domain. At the very least, with your help, the next compilation of edited chapters on this subject will be more representative of current practices and theories.

Steve Clarke, Elayne Coakes, Gordon Hunter and Andrew Wenn
Editors.

Please forward any comments in the first instance to the editors via:

Professor Steve Clarke
University of Luton Business School
Department of Finance, Systems and Operations
Park Square
Luton
LU1 3JU
United Kingdom

Email: Steve.Clarke@Luton.ac.uk

About the Authors

Steve Clarke received a BSc in Economics from The University of Kingston Upon Hull, an MBA from the Putteridge Bury Management Centre, The University of Luton, and a PhD in human centred approaches to information systems development from Brunel University–all in the United Kingdom. He is Professor of Management Systems at the University of Luton. Dr. Clarke has extensive experience in management systems and information systems consultancy and research, focusing primarily on the identification and satisfaction of user needs and issues connected with knowledge management. His research interests include: social theory and information systems practice, strategic planning, and the impact of user involvement in the development of management systems. Major current research is focused on approaches informed by critical social theory.

Elayne Coakes is a Senior Lecturer in Business Information Management at the Westminster Business School, University of Westminster, teaching mainly in the Strategies for Information Management and eBusiness fields. She received a BA in Public Administrative from Sheffield Polytechnic and an MSc in Information Systems from Brunel University in the UK. Her PhD (also under completion at Brunel) is concerned with the problem of boundary designation and stakeholders for the Strategic Information Systems Planning process. Her research interests lie in the socio-technical aspects of information systems. She is also involved in a research group, at Westminster, looking at Knowledge Management. As well as co-editing a number of books, she has also published a number of conference papers and articles in journals such as *Information and Management*, *Management Decision*, *CAIS*, *Engineering Requirements*, as well as several chapters in books.

M. Gordon Hunter is currently an Associate Professor in Information Systems in the Faculty of Management at The University of Lethbridge. He has previously held academic positions at universities in Canada, Hong Kong and Singapore. He has held visiting positions at universities in Germany, USA and New Zealand. He has a Bachelor of Commerce degree from the University of Saskatchewan in Saskatoon, Saskatchewan, Canada. He received his doctorate from Strathclyde Business School, University of Strathclyde in Glasgow, Scotland. Dr. Hunter has also obtained a Certified Management Accountant (CMA) designation from the

Society of Management Accountants of Canada. He is a member of the British Computer Society and the Canadian Information Processing Society (CIPS), where he has obtained an Information Systems Professional (ISP) designation. He has extensive experience as a systems analyst and manager in industry and government organizations in Canada. Dr. Hunter is an Associate Editor of the *Journal of Global Information Management*. He is the Canadian World Representative for the *Information Resource Management Association*. He serves on the editorial board of the *Journal of Global Information Technology Management* and the *Journal of Information Technology Cases and Application*. He has conducted seminar presentations in Canada, USA, Asia, New Zealand, Australia and Europe. His current research interests relate to the productivity of systems analysts with emphasis upon the personnel component, including cross-cultural aspects, and the effective development of information systems.

Andrew Wenn is a Lecturer in the School of Information Systems at Victoria University of Technology, Melbourne and is currently undertaking his PhD in the History and Philosophy of Science Department at the University of Melbourne. His main field of research is nexus between the social and the technical, particularly in the area of global information systems. Mr. Wenn has a number of publications in this area as well as in the area of Internet-based education and ecommerce and small businesses in Australia. He has recently been appointed to the Editorial Review Board, *Information Resources Management Journal*, and is currently editing another book, *Skilling the Electronic Commerce Professional* to be published in late 2002.

***

Michael Arnold is a Lecturer in the Department of History and Philosophy of Science at the University of Melbourne, where he teaches and writes about a variety of subjects relating to digital technologies in the social context. He completed a PhD at Deakin University with a thesis entitled, "Educational Cybernetics: Communication and Control with and of Logo," and he retains an interest in educational technologies. His current research, though, involves an examination of technologies employed in the context of residential communities, and in the context of urban development. He may be contacted at mvarnold@unimelb.edu.au.

David Avison is Professor of Information Systems at ESSEC Business School, Paris, France, after being Professor at the School of Management at Southampton University for nine years. He is also Visiting Professor at the University Technology,

Sydney, Australia, and Brunel University in England. He is joint editor of Blackwell Science's *Information Systems Journal*. He is also joint editor of the McGraw-Hill series of texts in information systems. So far, 18 books are to his credit (plus one translation from the French) as well as a large number of papers in learned journals, edited texts and conference papers. He is Chair of the International Federation of Information Processing (IFIP) 8.2 group on the impact of IS/IT on organisations, and was past President of the UK Academy for Information Systems and past chair of UK Professors and Heads of Information Systems. He has been joint programme chair of the International Conference in Information Systems in Atlanta, programme chair of the IFIP conference in Amsterdam, panels chair for the European Conference in Information Systems at Copenhagen, publicity chair for the entity-relationship conference in Paris, and chair of several other UK and European conferences. He also acts as consultant and has most recently worked with a leading manufacturer developing their IT/IS strategy. He researches on information systems in their natural setting, in particular using action research, though he has also used a number of other qualitative research approaches.

Aileen Cater-Steel is a Senior Lecturer in the Department of Information Systems of the Faculty of Business and Commerce at USQ Toowoomba, Australia. Prior to this, she worked in the IT industry on the Gold Coast, as IT Manager at the Gold Coast Institute of TAFE and at the Gold Coast City Council for 17 years, first as programmer, then analyst, project leader and EUC Support Manager. Having completed a Master's of Information Technology degree at USQ, she is now undertaking a PhD with the Australian Software Quality Research Institute at Griffith University (Brisbane, Australia).

Sandra Cormack is currently the Information Technology Manager at Lismore City Council in Northern New South Wales, Australia. She has extensive IT industry experience, gained from managing a diverse range of projects, and also from managing the IT function in a number of smaller organisations. Her skills also include business process reengineering. Ms. Cormack has recently completed her Master's in Information Technology with the University of Southern Queensland. Her specific area of interest was improving the IT-business relationship through cultural awareness.

Neil F. Doherty gained his PhD in software engineering from the University of Bradford, following many years practical experience as a programmer, systems analyst and project manager. He is currently a Senior Lecturer in Information Systems in the Business School at Loughborough University. His research interests include the treatment of organisational issues in systems development projects, success and failure in systems development projects, strategic information systems planning, and the uptake and application of e-commerce.

Paul Drake is Director of Security Services for GlaxoSmithKline PLC. In this role he has global responsibility for virus management, perimeter defence, intrusion detection, incident management and investigations. Principal activities include a full range of information security issues from strategy formulation through setting of run-time policies to full accountability for operational services. Mr. Drake has had a varied career in research and project management, and has spent the last 10 years in information security, as a consultant or senior manager. He holds a Master's Degree in Management (Information Security) from Anglia Polytechnic University in the UK, and is currently studying for a Doctorate at the University of Luton.

N. F. du Plooy worked as a physicist at various research institutes. In 1966 he decided on a career change, and was trained as a programmer and a systems analyst in a large corporation. Seven years later he joined the University of South Africa as a lecturer. At that university he was appointed Professor in 1982 and Head of the Department of Computer Science and Information Systems. In 1990 he joined the University of Pretoria's newly established Department of Informatics. He is now retired. He holds an MSC in Physics, an MBA and a Doctorate in Information Systems.

Julie Fisher is an Associate Professor in the Faculty of Information Technology at Monash University, Melbourne, Australia. She has a research interest in the area of systems development, and in particular how the development process might be improved to deliver systems that have a greater user focus. Professor Fisher is also interested in issues relating to usability, in particular website usability. She has had a number of papers published in *IEEE Transactions on Professional Communication*, reflecting her ongoing interest in the role technical communicators play in the systems development process.

Shirley Gregor is Professor of Information Systems at the Australian National University, Canberra, where she heads the Electronic Commerce Research Group. Her current research interests include electronic commerce and the theory of interorganisational systems, intelligent systems and information systems adoption. She has led several large projects in the e-commerce area funded by the Meat Research Corporation, the Department of Communications, Information Technology and the Arts and the Australian Research Council. She spent a number of years in the computing industry in Australia and the United Kingdom before beginning an academic career.

Abdul Samad (Sami) Kazi is a Research Scientist at VTT Technical Research Centre of Finland. His research interests and experiences involve: information integration, product and process modelling, process reengineering, knowledge management, Internet-based tools and technologies, liaisons with the industry, etc. He has experience in the construction IT-related EU (European Union) projects, PRO-CU-RE, I-SEEC, OSMOS, eLEGAL, and the multi-industrial IMS GLOBEMEN project. Furthermore, he is involved in European Commission-funded IST (Information Society Technologies) cluster projects, VOSTER and ICCI. Active roles in dissemination and deployment of developed solutions have been one of his focal activities. He has also recently served as an evaluator of IST project proposals and reviewer of ongoing IST projects. His relevant industrial experience spans South East Asia, Indo-China, the Middle East and Europe.

Malcolm King is the Professor of Management Sciences in the Business School at Loughborough University. As well as mathematical modelling, his research interests include the impact of information technology on all areas of management, and the organisational and political aspects of systems development. He has also written on the acceptance of information technology among users, and its application within small and medium-sized enterprises.

Lauri Koskela is a Senior Researcher at VTT Technical Research Centre of Finland. His research is presently focused on the generic theory of operations/production management and its application to production situations in project-based industries. He is a founding member of the International Group for Lean Construction.

Teresa Lynch is Head of the Computing and Information Systems School in the Faculty of Informatics and Communication at Central Queensland University. Her current research interests include the adoption and use of intelligent support systems in agriculture, user involvement in system development and web delivery of intelligent support systems. She has also published in the areas of participation of women in tertiary information technology courses, computer-mediated communication and computer-based learning.

Mike Metcalfe is an Associate Professor in the School of Accounting and Information Systems at the University of South Australia. He coordinates the research in the Information Systems Doctoral School using his argumentative methodology. His area of expertise is the use of 'argument' to assist project definition. He has been involved in IS and strategic planning for more than 30 years with the military, industry, education and the government. Editorships include

Associate Editor of *The Middle Eastern Business Review* and the *Journal of IT Education*, and Associate Publisher of the *Journal of Theory and Technology Applications*.

Jeffrey M. Stanton, PhD (University of Connecticut, 1997) is an Assistant Professor in the School of Information Studies at Syracuse University. His research focuses on organizational impacts of information technology, and he has published more than 20 articles and chapters. Dr. Stanton is the Director of the Syracuse Information Systems Evaluation project, an effort to understand and promote effective use of information technology in non-profit and social service agencies. His background also includes 17 years of business experience in consulting, management, research and software engineering positions.

Arthur Tatnall is a Senior Lecturer in the School of Information Systems at Victoria University in Melbourne, Australia. He holds bachelor's degrees in Science and Education, a graduate diploma in Computer Science and a research Master's of Arts in which he explored the origins of business computing education in Australian universities. His PhD involved a study in curriculum innovation in which he investigated the manner in which Visual Basic entered the curriculum of an Australian university. His research interests include technological innovation, information technology in educational management, information systems curriculum, project management, electronic commerce and Visual Basic programming.

Leoni Warne is a Senior Research Scientist within the Defence Systems Analysis Division of the Defence Science and Technology Organisation (DSTO) in Australia. She works in the Joint Systems Branch where she is the Task Manager and Team Leader of the research team responsible for researching and developing Enterprise Social Learning Architectures. Dr. Warne has been with DSTO for three years. Prior to this, she spent 10 years lecturing in Information Systems at the University of Canberra. Dr. Warne's research work is primarily focused on the social and organisational aspects of information systems.

Trevor Wood-Harper is Professor of Information Systems and Director of the Information Systems Research Centre (ISRC) at the Information Systems Institute, in the Faculty of Business and Informatics, University of Salford. The institute with 33 academic staff is one of the largest IS schools in the UK. He is also Visiting Professor of Management Information Systems at the University of South Australia, Adelaide, and has held visiting chairs at the University of Oslo, Copenhagen Business School and Georgia State University. Dr. Wood-Harper has co-authored 11 books and monographs, and more than 150 research articles in a wide range of topics including multiview methodology, software maintenance, electronic commerce, action research, business process re-engineering, ethics in systems development, fundamentals of information systems and doctoral education. Currently he is researching into information systems methodologies for business process re-engineering, total quality management, systems theory for electronic commerce, information systems ethics, organisations and IS doctoral education. Recently, he was appointed to the Library and Information Management panel for the Research Assessment Exercise (RAE) in 2001, the British Computer Society accreditation panel and the UKAIS board. He set up (in 1990) one of the first information systems doctoral schools (a combination of the European and American styles) in UK, which is attracting an increasing number of international as well as British students. Currently the school has more than 30 PhD students. Dr. Wood-Harper has successfully supervised 16 doctoral students and acted as an external examiner for more than 35 PhD theses in the UK, South Africa, Norway and Australia. In 1999, at the University of South Australia, he has started a new doctoral programme in information systems with a research fellow and six doctoral students.

Index

New Books on the Human Aspect of IT

Human Factors in Information Systems

Edward J. Szewczak, Ph.D., Canisius College, USA
Coral Snodgrass, Ph.D., Canisius College, USA

Many factors contribute to the way people view and use information, including task requirements, organizational settings, and personality characteristics. Today it is generally accepted that people are an integral element of an information system. System development methodologies include various kinds of people – managers, analysts, programmers, support staff – in the development process. IT could be wasted if various aspects of human behavior were not seriously accommodated. Human Factors in Information Systems addresses pertinent issues by including the most recent research in the discipline, which can be utilized by businesses and organizations when implementing information systems into their policies, procedures and daily tasks.

ISBN: 1-931777-10-1; eISBN: 1-931777-31-4; Copyright: 2002; Pages: 264 (s/c);
Price: US $59.95

Human Computer Interaction Developments and Management

Tanya B. Barrier, Ph.D., Southwest Missouri State University, USA

Organizations today realize that information systems must be managed. Management can no longer continue to introduce components into information systems without studying the effectiveness, feasibility and efficiency of the individual components of an information systems. The "latest, greatest and most powerful component is the one for our organization" perspective is no longer blindly accepted. Human Computer Interaction Development and Management contains the most recent research concerning IS evolution in organizations, including not only hardware, software, data, information, and networks but also people. Integration of these key components is paramount to the success of organizations today.

ISBN: 1-931777-13-6; eISBN: 1-931777-35-7; Copyright: 2002; Pages: 290 (s/c);

Managing the Human Side of Information Technology: Challenges and Solutions

Edward J. Szewczak, Ph.D., Canisius College, USA
Coral Snodgrass, Ph.D., Canisius College, USA

As the field of information technology continues to grow and impact the personnel and management of organizations, changes have occurred in the way that such people contribute and participate in effective business operations. Managing the Human Side of Information Technology: Challenges and Solutions addresses how to effectively manage the ways in which information technology impacts both human and organizational behavior.

ISBN: 1-930708-32-7; eISBN: 1-59140-021-X; Copyright: 2002; Pages: 364 (h/c); Price:
US $89.95

Human Centered Methods in Information Systems: Current Research and Practice

Steve Clarke, Ph.D., University of Luton Business School, UK
Brian Lehaney, Ph.D., University of Luton Business School, UK

The 1980s and 1990s saw a growing interest in research and practice in information systems design and development from a human-centred perspective. This is an interest that is accelerated by the increase in organizations in which the human resource provides the means to key competitive advantage. Human Centered Methods in Information Systems: Current Research and Practice addresses the relationships between human activity, organizational issues and technology.

ISBN: 1-878289-64-0; eISBN:1-930708-56-4; Copyright:2000; Pages: 241 (s/c);
Price: US $69.95

Human Computer Interaction: Issues and Challenges

Edited by Qiyang Chen, Ph.D.
Montclair State University, USA

As humans increasingly relate to and rely on interactions with computer systems, researchers, designers, managers and users continuously develop desires to understand the current situations and future development of Human Computer Interactions (HCIs). *Human Computer Interaction: Issues and Challenges* focuses on the multi-disciplinary subject of HCI, which impacts areas such as information technology, computer science, psychology, library science, education, business and management, human factors, industrial engineering and ergonomics. This book reflects the most current, primary issues regarding human computer interactive systems, by emphasizing effective design, use and evaluation of such systems.

ISBN: 1-878289-91-8; eISBN:1-930708-84-X; Copyright:2001; Pages: 268 (s/c);
Price: US $74.95

NEW Titles
from Information Science Publishing

- **Web-Based Education: Learning from Experience**
  Anil Aggarwal
  ISBN: 1-59140-102-X: eISBN 1-59140-110-0, © 2003
- **The Knowledge Medium: Designing Effective Computer-Based Educational Learning Environments**
  Gary A. Berg
  ISBN: 1-59140-103-8; eISBN 1-59140-111-9, © 2003
- **Sociotechnical and Human Cognition Elements of Information Systems**
  Steve Clarke, Elayne Coakes, M. Gordon Hunter and Andrew Wenn
  ISBN: 1-59140-104-6; eISBN 1-59140-112-7, © 2003
- **Usability Evaluation of Online Learning Programs**
  Claude Ghaoui
  ISBN: 1-59140-105-4; eISBN 1-59140-113-5, © 2003
- **Building a Virtual Library**
  Ardis Hanson & Bruce Lubotsky
  ISBN: 1-59140-106-2; eISBN 1-59140-114-3, © 2003
- **Design and Implementation of Web-Enabled Teaching Tools**
  Mary F. Hricko
  ISBN: 1-59140-107-0; eISBN 1-59140-115-1, © 2003
- **Designing Campus Portals**
  Ali Jafari and Mark Sheehan
  ISBN: 1-59140-108-9; eISBN 1-59140-116-X, © 2003
- **Challenges of Teaching with Technology Across the Curriculum: Issues and Solutions**
  Lawrence A. Tomei
  ISBN: 1-59140-109-7; eISBN 1-59140-117-8, © 2003

Excellent additions to your institution's library! Recommend these titles to your Librarian!